DYNASTY

50 YEARS OF SHANKLY'S LIVERPOOL

PAUL TOMKINS

REASSESSING SHANKLY, PAISLEY, FAGAN, DALGLISH, SOUNESS, EVANS, HOULLIER & BENÍTEZ

R
E

For my nieces, Lauren and Mia Purdy.

And also for Jason Lock, Mark Lynch and Robert
Radburn, my oldest friends.

Also by Paul Tomkins:

GOLDEN PAST, RED FUTURE
RED REVIVAL
THE RED REVIEW
ABOVE US ONLY SKY
AN ANFIELD ANTHOLOGY

DYNASTY: 50 YEARS OF SHANKLY'S LIVERPOOL
BY PAUL TOMKINS

Published By GPRF Publishing

First edition published 2008

DYNASTY
50 YEARS OF SHANKLY'S LIVERPOOL

CONTENTS

"Knowledge of history frees us to be contemporary."

LYNN WHITE, JR.

ACKNOWLEDGEMENTS

Special thanks to the excellent www.LFCHistory.net for all the appearance/goal statistics. Also, a big thank-you to Garreth Cummins, Chris Hadley, Adrian Mervyn, Andy Searle, everyone at www.liverpoolfc.tv, and especially to all those who contributed to the Brains Trust, who are listed at the end of the introduction.

Extra special thanks to Kate, and also to my family, for their love and support, for which I am eternally grateful.

"History with its flickering lamp stumbles along the trail of the past, trying to reconstruct its scenes, to revive its echoes, and kindle with pale gleams the passion of former days."

SIR WINSTON CHURCHILL

INTRODUCTION

*"You f*cking beauty!"*

MARK WRIGHT,
LIFTING THE 1992 FA CUP

Glamourous locations arrived at in global travels; power and money; unfeasibly big hair; silver ostentatiously displayed; success that peaked in the '80s with huge TV ratings; and warring silver-haired American tycoons — but not a Joan Collins or Heather Locklear in sight. This is the story of a different *Dynasty*. Liverpool Football Club's rise to the pinnacle of the game began five decades ago — 2008/09 is the 50th season since the appointment of Bill Shankly — and bar a brief exile, the club abides as a major English and European team. The eight men at the helm during that time have not been linked by blood, but they have all bled red for the club. Successful or not, skilled or not, they all cared.

Fifty years of unparalleled success. Thirteen league titles, five European Cups, three UEFA Cups, seven FA Cups, seven League Cups: 35 major trophies in five decades — the honours list speaks of unprecedented triumph. Add three European Super Cups and 15 Charity/Community Shields, and it's 53 pieces of silverware by the 50th year. (Any Newcastle fans reading this, you have my permission to weep uncontrollably; just don't damage the pages.) Of the eight men who got to manage the club during this time, four were former Liverpool players — and each landed at least one major honour.

Of course, the majority of those trophies were garnered in the first 30 years. The fourth decade of the dynasty saw a relative drought: Championship in 1990, FA Cup in 1992 and League Cup in 1995. And were it not for a new direction, courtesy of continental cousins, the dynasty may have ended there, with a drift towards mid-table mediocrity and a failure to revisit the scenes of so many cup successes. Gérard Houllier had his critics, and it's undeniable that the second half of his tenure was a massive disappointment after the positive reconstruction of the first, but he landed four major trophies and finally got the team back into the Champions League; throw in 'showpiece' silverware, and he can count one trophy for each year of his reign. Rafa Benítez, like his three predecessors, has yet to find the magic formula for a league title, but he put the Reds back into the very top bracket with two Champions League Finals and an FA Cup success, as well as coming within nine minutes and a Steven Gerrard own goal of landing the League Cup in his debut final. As with Houllier, add the European Super Cup and Community Shield, and the Spaniard was registering a trophy per season. The new millennium had seen the rebuilding of the club; its name back in lights. In the summer of 2008 it was announced that the Reds had risen to become the top-ranked team in Europe, based on results of the previous five years. But without the foundations laid five decades ago, it would almost certainly have been a club sinking into darkness.

It's always frightening to think about how different things might have been if only a certain decision wasn't taken; as George Michael noted in the song that was number one in the UK charts at the time Liverpool won their one and only double: turn a different corner and certain people might never have met (something he no doubt pondered when caught cottaging in a Los Angeles lavatory). In the case of Liverpool Football Club, that corner was turned, both figuratively and literally, by Tom Williams, the chairman, and Harry Latham, a fellow director, when approaching the lone figure of Bill Shankly late on Saturday 17th October 1959, as the then-Huddersfield manager left his team's home ground following defeat to Cardiff. Had that meeting not taken place, this book would not have been written. Liverpool may eventually have come good again, given the club had already won five league titles in its history, but it's unlikely that it would have been to anything near the extent subsequently seen. For that to happen, it needed key men, visionaries.

Shankly took up the offer made to him in Williams' car, and Bob Paisley, already a first team coach, became his assistant. In that moment, the future of the club was set on a course for the stars in a way that Williams and Latham could not have believed possible. It was as if they inadvertently created the world's first spaceship and sent it successfully into orbit. Shankly's fifteen years and Paisley's nine meant that almost all of the first half of the 50-year dynasty was overseen by just *two* managers. Unquestionably they were aided by the back-room men, oiling the wheels behind the scenes; a collective known for years as the legendary 'Boot Room', on account of the glorified kit cupboard within Anfield in which they gathered. But these men needed a leader to follow; at least until it came to their chance to take control.

Other clubs have possessed more than one legendary (or, at the very least, notably successful) manager in the last 50 years, such as Matt Busby and Alex Ferguson at Manchester United and Bertie Mee, George Graham and Arsène Wenger at Arsenal, but no club has employed undoubted geniuses in back-to-back appointments. Shankly possessed everything necessary to build a club up from a very humble starting point, and Paisley had the different kind of eye necessary to take things that one step forward.

But this is about much, much more than just two men. Joe Fagan won a treble of League, European Cup and League Cup in his debut season and was a beaten European Cup finalist in his second and final campaign; Kenny Dalglish won three league titles, one of them in scintillating style, and the club's only double — in his inaugural campaign at that; Gérard Houllier led the team to an historic three cup successes in one season; and Rafa Benítez oversaw the most remarkable night in the history of the club by winning the most memorable of all European Cup Finals in the time-span covered by all but the first year of this book. Indeed, even the other two won trophies: Graeme Souness punctuated a disappointing tenure with an FA Cup; Roy Evans, meanwhile, had just a League Cup to show for some fine attacking football — but unlike the much-heralded Newcastle United of the same era, or Leeds a few years later, at least it was *something*. You have to go back to the 1950s, before the dynasty was in place, to find the last Liverpool manager to leave the job empty-handed. And since the club returned to the top flight in 1962, the lowest the Reds have finished is 8th. (Unlike Manchester United, relegated in 1973, and with three bottom-half finishes in Alex Ferguson's first four seasons; and Arsenal, with a low of 17th and a further five finishes of 12th and below in that time). Not bad for a club languishing in the old Second Division when Shankly pitched up.

With the 50th anniversary of Shankly's appointment approaching, and the club approaching the level it was at in the years before the Scot's abdication — towards the top of the league, and making waves in Europe — the great institution experienced the previously unthinkable, and descended into civil war. Owned by two Americans — George Gillett and Tom Hicks — who acquired the club in 2007, the pair were at odds with each other in the world's media, dragging the manager, Rafa

Benítez, into the discord, and with chief executive Rick Parry publicly asked by Hicks to resign at the height of the squabbles. Whatever the rights and wrongs, and whoever's side you care to take, it was not a situation anyone involved in the running of the club could be happy about. It certainly wasn't the way the club used to do business, and a return to such values must be on the minds of all concerned.

Dynasty is not intended as some trip down memory lane purely to marvel in its delights, even if that is a most welcome part of the journey. "If you want to understand today, you have to search yesterday", said Pearl S Buck. In football, while much will change — indeed, *has* to change — there are plenty of universal truths that endure. Speaking of his time as manager at Real Madrid, and referring to what he learned from the Boot Room, John Toshack said "There are a lot of modern theories, but the most important things in football were important 50 years ago. And they'll be important 50 years from now."

Despite some obvious differences, there are some surprising and striking similarities between Bill Shankly and Rafael Benítez, the men at either end of the fifty year divide. For instance, the lessons of how Shankly got the ball rolling: the birth of modern Liverpool FC. There are a lot of parallels between what Shankly did and what Benítez attempts 50 years later. Shankly started from a lower position, but Benítez is working in an age where more is demanded, and where expectations are higher as a result of that unprecedented success between 1964 and 1990. Both missed out on a number of early targets deemed too expensive, as each worked with less funds than some rivals, but both eventually had far stronger squads than they inherited once they were four years into their reign. Both bought players who were impressive initially, but with better replacements arriving were later sold for a profit (Kevin Lewis and Momo Sissoko are just two examples). Character was vitally important to both managers when sizing up a transfer target. Then there were the two pairs of crucial signings with apparent similarities. In 1961 it was Ian St John and Ron Yeats, while 46 years later it was Javier Mascherano and Fernando Torres. All were 23 when they put pen to paper; each pair became the two most expensive players in the club's history; and one was a forward and the other there to stop the opposition. Then there was Shankly's belief in a large squad, his penchant for making notes (not during games, mind) and his belief that players could not repeat their usual level of intensity in games that were close together; it could almost be Benítez under discussion. Shankly was hauled over hot coals for making wholesale changes to his side just a matter of days ahead of crucial games in 1965 and 1973, with the club receiving a large fine for the latter incident when the manager made ten changes for the visit to Manchester City.

When Inter Milan narrowly overcame Liverpool in 1965, Shanks pointed out how pleased the unofficial world champions were to beat the Reds. "That's the level you have raised yourselves up to," he told his players. That is finally true once again.

The Past and the Present

Comparing different eras within football is notoriously perilous. The sport, and how we look at it, has changed in innumerable ways. Simply knowing the name of each division is in itself a complex matter: in 1992 the First Division became the Premiership, so the Second Division became the First Division. A few years later, the First Division became the Championship (which only confuses the issue of saying a team 'won the championship') and the Second Division (i.e. old Third Division) became the third different First Division in the space of a decade. Confused? You should be.

Different skills are more important in different decades, as the rules are amended to alter the influence of attacking play. Tactics, systems and formations have changed and developed, and the English game has become cosmopolitan in its personnel and global in its appeal. Priorities also change. In 1965, winning the FA Cup was almost the pinnacle of the game, on a par with winning the league title. Within 40 years it had become an afterthought. In the days of Shankly and Paisley, first was first and '2nd was nowhere'. But by the new millennium, 2nd, 3rd and 4th were of great importance. The relevance of the League Cup has never been that great, but in recent years it's almost become a youth/reserve competition.

The aim of this book is to compare the situations, prepare the context — within which framework accurate judgements can be made. For example, comparing a modern squad against one from 1964 is misleading, because back then, even though Shankly wanted a strong squad, it could be about 14 players at most over the course of a season. The allowance of a substitute was still a season away, and the lower pace and intensity meant fewer injuries, so fewer players were needed; these days, squads of 25 or more are commonplace, while up to 50 players may have squad numbers. The notion of the 'squad player' has expanded in recent years. In the first 30-40 years covered by this book, a club had players who played regularly for the first team, and who tended to be good or very good. Then you had those who didn't play very much, or not at all, and bar the odd exception, they were understandably viewed as being not so good. But nowadays clubs can see full internationals as mere bit-part players; they may not play too often, but in some cases their quality is undeniable — even if they don't get a lot of time to prove it. With the pace of the modern game, and the way athletes are pushed to the limit, strength in depth has become an important concept. In previous decades, a decent local lad would make up the numbers; these days, a manager has to try to buy two top-class players for every position. But of course, he cannot play both at the same time; as such, one could be seen as a failure, even if he provides a decent alternative.

Writing for *The Times* the morning after the Reds' remarkable 4-2 victory over Arsenal in the quarter-final of the Champions League on April 8th 2008, Oliver Kay noted how the game has changed over the last two decades: "When players of a certain vintage try to dismiss the 'nonsense' spoken by modern managers about the pace of English football these days, they should be given a tape — not a DVD, obviously — of this match to sit through. This was not football as they knew it. The worst thing that ever happened to that generation was the advent of nostalgia-based sports television channels. As classic matches from the archives are reshown, younger viewers can marvel at the talents of Kenny Dalglish or Liam Brady, but they can also see the outdated rules and the outlandish physiques that made for such a different spectacle.

"One station recently showed a rerun of the most famous Liverpool-Arsenal clash of them all: that on May 26, 1989, when the London club needed a 2-0 victory at Anfield in the final match of the season to beat the Merseysiders to the League championship. It is remembered as a classic, but it was a stultifying spectacle as Liverpool's defenders repeatedly passed the ball back to Bruce Grobbelaar to wind down the clock. With the back-pass rule still three years away, Grobbelaar would bowl the ball out and, within 20 seconds, it would be back in his hands. It was a misplaced sense of adventure that drew them out in the closing stages, only for Michael Thomas to score Arsenal's decisive second goal deep into stoppage time, thus providing the most dramatic climax to a title race that England has seen."

Of course, Liverpool were perfectly entitled to make use of the back-pass law — much of their European dominance had involved that very process. And if it was so easy to achieve success this way, why didn't every team adopt it and reap the rewards? But even so, much of the game's increased speed is down to the ball being in play — and out of the goalkeepers' hands — for greater periods of time.

Pitches nowadays are more like bowling greens and less like reenactments of the Somme; balls are like balloons; goalkeepers narrow their angles rather than stay rooted to their line; off-the-ball incidents are captured by a dozen cameras, as is every movement of the players (who are also monitored by tracking devices), while the internet, countless sports satellite channels and extensive newspaper coverage mean that the game is now endlessly analysed, shortening managerial careers in the process. The outlawing of challenges from behind has allowed more freedom to creative talents; the offside rule has evolved to the point where eight players can be in an offside position but, without a hint of logic, not 'interfering with play'; players and club owners are more likely to be from overseas than England (only 38% of Premiership players are currently English), while the Bosman ruling has altered how clubs trade players; while your average tackle from 1971 would result in a life ban if made three decades later. Other than that, it's still eleven versus eleven (at kick-off) on pitches marked out in the same manner, trying to score in goals that, despite some talk of expansion ahead of the 1994 World Cup, remain the same size. *Plus ça change...*, as the French say.

In an interview in March 2008, Rafa Benítez gave his views on how things differ. "Nowadays," he said, "in comparison to 20 years ago, we play 20 percent more games in a season. Players run 15 percent more than they used to and, even more importantly, they run 30 percent faster."

As a result, comparing fitness from decades ago is possible only against the competition of that era, not against the modern scientific methods (which, in 50 years' time, may seem as archaic as Shankly's dietary advice of eating steak and chips does now). Of course, everyone is usually in pretty much the same boat; no-one is ever that far ahead of their rivals for long, with good ideas quickly adopted as they are disseminated. With all this in mind, as well as the changes in the financial landscape and numerous other factors (including strength of squad inherited, development of players, tactical awareness, the support of the board, quality of the league at the time, and so on), I have devised a set of categories in which the analysis can take place, so comparisons between Shankly, Paisley, Fagan, Dalglish, Souness, Evans, Houllier and Benítez can be made in full awareness of the problems and luxuries they experienced in their own era. For example, in the late '60s and early '70s there were a lot of strong English teams capable of winning the league, such as Manchester United, Leeds, Manchester City, Everton, Arsenal and Derby, as well as Liverpool, while United were so strong they had become the country's first European Champions in 1968; as such, Shankly's failure to land a league title between 1966 and 1973 can be viewed in that context. Alternatively, United fell away to 18th in 1973, and were relegated in 1974, to remove one major rival. In the late '70s and early '80s, English football dominated Europe; in the early '90s, the country's national game was in poor health. Come forward to more recent times, and the arrival of Roman Abramovich at Chelsea in 2003 meant that Rafa Benítez had to try and overcome a rival team — the *nouveau riche* Blues — whose wealth was on an unprecedented scale.

An example of how the challenge of winning the league — or even finishing 2nd — has changed can be seen in the statistics of each of the managers' first 150 league games: a landmark Benítez reached two matches before the end of 2007/08, and as such, a nice figure to use by way of comparison. (Only Joe Fagan and Graeme Souness failed to reach the 150-game landmark, managing 84 and 115 league games respectively; Ronnie Moran, as a mere caretaker for nine matches in 1991, isn't counted, nor is Phil Thompson's leadership during Houllier's time in hospital with a ruptured aorta a decade later.)

Kenny Dalglish chalked up the most wins in his first 150 league matches, with 87. But Benítez and Houllier had the next-best record, with 81 wins each. Bob Paisley won 79, Bill Shankly 77 and Roy Evans 72. Bob Paisley's first 150 league games were spread across complete seasons where the Reds finished 2nd, 1st and 1st, while Dalglish's were chalked up during 1st, 2nd and 1st place finishes; both managers would see their Liverpool team finish 2nd in the fourth season, in which the 150th game occurred. So Paisley's two titles and two runners-up positions were achieved with fewer league wins than Houllier and Benítez managed when averaging between 3rd and 4th. Equally, it could be argued that bigger squads make it more possible to win a greater percentage of games in a single season.

Judging a manager purely on the silverware he wins ignores the challenges inherent in winning them. The key is not purely counting trophies — as important as they are — but discovering the context of each man's achievements or, in some cases, failures. What situation — and what players — did he inherit? What state was the club in, politically and financially? How expertly was he assisted by his coaching staff? How much money did he spend, in relative terms? How did each of his signings pan out? What legacy did he bequeath? How dominant, rich and/or well-managed were rival teams? And so on. All of these factors, and more, are considered when assessing the men concerned.

How the club now moves forward cannot be foretold — it's simply impossible. So much could change, and no doubt will change in the coming months and years. But the past 50 years is written in stone, with Liverpool's achievements inscribed upon marble and silver, and its modern founder, with arms outstretched in triumph, carved in gleaming bronze.

BRAINS TRUST

For the purposes of this book it was essential to have valid evaluations of all the players purchased by the club over the five decades, to help gauge each manager's activity in the transfer market. These, along with the contributions of those who emerged through the ranks, are also used determine how strong the squad was when each manager reported for his first day in charge — a crucial part of deciding how difficult his task was.

In order to have each player analysed as accurately as possible, I assembled a Brains Trust, where experts — including those who knew some of the key figures, as well as football writers, authors and editors of various LFC websites — along with a select few fans, have contributed marks out of 10 for every Reds' performer in the last 50 years, from which an average rating for each player has been ascertained. (Of course, 'expert' is always a subjective term. However, I have tried to make sure only those with real knowledge are included; anyone awarding Sean Dundee 9/10 would instantly be struck off and reported to the relevant mental health authorities.)

Once the quality of each player was rated, other factors needed to be analysed. It struck me how important it was to judge the 'value' of these players — as signings, and as part of a squad bequeathed to a managerial successor — as precisely as possible, with a set of criteria that could apply equally to 1959 and 2008. That process needs explaining.

Please note that this is not a statistical book by any means. However, when it comes to judging players — from the amount of games they played, through to their transfer fees, and on to rating their contribution to the Liverpool cause with a mark out of 10 — everything leads back to figures, or statistics. The use of numbers is inescapable. As an alternative, in order to be more colourful, the players' quality could perhaps have been compared with, say, aquatic life: Ian Rush a shark, Michael Owen a stingray, Jan Molby a whale, El Hadji Diouf a catfish and Torben Piechnik a plankton. But ultimately such comparisons wouldn't really provide the quantifiable accuracy required.

First and foremost, this is a book based on history, and what people saw with their own eyes. Achievements and anecdotes are a vital part of the assessment process for each manager, but when it comes to analysing their players more deeply than "he was great, he was rubbish", or "he was cheap, he was expensive", a different kind of evaluation is necessary. As such, *Dynasty* mixes subjective, eye-witness appraisals with objective statistical facts.

While this is a book about managers, it is undeniable that their contribution is largely measured through the strengths and weaknesses of their players. How successful a manager is depends on the abilities of those who cross the white line on his behalf. The true measure of a manager is in the games and, if all goes well, the trophies he wins; but getting it right in the transfer market is arguably the most influential factor in success. How successful a manager can prove to be clearly depends to a large degree on his budget, and how he invests it, but it's not the only consideration. The players he inherits and those graduating from the youth team are often as important, if not more so in some cases. All these are vital parts of the assessments herein.

While the idea was to be as fair as possible and rank the players for their quality and not their fee (seeing as the fee would be assessed separately), it's important to acknowledge that it's impossible to completely divorce the two. Had Gary McAllister cost £5m, then despite his influential displays he would have been viewed slightly less favourably; maybe people would have focused on the fact that, apart from two sensational months, the rest of his two years were steady rather than spectacular, and that £5m was a very high fee for a man of his age. Equally, had Paul Stewart been a free transfer, then perhaps he'd have been viewed more sympathetically. (Then again, any player lumbering about like an inebriated vagrant who's lost his can of Special Brew is never impressive, no matter how much or little they cost.) So any perception of a player is tainted by his transfer fee.

Transfers

Many experts claim that managers succeed or fail by the signings they make. Tactics, groundbreaking fitness regimes, special diets, sports psychology, etc, are all important, but will only get you so far if the quality of personnel is substandard; you can use these techniques to punch above your weight, but there tends to be a ceiling to the success, while consistency can be difficult to achieve. The best managers can get more out of limited players, but the greater the quality and the better the balance of personnel, then the more chance there is of succeeding over the course of a season.

Obviously modern managers spend far more money, in terms of pounds sterling, than their forebears, as fees have risen at a staggering rate since the post-war period. Clearly, football transfers do not follow standard inflation. It's pointless saying that Josemi cost four times as much as Kenny Dalglish — it needs to be looked at in terms relative to the year in question. You could add the values of all Shankly's signings together and, coming in at £1,329,250, still not attain the current asking price for a jobbing lower division player. But the question should be: in his day, how much did Shankly spend relative to his rivals? And how much did he spend, in relative terms, compared with his successors?

With this in mind, I have devised a system to rank the cost of each signing out of 10, based on the fee's relation to the English transfer record of the time; so that rather than use a financial figure to make comparisons — which becomes meaningless with the passing of time — the mark will show how large or small the fee was in *relative* terms. Outbound transfer fees, as debits, are rated as a minus number, up to -10; money coming into the club, as credit, is rated as a positive number, up to +10. The transfer record is taken only as what English clubs have paid.

Ranking signings against the record fee works back from a benchmark. It is not 100% accurate, and cannot escape the vagaries and arbitrariness of transfers, which don't always follow logical comparisons. After all, a player's value is set by how much the buying club is prepared to spend, and how much the selling club is willing to hold out for. Sometimes this eventual evaluation leaves pundits scratching their heads. All the same, comparing transfers with the record of the day is still the best way to judge how much each signing cost in real terms.

As an example, Peter Beardsley's transfer fee of £1.9m in 1987 was the equivalent of £2.9m in 1991, when the Reds broke the English transfer record again with the purchase of Dean Saunders. Both of these were -10 signings in terms of outlay — the most an English club had paid. By 1995 — the last time the Reds set the record, when signing Stan Collymore — that high-water mark had become £8.5m; therefore, another -10 outlay. As an example of how other players' values compare, Jason McAteer, signed for £4.5m that same year, was a -5.3 signing; roughly equivalent to a fee of £17m 13 years later.

Come forward to August 2008, and the English record stands at the £30.8m Chelsea paid for Andrei Shevchenko in 2006, whilst there are several other players who have been bought for fees in this vicinity: Rio Ferdinand, Juan Sebastian Verón and Wayne Rooney, to name just three. Given the cost of Shevchenko, Liverpool's record signing, Fernando Torres, is rated at a -7.5 fee. This is based on the price of £23m, which is the median fee quoted for the Spaniard, on account that reports differ, with some sources claiming it was as low as £20m and others as high as £26m, including possible add-ons for milestones reached by the player. One difficulty with assessing modern-day transfers is that an increasing number of fees are undisclosed, or involve such incentives to reward appearances or trophies won.

Going back to the summer of 1962, the point when Liverpool won promotion to the top flight as champions of the Second Division, Denis Law (a protege of Shankly's at Huddersfield) secured a move from Torino to Manchester United for £115,000, a new high-water mark; it would be 12 years before Liverpool topped that figure, when Shankly shelled out £180,000 on his very last signing, Ray Kennedy — at which point the new record became the £350,000 Everton paid for Bob Latchford. At the time of Law's arrival at Old Trafford, Shankly's record outlay was the purchase of Ian St John from Motherwell for £37,500 a year earlier. This was more than double what the Reds had previously paid for a player, but even so, it was still some way short of what United were able to afford.

However, that is not to say that Shankly didn't pay big money; in 1967 he paid £96,000 for Tony Hateley, which was 83% of the record (-8.3). Shankly, Fagan, Houllier and Benítez are the four managers who have failed to make a record-breaking signing, although each, bar Fagan, broke the club's own record on at least one occasion. Between 1977 and 1995, Paisley, Dalglish, Souness and Evans all broke the English record.

Ultimately, all clubs use the transfer record as a barometer. And paying large fees helps any club get the men they covet. A transfer fee may seem cheap five years after the event, but at the time it may have stretched the club's resources and, of course, seen off the hopes of any rivals in the market. This can be seen with someone like Gary Pallister, who cost Manchester United £2.3m (-8.5) in 1989; four years later, when they won the title, it was in no small part down to the giant centre-back. By spending big in 1989, Ferguson had taken Pallister off the open market; by 1996 the English record was £15m, but Pallister still has to be viewed as a very expensive player when considering United's double-winning side.

With every new TV deal comes a rash of extravagant spending. As soon as someone increases the record, the values of every other player, be they world-class or jobbing journeyman, are adjusted accordingly. Clubs turn around and say "well, if *he's* worth £30m, our reserve goalkeeper must be worth £10m", when the day before, they saw their player's worth as £7m.

The inward and outbound transfers of Stan Collymore, in 1995 and 1997 respectively, provide an example of how the transfer record affects other fees. In 1995, Collymore cost Liverpool £8.5m, a new English record. Two years later he was sold for £7.5m — only a £1m loss, on the surface. But in between, Alan Shearer had moved to Newcastle for £15m. Therefore, the going rate for a top striker had almost doubled, and should Roy Evans have wished to buy another top forward in England, he'd have struggled with what he received for Collymore. Had Collymore, with the exception of a few excellent games here and there, produced for Liverpool what he did at Nottingham Forest, or indeed, actually *improved*, then by 1997 his value should have risen to somewhere in the £15m ballpark. Instead, from being the country's record signing, he was sold to Aston Villa for only *half* of the new high-water mark — a more accurate marker for his dwindling value by 1997. The very reason Collymore was sold at all was down to his relative failure, and this was reflected in his price. Had he succeeded at Anfield, then the point may well have been moot, as Liverpool would not have sold him — at least not to another English club. So in relative terms, Liverpool lost a lot more than a million pounds.

On the whole, the transfer record has seen an increase every year or two, with the occasional longer period of stability. But 1979 was when English football went insane, as spending went through the roof — although interestingly, Liverpool, the champions, were not party to the craziness. In the year of Margaret Thatcher's first election success and as a prelude to English society's self-centred, spend-big culture of the next decade, it was a year when the record rocketed. The proof that my evaluation system has some validity can be seen in the events that followed David Mills — a run-of-the-mill (no pun intended) midfielder never capped beyond U23 level for England — moving from Middlesbrough to West Brom in January for a new record fee of £516,000. Trevor Francis, a far superior player, became the first million pound player a month later (after all, he had to be worth at least *twice* someone like Mills, surely?), and by then even average or totally unproven players became more expensive overnight. In September, jobbing England B international Steve Daley — another who never made the senior England side — moved from Wolves to Man City for a ludicrous £1.45m, and then Andy Gray, an effective but hardly world-beating centre-forward, was transferred from Aston Villa to Wolves for £1.469m. In eight months, the record fee had virtually trebled, and average players became far more expensive as a result.

So this is the level against which the transfer of Ian Rush in 1980 should be judged, and not against Dalglish's fee just three years earlier; Rush cost only £140,000 less than Dalglish, but by that time, rather than be close to the English record, it was only one-fifth (-2). In 1980, £300,000 was still a hefty fee for a teenager from the lower leagues, but it was nowhere near the kind of money being splashed by other clubs. The spending eventually slowed after Bryan Robson moved to Manchester United for £1.5m in 1981 — a minimal increase — and it wasn't until 1987 that the record rose again, with the Reds' procurement of Beardsley.

Other factors, like the Bosman and Webster rulings, have played a part in determining a fee since 1995, whereas before that there was the transfer tribunal, which would appear to pluck a figure out of the air for a player out of contract; Bosman subsequently resulted in such players moving for free. But this has just made it easier to buy players. Where it's cost Liverpool more than their rivals is in losing key personnel for far less than they were worth: both Steve McManaman and Michael Owen moved to Real Madrid, in 1998 and 2004 respectively, leaving Liverpool with a total of just £10m for two players whose combined value should have been four times that amount. As a result, it made it harder for the club to find replacements.

Value For Money
The key thing when assessing signings is the value for money they presented. In some ways it's easy to just go out and buy all the top

established stars — particularly if money is no object. It doesn't guarantee success, but it takes less skill and leaves less to chance. Unlike recent Chelsea managers, no Liverpool boss has ever had unlimited resources. And as such, it's not just the quality of the player that's important, but how much he cost, what service he provided, and how much he was sold for. While Chelsea can afford to see Shevchenko's value dwindle from £30.8m to £5m in a couple of years, as he heads towards retirement, Liverpool could never countenance such a move. When Liverpool buy a player, the club almost always needs to know that it can get some money back further down the line, to reinvest in the team.

First of all, each player's contribution to LFC was assessed by the Brains Trust. The *Quality* rating focuses solely on what they did in a red shirt (therefore, someone like Brad Friedel's resurgence at Blackburn is not a factor), and, in the case of the newer players, what they've had the chance to *realistically* achieve in the time allowed. At the time of writing, Fernando Torres has had only one season; therefore, that is all he can be judged on — and it just so happens that it was almost perfect. It's easy to say "well, he hasn't done it over five or six seasons" by way of criticism. While that kind of multi-season consistency is necessary when it comes to retrospectively judging the greats, you cannot hold the fact that he's only been at Liverpool for a year against him or Benítez, when trying to judge all eight managers on an equal footing.

The ratings are in many ways as expected, with the club's obvious greats — Dalglish, Gerrard, Clemence, Keegan, Hansen, Hughes, Fowler, Hunt, Torres, Souness, *et al* — at the very top of the list, and its embarrassing dross at the bottom; after all, it doesn't need a Brains Trust to separate Kenny Dalglish and Sean Dundee. But the list does help differentiate between the very good and the great, and the fairly good, the mediocre and the below average.

However, the *Value For Money* list looks a little different. Starting with each individual's *Quality* rating, a series of adjustments were made to arrive at a coefficient for every single player. His age, the fee he was purchased for, the fee he was sold for, and the number of appearances for the club all affect the *Value For Money* rating. As an example, even though David Burrows and Djibril Cissé — vastly different players from different eras — both scored 5.94 in terms of *Quality*, the former was a cheap player sold for a profit, while the latter was an expensive player sold for a loss. Add that Burrows played over 100 games more than the Frenchman, and you get a *Value For Money* rating of 9.17 compared with Cissé's 3.73.

The basic equation is as follows: the player's *Quality* rating (out of 10), plus 0.01 point for every game played, minus purchase fee (up to -10), and finally, the addition of the sale fee (up to +10) — or, if he hasn't yet been sold, his current transfer value (as estimated by the Brains Trust). So for Cissé, who played 79 games for Liverpool, having cost 49% of the 2004 transfer record and been sold for 19% of the 2007 record, it would be $5.94 + 0.79 - 4.9 + 1.9 = 3.73$; a fairly low score, although four players have the ignominy of a negative figure.

At the other end of the table, seven players scored over 20 for *Value For Money*, with a theoretical high of 30 points available if a player reached 1,000 games. For Benítez, whose first signings have not had the chance to play more than 239 games, and whose later signings, such as Fernando Torres, no more than the 59 games the club has faced since he arrived, a weighting for 'future game potential' has been added. Meanwhile, players like Rob Jones and Mark Lawrenson, who had to retire injured when in their pomp, receive additional points relating to how many games they might have otherwise gone on to play.

Time

Judging footballers is clearly dependent on the passing of time. Perceptions of players change throughout their stay at a club. In the winter of 2001, Emile Heskey, scoring goals and terrorising defences with his bulk, height and brute strength, seemed an inspired signing; three years later, despite a number of apparent attributes still in place, his limitations were only too clear to the watching faithful. Spanish right-back Josemi started well, and his no-nonsense approach to tackling made him look ideal for English football, but his game quickly fell apart. Glenn Hysen was imperious initially, then mistake-ridden afterwards.

In some ways Benítez is at a disadvantage in the comparisons, in that many of his signings have been younger players yet to mature, or senior ones who have not yet played enough seasons to be considered legends. Players like Krisztian Nemeth, Emiliano Insua, Jack Hobbs, Daniel Pacheco, Mikel San Jose, Gerardo Bruna and Damien Plessis have exceptional talent for their age, as evinced by their big influence in helping Liverpool win the Reserve League Northern Section in 2008 and then the overall English title via a play-off final, but at present it's about gaining experience and working their way through the second string; just as, back in 1980, Ian Rush and Ronnie Whelan (as well as Steve Nicol a year later) were Bob Paisley signings who were still virtual unknowns, as had been Alan Hansen in 1977. The current youngsters could end up being Benítez's best investments. Or they could end up like Florent Sinama-Pongolle and Anthony Le Tallec — young players with quality who didn't necessarily look out of place in the first team, but who never developed as hoped.

However, a lack of time to judge Benítez's signings works both ways. Ryan Babel has the potential to be a world-class star, but if he fails to build on the promise of his first season, then what at this point seems a good investment could turn sour; equally, and as unlikely as it seems, players like Pepe Reina, Javier Mascherano and Fernando Torres could end up seeing their reputations tarnished if they don't maintain their high standards in the coming years. Then there's Daniel Agger, whose potential seems limitless, but who needs to overcome the injury problems that dogged him in 2007/08. But as all are still young, even if they fail to develop as hoped they should retain, if not increase, their value — as was seen with Momo Sissoko in 2008. Even when players lose their way after a couple of excellent seasons, if they are young enough then they can be sold for a profit and the cash reinvested in the side. The £9m the club received for the Malian from Juventus, for a player who originally cost £5.6m, allowed Benítez to tie up the superior Mascherano on a permanent deal. So while the final impression of Sissoko was one of disappointment after his initially high standards slipped, in every way you look at it he remains an excellent *signing*.

Age and Adjustments

Once the players were rated out of 10 in terms of *Quality*, a number of adjustments were made to deal with the slight anomalies that occurred. For example, it struck me that age needed to be taken into account when it comes to transfers involving players aged 28 or over, given that their values drop as they approach 30, and dwindle rapidly once they hit 31/32. So while Graeme Souness left in 1984 for £650,000 — 43% of the English transfer record — it was a huge amount for a 31-year-old, and testimony to Paisley's judgement in buying the Scot. So that signing scores double (+8.6/10), on account of the fee recouped for his age.

Of course, some players get the chance to see out their time at Anfield, rather than embark on one last transfer into the sunset. Some may receive the opportunity to move on, but also be given the option to stay as part of the squad. But only the best last into their mid-30s, and even then, it takes someone special to still be a regular after more than a decade in the first team, as was Alan Hansen. And this also needs acknowledging. Anyone who manages five years or more as a regular in the first team that takes them into their 30s gets points for *Value For Money*, to compensate for a loss in transfer value; they are giving value in terms of appearances rather than transfer fee.

A key to managing a successful team is also knowing when to sell. Graeme Souness raised a lot of funds in his first 12 months, but later admitted he should have hung on to some of those players for longer; while in other cases, managers kept ageing stars too long. Of course, the transfer values of those Souness sold relied on their success before he arrived, which made them valuable commodities even though many were getting on in years; in addition, there's the negotiating skills of the chief executive in getting the desired price. It didn't take a genius to get £1m for Peter Beardsley, who was still such a bright talent (and indeed, one who was sold for £1.3m two years later), although to get £925,000 for 31-year-old Gary Gillespie was fairly incredible, while the £900,000 Manchester City paid for the fading force that was Steve McMahon was another acceptable deal for Liverpool. Compared with a lot of other managers, Bob Paisley was a master at releasing players at just the right time. Talking of his time at Liverpool in the '80s, Paul Walsh said "There's no sentiment at Anfield. When your number's up your number's up." Ronnie Moran explained the thinking: "All the lads who have played for Liverpool are more than welcome to come back here [to visit] any time. They know that. But as far as the team goes, once they leave, they are forgotten. They have to be."

A recent example of the perfect transfer, and how a manager without a big reserve of riches can continue to improve the team, would be Patrick Vieira at Arsenal. He was bought from AC Milan's reserves aged 20 in 1996, for a fee that wasn't cheap but which, at £4m, wasn't going to destabilise the London club. He played 426 games at an incredibly high standard as the Gunners won plenty of trophies, and crucially, was sold when on the cusp of 30, when injuries were catching up with him, for a whopping £13.7m. Had Arsène Wenger held off for another couple of years, as pundits felt he should, he might have got some (faltering?) service out of the French midfielder, but would have been left with a player with no resale value — which would make it harder to either find a replacement or reinvest to strengthen other areas of the team. Much of Manchester United's success of late, despite their large revenue streams, has been based on selling players like Jaap Stam, David Beckham and Ruud Van Nistelrooy for large fees as the clock starts to run down on their careers, and reinvesting the money in the next wave of talent. It seems that Rafa Benítez is working in a similar way, albeit so far when it comes to selling his fringe players, like Momo Sissoko, Peter Crouch, Scott Carson, Mark Gonzalez and Craig Bellamy, for a significant profit. For too long, anyone who wasn't a regular in the first team at Anfield had a value that depreciated rapidly, until they were worthless; plenty, like Diao, Cheyrou and Le Tallec, were released or sold for pittance. While neither he nor the club would want to sell his best players, many of those Benítez has signed, such as Torres, Reina, Alonso, Agger, Skrtel, Babel and Arbeloa, are worth much more now than when they first arrived.

Home-grown players

At times it's hard to know which manager to accredit when a young player comes through the ranks. For instance, Robbie Fowler was personally enticed to Liverpool by Dalglish, given his debut by Souness, played his best football under Evans and, after some serious injuries, was sold by Houllier for £11m after becoming third choice. Ian Callaghan and Gerry Byrne were already at Liverpool when Shankly pitched up, but Byrne was transfer-listed at the time. Houllier gave Steven Gerrard his debut in his first game in sole charge, but he didn't 'discover' the youngster; Gerrard's talent had been well known at the club for a number of years.

What is true is that any manager who has such players coming through during his time in charge is blessed; Rafa Benítez must be wondering where the type of talents that emerged during the '90s have gone. It's not like Liverpool have been releasing players like McManaman, Fowler, Carragher, Owen and Gerrard simply because the team is now full of foreigners. The best home-grown players — the big hopes — of the last decade (since Gerrard's debut in 1998) have yet to prove they are anything but lower league standard, with the exception of Stephen Warnock and Danny Guthrie, both of whom have been sold because of better players ahead of them. Richie Partridge, John Welsh, Jon Otsemobor, Neil Mellor, Stephen Wright and Darren Potter have all failed to reach anything near the standards expected at a top club, and yet these were the cream of the Academy system. Then again, between 1972, when Phil Thompson broke through, and 1990, when Steve McManaman emerged, only Sammy Lee and David Fairclough made the grade, and even then, unike Gerrard, Fowler, Owen and Carragher, they were not in the very top bracket of Liverpool players. The talent just wasn't there in those years, so the Reds had to look further afield to find it; albeit not as far and wide as today's top teams need to cast their net. The sad fact is, in the '90s Liverpool spent a lot of money buying players, and had its greatest success in producing top class players via the youth team, but won only two trophies and averaged 5th in the league.

Inheritance

When comparing the managers' records, it has to be acknowledged that while some were fortunate enough to inherit majestic galleons ploughing imperiously through the waters, others took charge of punctured dinghies ailing in the open ocean.

We can all get an idea of how good certain players were over the course of their careers, but it's one thing for a manager to inherit a player freshly in his prime and at the peak of his powers, and another entirely inheriting a fading great whose best days are well behind him.

Most managers would like to be given at least five years to have a proper stab at things; often such time is seen as a luxury, but for those who have had to immediately overhaul a squad — Shankly, Souness, Evans, Houllier and Benítez — any less time usually isn't long enough. In such circumstances, a manager needs to work through the process of signing players, keeping the successes and moving on the inevitable flops (if 50% of any manager's signings are roaring successes, he's a genius); bringing through the kids, who need time to adapt, and replacing the stars who grow too old; and repeating each summer, to the point where the wheat remains and the chaff is scattered to the wind.

It's no bad thing inheriting a great player who's 34 and has a year left at the top, in that the team will have that strength to call upon over the next 12 months. But finding a replacement is clearly the new manager's problem, and a pressing one at that, given the time it takes to identify targets and negotiate deals. Clearly Kenny Dalglish, in 1985, inherited a better Ronnie Whelan than did Graeme Souness six years later, while the version Roy Evans received was 33 and well over the hill. Same man, very different version of a top player. However, while some players are washed up at 31, others, who have kept themselves fit, can bring their experience to bear — at least for two or three years. This applies mostly to thinking players, rather than those who rely on athleticism. This is true of Alan Hansen; although his knees were like a collection of loose pebbles in a sock, his experience and positional sense alone made him as invaluable at 35 as he was at 25.

There are several factors in judging the squads that formed each manager's *Inheritance*. The process applies to the squad as a whole — because a manager doesn't deal with just eleven players — and also the strength of what would probably be the strongest XI they could field, before they even think of dipping into the transfer market. (Of course, the ratings are based on individuals; as such, they do not take into account the team exceeding the sum of its parts. That becomes evident in the success or failure of the team.)

To start with, there's the *Quality* of the player. Then there is his age, and as with transfers, points are penalised for every year from 28 onwards. So while the great Billy Liddell, in the squad Shankly encountered on his first day, had a near-perfect rating due to two decades of sterling service, he was 37 years old. As such, Shankly was not inheriting a 9.90 player, but a 1.90 player; he'd be lucky if he got a season out of him.

At 28, a player is in his prime, but his transfer value is starting to depreciate; as such, every subsequent year limits the chances of cashing in and reinvesting that money, which will be part of any new manager's considerations. While there will always be exceptions, players tend to peak at around 27/28. That hasn't really changed — the game has grown far faster and more injuries occur; but improvements in diet, professionalism and fitness, and superior medical treatment balance out any differences. Once a player hits 29, it clearly creeps into the thinking regarding transfers.

Age-balance is vital to a successful side. It can be a mix of young and old, or simply eleven players in their prime, but the average age of a successful side is almost always 27/28, in keeping with the peak period of an individual. With this in mind, it's interesting to observe the first XI Kenny Dalglish bequeathed Graeme Souness. As a team, it was still very strong, averaging out at 8.03 for *Quality*. This makes sense; it wasn't as strong as the team of European Champions-elect that Bob Paisley handed over to Joe Fagan, which averaged at the high-water mark of 8.86, but they were still the reigning champions of England and still in the running for the 1991 title. But as soon as 'weighting' is added to take age into account, it drops to 5.67: the worst inherited XI in the 50-year history of this book. That damning conclusion is due to its average age of 30 — an incredible two-and-a-half years older than any other squad at the point of a managerial changeover. The other seven managers each inherited sides with an age between 25 and 27.5, while the current team also falls neatly into that range — but Souness clearly had his work cut out. So while Souness' time would prove a disaster, it wasn't quite an *unmitigated* disaster; he at least had some valid excuses. And that, to a large degree, is the purpose of this book: to look deeper into the reasons behind the success or failure of each manager, considering whether they were blessed or handicapped, and to see if their decision-making improved their fortunes or merely compounded their fate.

CONCLUSION

Above all else, the findings of the Brains Trust are there to give an indication of quality; their conclusions can only ever be opinion, and not fact. Just because Steven Gerrard marginally edges out Graeme Souness does not mean he is *definitely* better. Some felt the opposite, but the current captain's overall average was fractionally higher. Also, there is a little misty-eyed nostalgia that naturally occurs when assessing players, with some of Shankly's total rejects scoring better than those who fared just as badly decades later. Where possible this bias has been kept to a minimum, but it is of course the nature of any retrospective analysis.

Hopefully the results of the Brains Trust will prove entertaining and prompt some debate; while they can never be 100% correct, in most cases the findings should be close to the truth.

BRAINS TRUST TRUSTEES

1959 - 1974

BILL SHANKLY

"The socialism I believe in is not really politics. It is a way of living. It is humanity. I believe the only way to live and be truly successful is by collective effort with everyone working for each other and everyone helping each other and everyone having a share of the reward at the end of the day. It is the way I see football and the way I see life."

BILL SHANKLY

INTRODUCTION

It's impossible to imagine what Liverpool Football Club would now be like had Bill Shankly never arrived; his imprint remains so undeniably unique. Sleeping giants tend to awake sooner or later, but the man from Glenbuck was like a thousand alarm clocks sounding within the club's inner halls. He took a tired team and a run-down institution and made them great. He did so on a relatively tight budget, and although the club would go on to even better things in his absence, he set the ball rolling. It was as if he took a tiny sphere of impacted snow, and released it down the side of an Alpine mountain; in time it grew and grew, until it was a giant snowball that caused an avalanche.

Having lost his way a little in the middle-to-latter part of his reign — seeing his ageing team hit a wall — Shankly faced something many great managers have encountered: the need to start again and rebuild. Few managers build one great side, let alone two. But that's just what he did.

Whether or not Shankly ever stopped to consider that he was building a dynasty that would last well after his death is debatable, but there's no doubting he wanted the club to be the best during his time in charge — a 'bastion of invincibility', as he famously put it.

Situation Inherited

Overgrown, unkempt and tired: the Melwood training ground that greeted Bill Shankly in December 1959. It had been five years since the club lost its top division status — after a half-century spent continuously in the big league. He didn't need to think too deeply to see the disrepair behind the scenes as a metaphor for the club as a whole. Beyond implementing anything too fancy, it simply needed some care and attention, and the installation of a little pride. Anfield itself wasn't in much better shape. There was not even any plumbing to enable the pitch to be watered — something Shankly rectified, to the tune of £3,000.

It's a truism in football that a manager doesn't take control of a side where all is well; rare are the appointments when everything is rosy, but of course, even those exceptions bring their own problems: replacing a retiring great can be more difficult than taking over from a sacked halfwit. Calling it quits while at the top would be the situation Shankly would ultimately present to his successor, Bob Paisley. But for Shankly in 1959, the problems were rife. Liverpool, league champions as recently as 1949, were now in the old Second Division. Phil Taylor had grown tired trying to get a big club back into the top flight, and resigned four years into the job.

Players Inherited

The squad Shankly inherited was not without talent and hope for the future. Of course, its most famous name was that of the legendary Billy Liddell, but he was just a month short of his 38th birthday when Shankly took charge. Alan A'Court was a fast and tricky outside-left in his mid-20s, and Ronnie Moran, at the same age, was a strong leader from right-back. Jimmy Melia was a talented ball-player capable of scoring goals as an inside forward, and played twice for England. Up front, Dave Hickson was a brutish centre-forward who had been signed from Everton, for whom he'd scored 111 goals in 243 games. Hickson had previously played under Shankly at Huddersfield, and although he scored 38 times in 67 appearances for the Reds, his disciplinary record proved problematic. At 30, he was not one for the future — but Roger Hunt, who had started to force his way into the first team picture, clearly was. Gerry Byrne was another future England international who had already made the breakthrough, although he was transfer listed when Shankly arrived. Then there was Ian Callaghan — the 18-year-old midfielder given his debut by the new manager five months into his reign. Callaghan would be twice that age when he played his final game for the club. Players like Hunt, Byrne and Callaghan meant that the strongest First XI had an average age of just 24. Clearly there was potential for the team to develop, but of course, it needed the right leadership.

It's a myth that Shankly completely overhauled the squad almost overnight. If large squads are seen exclusively as part of the modern game, it may surprise younger readers to know that the playing staff in 1959 amounted to 40. The minimum wage of £20-a-week meant it was possible to have more players than were actually needed; unlike the present day, far fewer of the squad were actually part of the first team picture. It was a big playing staff containing a lot of dead wood. Shankly reckoned that 24 of them had to be got rid of, and within a year he had done so; but these were largely peripheral figures. Some of the older players, such as Liddell, retired, leaving a core of those Shankly inherited who would help the club regain its First Division status, and, before long, lead the charge to becoming champions of England.

Squad

Player	Quality	Age	Adj	Inheritance	Year	Age
Roger Hunt	9.50	0	0	9.50	1959	21
Ian Callaghan	9.08	0	0	9.08	1959	17
Alan A' Court	8.32	0	0	8.32	1959	25
Gerry Byrne	7.92	0	0	7.92	1959	21
Jimmy Melia	7.91	0	0	7.91	1959	21.5
Ronnie Moran	7.10	0	0	7.10	1959	25.5
James Harrower	7.06	0	0	7.06	1959	24
John Morrissey	6.92	0	0	6.92	1959	19
Alan Arnell	6.44	0	0	6.44	1959	25.5
Tommy Leishman	6.32	0	0	6.32	1959	22
Bert Slater	6.03	0	0	6.03	1959	23
Dick White	7.01	-1	0	6.01	1959	28
Robert Campbell	5.89	0	0	5.89	1959	18
Average	**6.73**			5.42		**24.4**
Dave Hickson	7.89	-3	0	4.89	1959	30
John Molyneux	6.23	-1.5	0	4.73	1959	28.5
Alan Jones	4.60	0	0	4.60	1959	19.5
Willie Carlin	4.40	0	0	4.40	1959	18.5
Reginald Blore	4.20	0	0	4.20	1959	17
John Nicholson	4.10	0	0	4.10	1959	23
Louis Bimpson	6.88	-3	0	3.88	1959	30
Fred Morris	6.11	-3	0	3.11	1959	30
Johnny Wheeler	6.85	-4	0	2.85	1959	31
Doug Rudham	6.23	-4	0	2.23	1959	33
Billy Liddell	9.90	-8.5	0	1.40	1959	37.5

First XI

Player	Quality	Age	Adj	Inheritance	Year	Age
Bert Slater	6.03	0	0	**6.03**	1959	23
Ronnie Moran	7.10	0	0	**7.10**	1959	25.5
Dick White	7.01	-1	0	**6.01**	1959	28
John Molyneux	6.23	-1.5	0	**4.73**	1959	28.5
Gerry Byrne	7.92	0	0	**7.92**	1959	21
Ian Callaghan	9.08	0	0	**9.08**	1959	17.5
Jimmy Melia	7.91	0	0	**7.91**	1959	21
Alan A' Court	8.32	0	0	**8.32**	1959	25
James Harrower	7.06	0	0	**7.06**	1959	24
Roger Hunt	9.50	0	0	**9.50**	1959	21
Dave Hickson	7.89	-3	0	**4.89**	1959	30
Average	**7.64**			**7.14**		**24**

Key: *Quality 0-10; Age = -1 point for every year from 28 onwards, eg -4 for 31 year-old, and -1 point from 30 onwards for keepers, eg -4 for 33 year-old; Adj = adjustments for players either exceptionally fit/unfit for their age, or soon to leave; Inheritance = total out of 10. Excludes players not part of first team picture.*

State of Club

Although the board promised Shankly a handsome war chest — £60,000 — in order to entice him into the role, the main reason they appointed him was his ability to work on a shoestring budget. At Huddersfield he had generated more money than he spent. The Liverpool board's mentality was strictly small-time, and frugality appealed to them. While Everton's manager Johnny Carey was spending £82,000 on three players — before receiving an interest-free loan from John Moores to further strengthen the side — Shankly found himself working on a budget that had yet to stretch to the far lower amount he'd originally been promised.

The board also began interfering in team selection. As unthinkable as this seems in the modern age, the time had not long passed when the directors of football clubs were responsible for selecting the side; in that sense, Shankly was distinctly new school — no-one from the boardroom was going to be involved in the running of *his* team. "At a football club," he once said, making his thoughts as plain as ever, "there's a holy trinity — the players, the manager and the supporters. Directors don't come into it. They are only there to sign the cheques".

John Moores, owner of the multi-million pound Littlewoods empire, was a shareholder at Anfield, but a board member across the park at Everton. It was the Toffees who were on the receiving end of his generosity from 1960 onwards. He was not allowed to sit on the board of both clubs, even if he wanted to, but he could nominate someone to sit on Liverpool's. He chose Eric Sawyer, the accountant in charge of Littlewoods' finances. It would prove to be the turning point in Shankly's time at Liverpool. Suddenly he had someone willing to loosen the purse strings and agree with his vision of investing in top-class players. If the *crème de la crème* of the the British game were not going to join a Second Division outfit, even if the club could afford them, then at least Shankly could be competitive in the transfer market for the standard of player he felt was needed: those with real quality, and who were up-and-coming. Unlike the other board members, who were stuffy and aloof, Sawyer was a man to whom Shankly could relate. Indeed, the two would share cups of tea and have two-way discussions, rather than Sawyer, as was the wont of his fellow board members, telling the manager how to run the team. Without the arrival of Sawyer, it's hard to see how Shankly would have survived, let alone thrived. The Scot was constantly talking about resigning; without the intervention of the new director, he might well have been true to his word.

It also helped that Shankly began selling players for reasonably considerable fees — raising £20,000 — while his culling of an oversized playing staff reduced the wage bill. So while he demanded more money to spend, he wasn't proving to be some reckless maverick with no appreciation of monetary matters.

In May 1961, with the help of Sawyer, Shankly took things to the next level. Ian St John was signed from Motherwell for £37,500 — more than doubling the previous club record. St John had been a target of Shankly's when at Huddersfield, and now the diminutive striker was looking for a move. Another player Shankly had coveted while in charge at Leeds Road was Ron Yeats, the giant Dundee United centre-back. Unlike St John, Yeats wasn't looking for a move, but Shankly persuaded him to swap life in Scotland for a team he mischievously described as a "First Division side"; when Yeats quibbled, the manager pointed out that they would be, with him in the team. The fee was £30,000. Shankly famously told the journalists gathered at the press conference to "Just walk around him. He's a colossus!"

Problems with the board did not end, however. In 1962, with Liverpool about to start the new campaign in the top division \ decade away, left-winger Johnny Morrisey was sold to arch-rivals Everton, against Shankly's wishes, and for just £10,000, to add insult to injury. (A year later, Morrissey was a league winner at Goodison, to rub salt in the wounds.) Shankly was irate, but having steered the club back into top flight he was not about to walk away in a huff.

As the trophies started arriving in the mid-'60s, and as Shankly continued offloading players to balance the books, the problems died down, and an uneasy truce was generally maintained.

Assistance/Backroom Staff
Unusually for a football manager, Shankly chose not to bring in his own men when he moved to Anfield from Huddersfield. Trust is a big part of

football management, and no manager can work with the feeling that someone in his direct command is not pulling in the same direction. As such, relationships built up in the early days of a manager's career become cemented, to the point where it's often actually a management *team* that is appointed. There's always the likelihood that a manager joining from outside will put the noses of those already at the club out of joint, particularly if they had harboured hopes of landing the job themselves. But Shankly was happy to work with those employed by the club when Phil Taylor retired.

It proved to be an inspired decision; the entire future of Liverpool Football Club, long after Shankly's retirement and even after his death, rested with those Shankly agreed to keep on. Bob Paisley, the former physio who would go on to win six league titles and three European Cups as manager, had just been appointed first-team trainer; meanwhile, running the reserves was Joe Fagan, who'd win the club's fourth European Cup as part of an historic treble.

Paisley acted as an important buffer, keeping problems with the players away from the manager. Shankly totally ostracised those with injuries — they were no use to him, and he wanted them fighting to be fit again — and on one occasion Paisley had to placate a young Kevin Keegan, whom the manager had called a malingerer. Paisley felt Keegan, who would later become famous for walking away from management roles when upset, was prepared to quit football on the spot. But the assistant manager dealt with the problem, without Shankly getting wind of the player's distress.

Reuben Bennett had been appointed as the head of training the year before Shankly's arrival. Bennett had played for Dundee with one of the other three Shankly brothers plying their trade in professional football, so Bill was aware of him prior to their working together. It just so happened that the two Scots hit it off brilliantly. Perhaps because he never went on to manage the club, Bennett is one of the less-heralded members of the original Boot Room. Finally, Albert Shelley was still at the club, albeit in an unofficial capacity, having been a trainer under George Kay in the 1940s. Shelley retired in 1959, at which point Paisley was promoted, but it didn't keep Shelley from turning up to help with the more menial tasks.

Clearly Shankly was taking a gamble by retaining the existing staff. It's easy with hindsight to see it as the exact opposite, given what we now know about the men at his side. But the club was underachieving when he arrived, and no-one on the staff had yet done much to prove himself, so a clean sweep could possibly have been justified. Instead he chose to keep them on and give them a chance, in the confidence that they would all move onto his wavelength; all he wanted in return was their absolute loyalty. "I don't want anyone to carry stories about anyone else," he told his new coaching staff. "If you come and tell me a story about someone else, whoever you're telling the story about won't go, the one who carries the story will go. I want everybody to be loyal to each other. We'll all get together and have that one big strength."

On the books in 1959 was 25-year-old left-back Ronnie Moran, another Boot Room legend in the making. Seven years later Moran, having lost his place in the team to Gerry Byrne, was appointed onto the coaching staff. Moran remained a player for another two years, both of which were spent in the reserves, helping the development of the younger players. In 1968 his appointment to the coaching staff became full-time, and he would remain there for another 30 years.

Then there were the men entrusted with finding future Liverpool players. Geoff Twentyman, a player who had left the club shortly after Shankly's arrival in 1959, was recruited in 1967 as chief scout. His contribution in that role cannot be overstated. In the next six years Twentyman recommended Ray Clemence, Steve Heighway, Kevin Keegan, John Toshack and Jimmy Case, all signed during Shankly's time, although Case would make his debut under Paisley. Twentyman was told to focus on the lower leagues, to spot up-and-coming young players who could acclimatise to Liverpool's methods in the reserves. Quickly spotted in these insalubrious locales was 19-year-old Ray Clemence of Scunthorpe United, and within a couple of years, two 21-year-olds — Alec Lindsay of Bury and Larry Lloyd of Bristol Rovers — were added. Twentyman was absolutely crucial in the building of Shankly's second great Liverpool team. Although Shankly almost always wanted to see those recommended to him for himself before committing to a transfer, without Twentymen recommending such talented prospects the club might never have prospered for a second time under the Scot, and the legacy could have petered out like an infertile bloodline.

One more vitally important appointment was made by Shankly. In 1968 Tom Saunders, a teacher and trainer of the Liverpool Boys team, was recruited as youth development officer — the first appointment of its kind in British football. Saunders remained in the role for almost two decades, with David Fairclough, Jimmy Case, Phil Thompson, Sammy Lee and Steve Heighway amongst those local lads who were under his command, either rising through the youth ranks or procured from local clubs as teenagers.

But the key to it all was when Shankly joined forces with Paisley — akin to John Lennon meeting Paul McCartney across the city two years earler. The best double acts operate on the same wavelength, but with different skills and attributes. They share a common ground, but one veers to the left, the other to the right. They balance each other out, and harmonise; singing different notes to make one cohesive voice.

Management Style

With an up-and-coming side that didn't have the experience, and perhaps lacked the overall quality of the established First Division teams, Liverpool needed a point of difference to compete at the highest level upon promotion; something to elevate them to the top. And the Reds had three things that gave them the edge.

For starters, Liverpool were believed to be the fittest side in the league. That instantly gave them an advantage. Phil Chisnall, the last player to make the move from Manchester United to Liverpool, described Shankly's training as 'back breaking', as opposed to Sir Matt Busby's leisurely routines at The Cliff.

Next was the style of play: pass and move. "Liverpool are the most uncomplicated side in the League," Joe Mercer, the former Aston Villa and Manchester City manager, once said. "They drive forward when they've got the ball and get behind it when they haven't." Endless five-a-sides honed technique and awareness. Keeping the ball worked the opposition, and the Reds superior fitness could have a double impact late in game — they got stronger as the opposition wilted. "Never pass to a red shirt in one direction when there are two in the other," Shankly would say. "Support the man, but look to the ball. If you lose the ball work twice as hard as the opposition to get it back." When trying to get to the heart of the simplicity inherent in Liverpool's game, he said: "Our approach was to use the ball like a baton in a relay race. You pass it to me, I pass it to him, he passes it on. It's the ball that is covering most of the ground — not the players." And when the players got into the penalty area, it remained simple: "If you are in the penalty area and aren't sure what to do with the ball, stick it in the net and we'll discuss your options afterwards."

On the whole, Shankly was the more distant, authoritarian character, with Paisley the approachable one. Shankly was very encouraging to the youngsters, but once players were in the senior side he became more standoffish, in order that no favouritism be showed.

In terms of the style of football, Liverpool were also patient; happy to contain teams and sit on slender leads, an understanding which grew in time with the lessons of European football. If no lead had been built up, the team would keep going until the death, often stealing late goals like a lot of the best teams, once the opposition is worn down. Despite the pass-and-move philosophy, which was in keeping with purist theories, they weren't regarded as a beautiful side to watch. The passing was simple but effective — find the nearest red shirt, give him the ball, move into space, get it back. There were elements of Total Football that the Dutch pioneered in the '70s, in which full-backs attacked and no-one stayed still. But the passing wasn't as elaborate or imaginative as some '60s rivals, particularly the two from Manchester. Liverpool's was an incredibly effective style of football, rather than one about aesthetic merits.

Above all else, Liverpool were driven to succeed by the man on the sidelines, for whom second place was nowhere. "In a way the worst sort of footballers become managers," Steve Heighway once remarked. "Only the fanatical would be silly enough to do it. They have to have the drive of Hitler. Our guy never lets you relax. The constant need is to win trophies. He never lets up."

Unique Methods

In these days of 'notebook managers', scribbling thoughts throughout games, it is interesting to note that Shankly himself carried a little book everywhere he went, jotting down every idea or useful piece of information he was party to. Clearly information was seen as power to the Scot. Training systems were tabulated, players' fitness levels were scrupulously monitored, and Shankly began having opponents watched — which in the very early '60s was relatively unheard of. But while he thought long and hard about the game, Shankly wasn't the expert tactician in the ranks; by general consensus that was Bob Paisley. Shankly was more of a motivator, an expert in sports' psychology, in the days before such a thing was taken too seriously.

Shankly's methods often involved building up his own players while belittling the ability of the opposition — before the game, at least. It's obviously not much of a boon for a player to get the better of an opponent who, if Shankly was to believed, wasn't far off being a one-legged alcoholic midget with leprosy — so only after the match would the true assessments come out. He famously told a young Kevin Keegan, who might otherwise have been overawed in his first encounter with the great Bobby Moore, that the West Ham skipper had bags under his eyes, was limping and also had dandruff, implying that the England captain, who was known to have a 'healthy' social life, had been out on the town again. Instantly Moore was demystified in Keegan's eyes, and Liverpool strolled to victory. But Keegan, while no longer overawed, soon knew he was up against a masterful defender in Moore, as England's World Cup-winning captain gave him his sternest test to date. "You'll never play against anyone better than him," was Shankly's post-match admission. Another famous assessment came at Old Trafford — Shankly writing off United's best trio as "one's too old, another's got a dicky knee and the other's a drunk." Privately, of course, Shankly had plenty of respect for the players in question.

In many ways Shankly was the forefather of the squad system. "We don't have eleven players here," he would often say, "we have twenty." Some players featured more prominently in Europe, while others were used more in the league; as an example, in 1964/65, Tommy Smith, then aged 19, played only 25 of the 42 league games, but all but two of those in the European Cup. Having inherited a massive squad in the days of the minimum wage, it was fair to say that most of them would not be involved at any point; their presence was almost pointless. Shankly culled the squad, but kept enough players to have a meaningful extended group to choose from. And while not all of them would be needed throughout the season, he liked to know he had strength in reserve. And that was a key thing — the reserve team, which he famously described as the second-best team on Merseyside (after Liverpool's first-team), needed to be strong. New signings — experienced senior players, at that — were consigned to the second-string, but not as punishment. The reserve team was there to provide an education: to allow players to adapt to the Liverpool way, and be brought through slowly.

Shankly was also trying to innovate in terms of diet. Without the scientific knowledge today's managers routinely call upon, he had to improvise. Having discovered that the legendary American boxer Joe Louis trained on steak, Shankly made it the mainstay of the Liverpool diet. Wherever the team travelled, the meals were always steak, chips and salad, followed by fresh fruit and cream. Players joked that they ate so much steak they became vegetarian after retiring.

Rather than flog the players ceaselessly after the summer break, the training regime was designed to ease them back to full fitness, to avoid injuries. "Some people think we're lazy, and that's fine," Shankly later said. "What's the point of tearing the players to pieces in the first few days? We never bothered with sand dunes and hills and roads. We trained on grass, where football is played." After precisely five weeks and two days of training, the players were ready to start the season in style.

It became a Liverpool tradition to not practice set-pieces. It was taken for granted that the players were intelligent enough to improvise. Tommy Smith said that they never practiced a single corner during all his years at the club. However, as often as not the team simply appeared clueless; wasting a series of set-piece deliveries. In the days before set-pieces were so seriously scrutinised with video and computer technology — and as such, before their importance grew — it was understandable that the staff focused on other areas. There is only so much time in the week to prepare for matches, and only so much energy players can expend in training. It is about finding an emphasis and prioritising, because the coaching staff cannot cover everything. 'Footballing' sides tend to practice with the ball, while teams lacking skill will focus more on set-pieces, given that they are the easiest route to a goal if individual brilliance is at a premium. Limited teams can hit balls over the defence and into the channels in order to try to force corners, at which point the giants parade forward as a rehearsed routine is put into practice. Over the years (and even now), Liverpool fans see their team as notoriously poor at scoring from corners; so much so that a fanzine called *Another Wasted Corner* was launched in 1990. A short corner was always a commonly used ploy, because the instinct of a footballing side is to get the ball and, without wasting time, pass it to feet; work the space, create angles, rather than deliver into the 'mixer'. (However, part of the belief in the Reds' failings at corners is fan perception; even now, despite some teams scoring almost 50% of their goals from set-pieces — true of Aston Villa in 2007/08 — the vast majority of situations end up coming to nothing.)

Stamina was built via the 'sweat box', a device in which players would kick and dribble the ball, continually on the move within boards assembled like the wall of a house; taking the ball from one end to the other, striking it against a board, controlling the rebound and turning to head to the other end. Initially Roger Hunt, the guinea pig, could manage only 45 seconds; soon, two minutes was no problem. The routines changed, with players having to strike the ball first time, and if they missed the board another player would come in, and the first player had to win the ball back.

The standard football exercises of the day were employed in a type of circuit training, with Paisley blowing his whistle to move them onto the next of the six stations. These included sprints, sit-ups, squats, press-ups, some work with weights, and the boxer's tool for aerobic stamina: a skipping rope. Two minutes of exercise would be followed by 30 seconds' rest. Next came football-based routines, such as heading, chipping and shooting, but always done at a high tempo without a lull in proceedings; these were not casual technical lessons where everyone stood about judging artistic merit — *bravo, Saint, lovely shot!* — but intense exercises that replicated some of the pace of an actual game, building fitness as well as honing technique. There was also 'Little Wembley', a 50-yard stretch of immaculate Melwood pitch reserved for shooting, with a boarded-up goal at the end. Drawn on the boards were a series of numbers, and these were for target practice.

But it all culminated in five-a-sides, with the final hour of training given over to various small-sided games. Groups were worked out before the start of the season, to keep the teams evenly balanced. It was football based on technique, ease on the ball, ability in tight spaces. Pass and move. While the senior players faced one another, the management team often played against youngsters, either home-grown or on trial from other clubs. This gave the old heads a chance to assess the young guns, while also helping to make them feel part of the set-up. The first-team five-a-sides were ultra-competitive. Ron Yeats described them as 'deadly'. Shankly wanted to see players giving their all, with no holding back. Fortunately, according to Yeats, there was only one serious injury from these games during his decade at the club.

This notion of fitness in small-sided matches was taken to its extreme in three-a-side encounters spread across a pitch 25 yards wide and 45 yards long. Whereas five-a-sides worked on technique in tighter areas, as well as enhancing stamina, these games prepared players for the longer sprints and wide-open areas more in keeping with a proper match. Initially players were almost instantly exhausted, but in time they managed to last longer and longer. Shankly and his assistants were promoting fitness but unlike a lot of clubs, achieved *with* the ball. Perhaps crucially, it honed the specific type of stamina needed for football.

(I am reminded of a story told to me by a player who had been at Crystal Palace in the late '70s. A top British long-distance runner was invited by Terry Venables to take a few training sessions. First on the schedule was a gruelling run. The athlete was appalled at how poorly the players coped, trailing miles in his wake. In a role reversal, he was then invited to join in with a training match. This time the players were in their element, while the athlete was choking for breath. And it is this unique kind of fitness — jogging, sprinting, turning, jumping, sprinting again, and then being kicked up in the air by some hairy-arsed thug — that Liverpool were focusing on over a decade earlier.)

"The system is based on exhaustion and recovery," Shankly explained, "building up players' stamina to enable them to produce their inherent skill and footballing ability, despite the speed of the game, from the first minute to the 90th."

After training, Shankly felt it was important that the players were given time to cool off before showering. A bus took them from Melwood to Anfield, during which time that cooling down took place. (Years later, this process would be taken to its scientific zenith by Rafa Benítez and his coaching staff, as Ryan Babel explained: "After a match we have to stand in an ice bath for five minutes. You can be affected with cramp or lactic acid, and that causes small tears in the muscles, but by applying cold water it repairs the damage immediately. In the beginning I could only suffer it for half a minute. Even during training I was thinking about the dreaded cold water, but now I'm used to it — and it certainly works as I'm more flexible and feeling a lot better the next day.")

Strengths

Arguably, Shankly is most famous for his renowned motivational powers. Perhaps it is because examples lend themselves to anecdotes, which become part of the folklore. Shankly made his men feel ten feet tall. To improve a player's psychology is to equip him for battle. But it only works for so long with limited players. The technical side of the game was not overlooked.

If a player wasn't as good as the star of a rival team, Shankly gave him a chance to believe he was. So much of success or failure in any sport is psychological. Confidence, belief, desire — they are all mental traits, not physical. Shankly tried to put his players at ease by having them share the burden. In his autobiography he detailed his instructions: "Don't think any individual is expected to win the game by himself. Don't worry that we are depending on you too much. Share out the worries. We want all of you to do something. So don't take too much on your plate or put too much in your thoughts and frighten yourself to death. You are as much responsible as the next man for winning, or losing." Shankly also introduced a new wage structure that was based around win bonuses — so players had to earn what they took home. There was an extra incentive to win; players could no longer coast their way to a living.

In 1973, Phil Thompson, who'd made his debut a year earlier, had been left out of the side to face Arsenal at home. Upset, he went to see Shankly for an explanation. The manager's response was typical of his unique gifts. "Christ, son, you say you're upset because I left you out? Son, you should be thanking me. That side on Saturday was rubbish, absolute rubbish. You should be thanking me for leaving you out. One day you'll captain this club, play for England, and maybe captain England too. [All of which came true.] And then one day you'll realise and you'll thank me for leaving you out." How could any young player not be inspired in the circumstances? Thompson, still aged just 18, probably felt like he could captain his country there and then.

A player's character was vitally important to the manager. Geoff Twentyman explained that "Shankly wanted, above all, to know about the lad's private life, what he was like, did he go out drinking every night, what his home background was, and so on. He wanted to know if the lad had the heart to play for Liverpool. Shankly wanted players who loved the game and were passionate about it. He liked players with character and commitment." Shankly had even been known to let apprentices go if they didn't scrub the floors with gusto; often, less talented kids who put their all into it were given contracts at the expense of more gifted individuals. "If I've got players on my books," Shankly said, "I search into them to see what they are, what they're made of, and I can tell you within a month what he is. Whether he needs to get bollocked or needs to get encouraged or he needs to get shifted altogether."

By getting the right characters, he could rely on leaders on the pitch. Ronnie Moran explained that it was vital that players could think for themselves: "Shanks always preached that we had eleven captains. He wanted to see players think things out and rectify things if they were going wrong. You never got shouted at for trying to change something out on the pitch. You were always taught to work things out for yourself. Mind you, if you tried something stupid and it didn't come off, we had a saying that we would 'hit you on the head with a big stick from the touchline'."

Togetherness was also crucial. "We have a family atmosphere with players that most other clubs don't have," Ron Yeats said. "It's a bit like being an orphan and then you join a good family." At times it was even more literal: Tommy Smith, who had lost his own father while in his mid-teens, saw Shankly as a father figure. Smith's mum entrusted her boy to the manager, and Shankly did not let her down.

Weaknesses

In football, strengths can easily double as weaknesses. Shankly's loyalty to his players could overstretch itself. When the time came for his favourite players to be moved on, he was hesitant. Joe Mercer explained: "They say he's tough, he's hard, he's ruthless. Rubbish. He's got a heart of gold. He loves the game, he loves the fans, he loves his players. He's like an old collie dog. He'll drive them, certainly. But bite them, never."

It was in 1970, when defeated at lowly Watford in the FA Cup, that Shankly bit the bullet and rebuilt the side that had brought him so much success. His players had achieved pretty much everything they dreamed of, winning two league titles, an FA Cup, as well as experiencing extended European runs and gaining international honours. In some cases a bit of the hunger had gone, whereas in other cases it was the legs. He hated doing it, but eventually it was taken care of. Perhaps it took longer than was ideal, but he wanted to know that the players were past their best before they were disposed of.

Unlike at Manchester United, at Liverpool there wasn't a great tradition of youth development. During Shankly's 15 years, only Chris Lawler, Ian Callaghan, Gerry Byrne, Tommy Smith and Phil Thompson were established youth graduates, and Byrne had come through the ranks before he took charge. Callaghan was more or less ready to make the breakthrough in 1959, but top-class locals were thin on the ground over the next decade and a half. Roy Evans, Phil Boersma, Doug Livermore, John McLaughlin and Steve Peplow failed to make the grade after breaking into the senior set-up, and the first three experienced far more games for Liverpool as coaches than players.

But those youngsters who did emerge were given a helping hand by the older pros, who showed a sense of community. Ian Callaghan spoke of his admiration for Ronnie Moran, who helped his development. "I don't know how I would have managed without him. It was a big step up playing in the first team, and I don't know how I would have coped without someone keeping an eye on me and helping me out of difficult situations. I soon learned that at Liverpool, we were essentially part of a team and depended on each other."

Historical Context — Strength of Rivals and League / Bête Noire

Such was the nature of the First Division in the '60s and early '70s that there were plenty of rivals pitting their wits against Shankly during his time as Liverpool manager. It's worth noting the time these rivals spent in charge of their clubs, and the honours they won. It's almost unthinkable in the modern age to see so many big clubs run by long-established managers; in the 21st Century, Alex Ferguson and Arsène Wenger are the two who stand out, but three and four decades earlier there were numerous men entrenched in their role.

First and foremost among the managerial stars of the era was Matt Busby, survivor of the Munich air disaster in 1958, and someone who, a decade later, became the first man to lead an English team to the European Cup (something Shankly felt robbed of three years earlier). Busby, a former Liverpool captain and a fellow Scot, was a friend and confidant. Busby was less of a *bête noire* and more a hugely respected older statesman — almost a father figure.

An obvious rival was Harry Catterick of neighbouring Everton. Catterick took charge at Goodison in 1961 and led the Toffees to the title two years later. The FA Cup followed in 1966, and they narrowly lost the 1968 final. In 1970 Everton romped to another league title, one point shy of a record points tally. Weirdly, a season later they were 14th, with roughly half as many points, and a decline had set in; finishing 15th in 1972, with an equally low tally. It was in this season that Catterick suffered a heart attack, and was "moved upstairs" (by the Everton board, not God) a year later.

Next up was Bertie Mee, the former Arsenal physiotherapist who, like Bob Paisley years later, became a top manager. In the case of Mee, it was not with a transition through coaching, running the reserves and being assistant manager, but straight from sponge man to main man. Mee recruited Dave Sexton and Don Howe, two coaches whose reputations would continue to prosper in the coming decade, as his assistants. Arsenal reached two successive League Cup finals in 1968 and 1969, and won their first trophy for 17 years a year later, beating Anderlecht to claim the Inter-Cities Fairs Cup. But Mee's big success came in 1971, winning the league and FA Cup — beating Shankly's Liverpool 2-1 after extra-time at Wembley to complete the double. Mee's Gunners lost the FA Cup Final a year later, and ran Liverpool close for the title in 1973, but spent the next three years in the bottom half of the table.

Another illustrious name was that of Bill Nicholson at Tottenham

Hotspur. In 1961, with Liverpool still in Division Two, Spurs became the first club of the 20th Century to win the league and FA Cup double. A year later, as Liverpool won promotion to the top flight, Spurs repeated their success at Wembley but failed to land the league title, dropping to 3rd. With Shankly now managing in the top flight for the first time, Spurs were runners-up, but also won the UEFA Cup-Winners' Cup. Finishes of 4th, 6th, 8th and 3rd followed, at which point another FA Cup was secured. Unlike a lot of the successful clubs of the time, Spurs spent most of their time comfortably in the top half of the table. In '71 they won the League Cup, in '72 they won the UEFA Cup, and in '73 the League Cup was won yet again — a pattern that was almost continued in '74, but the Londoner's were defeated by Feyenoord in the UEFA Cup Final. Just months after Shankly retired, Nicholson followed suit.

Manchester City were another force in the '60s, with Joe Mercer, the former Aston Villa manager, in charge from 1965 to 1972. Like many of the forces of the day (Shankly, Revie and Clough), Mercer led his team from the Second Division into the top flight (in his case, in 1966) before going on to win the title soon after — City were crowned English Champions in 1968. Success didn't end there: an FA Cup (1969), a League Cup (1970), and a European Cup-Winners' Cup (1970) soon followed, although those seasons were also spent in the bottom half of the division. By 1972 City were up to 4th, just a point behind champions Derby County in one of the tightest finishes ever seen. But following a dispute with his flamboyant assistant Malcolm Allison, who was looking for more power, Mercer was cast aside; Allison, known for his fedora hat, fat cigars and sheepskin coat, was all bluster but no silverware during his time as a manager.

A new kid on the block in the early '70s was Brian Clough, leading Derby County to the title in 1972; winning the league by one point from Leeds, Liverpool and Manchester City, who were separated only by goal difference. But Clough's greatest impact came after Shankly retired.

However, Shankly's *bête noire* was clearly Don Revie of Leeds United. The two, who would become friendly off the pitch, first locked horns in 1961, when Leeds, recently relegated, appointed Revie as player-manager. Shankly led Liverpool to promotion in 1962, two years before Revie repeated the feat. In 1965, Leeds instantly overtook deposed Champions Liverpool, finishing 2nd in their first season back in the top flight; although Shankly got the upper-hand in the FA Cup Final, his side defeating Revie's 2-1 after extra-time. Leeds spent their first four seasons well-placed in the First Division — 2nd, 2nd, 4th and 4th — before, in 1969, landing the title. The consistency of Revie's team could be seen over the next five seasons, with Leeds finishing 2nd, 2nd, 2nd, 3rd and, in Shankly's final season, winning another league title. Like many of the other strong teams of the day, they also had their share of cup success: losing two more FA Cup finals, but winning the trophy in 1972; winning the League Cup in 1968, for Revie's first silverware; ending up as beaten finalists in the 1973 Cup-Winners' Cup Final; plus three Fairs Cup/UEFA Cup Finals, winning in 1968 and 1971, and losing in 1967. Revie also matched Shankly's feat of taking a team to the semi-finals of the European Cup.

Don Revie had just left Leeds to become England manager when Shankly decided, out of the blue, to call it quits. His great adversary was no longer there to pit his wits against.

Pedigree/Previous Experience
Prior to taking charge at Anfield, Bill Shankly had never managed at the highest level, nor had he ever won promotion in his previous positions at Carlisle, Grimsby, Workington and Huddersfield. In some ways, the Liverpool board's lack of ambition when appointing Shankly — opting for him on account of his ability to run a tight ship, rather than steer it successfully to a desired destination — ended up being a serendipitous decision; on a par with Newton deciding to eat his lunch under an apple tree. Had the Liverpool board been truly ambitious, they would have sought out a bigger name, a man with an enviable CV. Appointing Shankly was a gamble, and after a difficult initial few years it would prove to be an inspired one. Clearly they thought they were getting a good manager, but it's unlikely they thought they were getting a great one, let alone a legend in the making.

In the early days, fans weren't convinced; unlike now, the disgruntled and the naysayers were confined to pubs, and as such their views were kept mostly private, with the exception of the letters pages in the local papers. There was a lot of inspiring talk from Shankly, but the first two seasons saw a continuation of what had gone before. However, without the endless football coverage and the instant damnations of radio phone-ins and internet fora, he was free to continue building towards a greatness that, to the fans at least, wasn't readily apparent.

Defining Moment
Two of Liverpool's greatest lessons were harshly learned in the mid-'60s, at which point the club had entered the European Cup for the first time. Getting into the top division, winning the league — these were both things Liverpool had done before. But it was the education the Reds received in the idiosyncrasies of European football — the travelling, the food, the gamesmanship, the refereeing, the style of football, and at times, the sheer outrageous talent — that would have the greatest bearing on the future of the club and help make Liverpool one of the most famous teams in the world. As so often happens, pupil became

master; in Europe, Liverpool would eventually eclipse the records of those two superpowers who had supplied that initial education.

The tutorials could not have been more contrasting. Against Inter Milan in 1965, it was a lesson about all that was wrong with the continental game — how you could find yourself playing not just a great team in a hostile arena, but the officials too. Reaching the semi-finals showed how good Liverpool could be. Until that point, managers made their reputations building up lower division clubs, and winning league titles and FA Cups — but Europe had not been taken as seriously in England. It's easy to forget how small the world seemed back in the '60s. Football fans who grew up in later decades, irrespective of their attention span during geography classes, would get to know cities all across Europe courtesy of the teams their side faced. But in the '60s there was a lot of cynicism, and no little xenophobia borne out of ignorance. The European Cup was only nine years old when Liverpool first participated. And, but for some hugely contentious refereeing, Shankly would have become the first British manager to take his team to the final, and, of course, a chance to be the first to win it. Two years later Jock Stein would lead Celtic to such a triumph, and a year after that Sir Matt Busby achieved the same feat with Manchester United. Neither faced refereeing as questionable as that seen in the San Siro against Inter Milan on May 12th 1965.

Liverpool took a 3-1 lead from Anfield over to Italy, but the actions of Spanish referee, Jose Maria Ortiz de Mendibil, would contribute to a 3-0 reverse that sent the Milanese through. Subsequent evidence of the systematic bribery of referees by Italian officials from the 1960s has only added to the legend over time, although de Mendibil, who is now deceased, never admitted any wrongdoing. Holding out in front of 90,000 passionate supporters was not going to be easy, particularly as the Reds had beaten Leeds, after extra-time, in the FA Cup Final just three days earlier — a game in which Gerry Byrne cemented folk hero status by playing for 117 minutes with a broken collarbone. The atmosphere in Milan was intense. "Purple things — smoke bombs — landed on the steps in front of us and Bob Paisley's clothes were covered in smoke," Shankly noted in his autobiography. Even with a straight referee, it was not going to be an easy night.

"We didn't seem to be getting anything in our favour," Ian St John recalled. "Not a throw-in or a free-kick. It [the referee's bias] was so obvious. We just couldn't get on the ball." Inter's first two goals were hugely contentious. The first was from an indirect free-kick that sailed straight in from Corso without another player getting a touch. The second goal was when Tommy Lawrence was bouncing the ball in his area, and Peiro hooked it away from the irate keeper to put it in the net. The legitimacy of this goal was more of a grey area; did Lawrence have the ball under control, or was it simply quick thinking by the Italian striker? If the first goal was blatantly illegal, the second was one of those decisions that can go either way. But that wasn't the end of the controversy. Ian St John, who said the referee refused to look him in the eye all night, also had a goal mysteriously disallowed. "I just remember running through and putting the ball in," the striker said. "I don't know what the infringement was supposed to have been." With an away goal from the first leg, Inter were going to progress even before Facchetti wrapped things up with a goal whose legality was never in question.

A handful of years after the game, evidence of the systematic bribery of Italian officials emerged, with many of the accusations centring around Inter Milan between 1964 and 1966. According to the testimony of a number of officials, Dezso Solti, a Hungarian fixer, worked with Inter's secretary Angelo Moratti to entice referees to corrupt the result in Inter's favour. The year before Liverpool's night of despair, Borussia Dortmund had a key man sent off in a semi-final at San Siro, while in 1966 the linesman Gyorgy Vadas claimed he was "offered enough dollars to buy five Mercedes" to help Inter overcome Real Madrid in the European Cup Final. So it stands to reason that the same efforts were being made in 1965. Perhaps most interesting is how Tommy Smith assaulted de Mendibil just after the final whistle, but the referee, who now had good cause to punish Liverpool, simply ignored it. Perhaps his sudden sheepishness was borne out of guilt, and a need to have the game end without a red card, the cause of which would need explaining. "I hoofed him in the left ankle," Smith recalled, "but he just kept on walking, just as he did when I was screaming 'el bastido' at him."

The second European lesson, 18 months later, was received from an up-and-coming Ajax side who would go on to become legends. As such, it's hard to say which lesson was the more galling to Shankly — being cheated, or being outclassed. Liverpool went to Holland in the second round of the competition and on a foggy night were on the receiving end of a 5-1 drubbing. The star of the show was 19-year-old Johan Cruyff. Shankly, in ebullient mood, felt the deficit could be overturned in the return leg at Anfield, but Cruyff, dubbed "Pythagoras in boots" by the sportswriter David Miller due to the angles he could spot, scored twice as Ajax drew 2-2. Shankly learned a lot from Dutch, which served him good stead as he began building the second great team from the late '60s onwards.

Crowning Glory

In 1973, Liverpool became the first English team to win a European trophy at the same time as landing the English league crown. But was it Shankly's greatest achievement? What about getting the team out of the old Second Division? Or winning his first league championship? Then there was beating Leeds in the 1965 FA Cup Final, at a time when it was seen as the most important day in the English football calendar. Any of these feats would be worthy of recognition, but the then-unique double of 1973 stands out, given that it was also achieved with a rebuilt side.

Legacy
While he may have regretted resigning almost as soon as the ink was dry on Bob Paisley's managerial contract, Shankly left the club in great health. Having only recently rebuilt his side, there were only two players — Callaghan and Lawler — on the wrong side of 30. The foundations were set for Paisley to take things to an even higher level. Paisley's job would have been that much harder had Shankly not had the foresight to sign so many talented young players to replace his first batch of stars.

Above all else, Shankly, aided by the men alongside him, was an innovator. Liverpool did not stick with tried and tested, and Shankly wasn't positing the methods and techniques of the 1930s. He took the club forward with foresight; unfortunately, part of the legacy of his success was that it became extremely difficult for subsequent managers to introduce new techniques, so successful had his own proven.

TRANSFERS

Transfers In
In many ways Shankly's signings were the most mixed of any Liverpool manager. There were a high number of resounding successes — the names now prominent in the club's folklore — but also, despite trophies making them easier to forget, an equal number of flops. The successes clearly obviated the need to rely on the flops. After all, it's not the signings a manager gets wrong that count when silverware is accrued, but the ones who contribute to that success. Getting the right players was a serious business to Shankly, and a lack of backing from the board tempted him to resign on a number of occasions. Ray Wilson, the England World Cup winner who made his start in the game under Shankly at Huddersfield, said "You felt Shankly was the only manager in the world who might spend his own money to buy players."

It started so inauspiciously for Shankly at Liverpool, with the transfer of Sammy Reid from Motherwell. Reid, who cost £8,000, never played a single game for the club. Kevin Lewis, signed from Sheffield United, was an altogether better signing. He cost a club record £13,000 in 1960 — 20% of the overall English transfer record at the time. Lewis, a tricky winger who was still not quite 20, went on to score 22 goals in his first 36 games, and was an important part of the team that finally escaped the second tier of English football. Once promoted to the top flight, he scored ten goals in 19 First Division matches, but was sold to Huddersfield in August 1963 for £18,000.

Two months after landing Lewis, Shankly broke the club record again to sign Gordon Milne from Preston for £16,000. Milne, the son of Shankly's friend and former colleague Jimmy, and known to the Liverpool manager since birth, went on to play almost 300 games for the Reds. As a result of his form at Anfield he was capped 14 times by England; he was in Alf Ramsey's provisional 27-man squad for the 1966 World Cup but missed the cut when it was reduced to the final 22. In 1967, at the age of 30, he was sold to Blackpool for £30,000 — a substantial fee for a player in the twilight of his career.

Promising striker Alf Arrowsmith, aged 17, cost just £1,250 from Ashton Utd in August 1960. He initially developed his scoring instincts in the reserves, netting 65 times in two seasons. By 1963/64 he had broken into the first team, and scored 15 goals in 20 league games as the Reds won their first league title for 15 years. But a serious knee injury sustained in the ensuing Charity Shield limited his effectiveness, and he started only 19 games in the next four years before being sold to Bury for £25,000 at the end of 1968. Although it didn't quite work out as anticipated after he burst onto the scene in such spectacular fashion, Arrowsmith proved to be a shrewd investment.

Having missed out on Brian Clough in 1960, a year later Shankly had the chance to bid for another striker he'd been trailing: Ian St John. The centre-forward was only 5ft 8, but had a wonderful leap and was deceptively strong, as well as being a talented technician. A fee of £37,500 was agreed with Motherwell, and then St John was on the receiving end of the 'Shankly sell'. St John was suitably convinced that the club was heading in the right direction. Originally prolific — scoring 22, 20 and 22 again in his first three seasons at Liverpool — 'Saint' would not maintain such a strike rate throughout his decade at the club, averaging only 11 over the next three campaigns and then falling well below that. Roger Hunt was the main goal threat, with St John dropping into deeper areas to create for his partner. St John, whose overall statistics were 118 goals in 425 games, left at the start of 1971, when he moved to Coventry.

The next key signing came in July. Liverpool agreed to pay Dundee Utd £30,000 for 23-year-old centre-back Ron Yeats. As with St John, Shankly had coveted Yeats in the past, hoping to sign him years earlier at Huddersfield. Yeats became the Reds' captain, and spent ten years at the heart of the defence, playing 454 games and scoring 16 goals. No-one has captained the Reds for as long as Yeats did — wearing the armband for almost a decade. In 1971 he was released, and moved to

Tranmere Rovers.

Teenager John Sealey arrived on a free transfer from Warrington in January 1962; he played just one game, three years later, and although he scored he was released in 1966. Jim Furnell, the Burnley keeper, was signed for £18,000 in February, and took over from Bert Slater as the Reds won promotion. The emergence of Tommy Lawrence shortly after would lead to Furnell being sold to Arsenal for £15,000 18 months after his arrival.

Skilful left-midfielder Willie Stevenson was purchased from Rangers for £20,000 in October. Almost 23 when he signed, Stevenson went on to play 241 games, scoring 18 goals, before the arrival of Emlyn Hughes made him surplus to requirements. Shankly sold Stevenson to Stoke, for £48,000, in 1967. He had been a key element in the successes of the '60s, and the profit only highlighted what an astute signing he was.

Shankly then went out and bought a Thomson and a Thompson. The first, Robert, was a £7,000 capture from Partick Thistle in December 1962. The full-back spent two-and-a-half years at Anfield, but only made eight appearances before being sold to Luton for £3,000. The second, Peter Thompson, proved an entirely different proposition. In August 1963 Shankly paid £37,000 for the fast and tricky Preston winger, still only 20, who had previously been courted by Juventus. Thompson played 416 games in nine years at Liverpool, scoring 54 goals. But Thompson almost sabotaged his move to Anfield. "I had a friend whose father was a coach at Preston and he told me to ask for signing-on fee," he recalled. "It was illegal at the time, but I knew a lot of players who'd got one." Shankly was not at all pleased. He turned to club chairman Tom Williams and snapped: "I don't want him. There's a flaw in his character." Thompson quickly insisted he was only joking, and Shankly withdrew his objection. "My whole body was shaking and I couldn't sign quick enough," Thompson said. "I never got a signing-on fee, but I was so relieved just to have completed the move in the end."

Reserve keeper William Molyneux arrived in November 1963 on a free transfer, but was released four years later after just one game. Then, in May 1964, Phil Chisnall became the last player Liverpool signed from Manchester United. Costing £25,000, he only played nine times and was sold to Southend for £12,000 three years later. Another 1964 signing, Geoff Strong was bought from Arsenal for £40,000. Brought in as a forward to replace the injured Arrowsmith, the 27-year-old ended up playing in virtually every outfield position in his six years at the club, ending up at left-back in his last two seasons following Gerry Byrne's retirement. Strong was sold to Coventry for £30,000 in 1970, a very substantial fee for a player aged 33.

Following a few successes, Shankly's next four signings proved a rather more mixed bag. John Ogston can be exempted, as a keeper bought as back up, costing £10,000 from Aberdeen in September 1965. Peter Wall, who cost £6,000 from Wrexham in October 1966, was a full-back who played 42 games in his four years at Anfield, before being sold to Crystal Palace for a good fee: £35,000. But Stuart Mason, signed from Wrexham at the same time, never made an appearance after his £20,000 move. David Wilson, a £20,000 purchase from Preston in February 1967, was another failure, returning to Deepdale a year later for just £4,000 at the age of 26.

But after a run of signings that never made the grade, Shankly secured one of his greatest: Emlyn Hughes. Shankly had previously bid for the teenager following his first game for Blackpool, offering £25,000 on the spot. Blackpool, then a top flight club, were not willing to sell, but a year later, in February 1967, with the Lancashire club facing relegation, they asked for £65,000 — far more than anything Liverpool had ever paid. Shankly had no doubts, and a deal was quickly struck. Hughes, just 19, had played only 28 games for Blackpool. Within weeks he was making his Liverpool debut in midfield, although he was an incredibly versatile player, going on to play at centre-back and left-back. An ebullient character, Hughes earned the nickname 'Crazy Horse' after an illegal rugby tackle on Newcastle United winger Albert Bennett. In total he'd make 665 appearances in a variety of positions, scoring 49 goals.

Having paid a club record fee for Hughes, Shankly would top it with his next purchase — albeit a far less successful one. However, the failure — Tony Hateley, who cost £96,000 in June 1967 — was followed by the arrival of another legend in the making. In a bizarre sequence, Shankly then broke the club record again, on another expensive mistake, in Alun Evans, before bringing in another of Anfield's enduring names in Alec Lindsay. His forays into the transfer market at this time were hugely mixed, but of course, the overriding factor was that the good purchases ensured success at Anfield for years to come.

Hateley did okay, and scored a more than respectable 28 goals in his 56 games, but he did not suit the Reds' style of play. A big, powerful centre-forward, he looked awkward in possession and out of place. A year later he was sold to Coventry for £80,000. But soon after signing Hateley, Shankly had moved to secure the services of Scunthorpe's young goalkeeper, Ray Clemence, for £18,000. Clemence, about to turn 20, made his debut a year later, but had to wait three years to fully displace Tommy Lawrence. Once he did, he would go on to become a Liverpool legend, registering 335 clean sheets in 665 appearances. He played an astonishing 337 consecutive games from September 1972 until March 1978. In 1981, when about to turn 33, he was sold to Spurs for £300,000 — 20% of the current English transfer record, but a far bigger fee in real terms when considering his age.

He is widely regarded as the Red's best-ever goalkeeper.

Having spent £110,000 on Alun Evans, only for the youngster to fail to live up to his potential, Shankly signed Alec Lindsay from Bury for £67,000. Arriving in March 1969 at the age of 21, Lindsay originally struggled in his left-midfield role, and even had a transfer request accepted, before finding success when moved to left-back. From there he displayed his strong attacking abilities as, in the Liverpool way, he overlapped down the flank. He played 248 times for the Reds, scoring 18 goals, before being sold to Stoke for £20,000 in 1977, at the age of 29.

Another wise investment came in the April of 1969, when Larry Lloyd, a centre-back in the mould of Ron Yeats, was bought from Bristol Rovers for £50,000. Lloyd lasted five years at the club; having lost his place to the more mobile and skilful Phil Thompson in 1974 he impetuously handed in a transfer request, and was sold to Coventry for a hefty £240,000. But Lloyd's career would undergo a remarkable renaissance years later, ending up as a double-European Champion with Nottingham Forest.

Continuing his run of successes and flops, in the spring of 1970 Shankly spent £57,000 on Jack Whitham, who failed to make the grade after moving from Sheffield Wednesday. The deal was quickly followed by the free signing of Steve Heighway from Skelmersdale, a far more inspired move. Whitham wasn't a bad player, and scored seven times in his 18 appearances, but injuries curtailed any real progress he might have made. He left for nothing four years after arriving. Heighway's story, however, could not have been more different. He made his debut later in 1970, and spent eleven years at the club, playing 475 times and registering 76 goals. An exciting winger with pace and an unusual gait that made his intentions hard to read, he was already 22 when he arrived from non-league football. Bob Paisley released him in 1981, when Heighway, by then aged 33, moved to play in America, before returning to Liverpool as head of youth development five years later.

Steve Arnold, signed from Crewe for £12,000, only made two appearances for the Reds, one of which was in a heavily 'rotated' side when Shankly made ten changes for a league game at the end of 1972/73, with two important cup fixtures still remaining. Arnold was released to Rochdale shortly after. But another signing from 1970 proved to be a resounding success: John Toshack. The big Welshman, who cost £110,000 from Cardiff, played 247 games in his seven and-a-half years at Anfield, and scored a respectable 96 goals. But it was more for how he linked with Shankly's next signing — and arguably his best — that Toshack is best remembered. Kevin Keegan cost just £33,000 from Scunthorpe in May 1971. Keegan proved nothing less than a sensation during his six years on Merseyside.

Frank Lane, signed from Tranmere for £15,000 in September 1971, was another back-up keeper. He only played twice for the club, but that was enough — on his debut he had the ignominy of safely catching a deep cross from Derby's Alan Hinton and then stepping backwards over his own goal-line. He was released in 1975. Central defender Trevor Storton, 22, was purchased from Tranmere for £25,000 in July 1972. He never made much of an impact, playing just 12 times, only five of which were in the league. In 1974 he moved to Chester for £18,000, and made 396 appearances for them in the lower divisions. Returning to players with real class, Shankly snapped up Peter Cormack from Nottingham Forest for £110,000. Recommended to Shankly by his brother Bob, who was in charge of Cormack during his days managing Hibernian, the 26-year-old was a skilful midfielder with an eye for an incisive pass. He was sold to Bristol City for £50,000 in November 1976, after 26 goals in 178 games.

In March 1973 Peter Spiring arrived from Bristol City, costing £60,000, but never playing a single game for the Reds — only twice making the bench. Spiring moved to Luton 18 months later for £70,000. Shankly then returned to the local game, as he had with Heighway, when picking up 19-year-old Jimmy Case from South Liverpool for an almost insulting £500. In 1981, after 46 goals in 279 games, Case was sold to Brighton for 7,000 times that amount. A ferocious competitor with a fierce shot, Case was one of the few players who excelled after being moved on from Anfield.

Shankly concluded his business with two more mixed signings. The first, Alan Waddle, was a 19-year-old signed from Halifax Town for £40,000 in June 1973. Waddle, the cousin of '80s England international Chris, played 22 games in his four years at Liverpool and only scored one goal — albeit a special one: the winner in a Merseyside derby. He was sold for £45,000 in 1977, and although that technically resulted in a profit, inflation in transfer fees meant otherwise. But Shankly bowed out on a high in terms of transfers — signing Ray Kennedy from Arsenal for £180,000, before swiftly resigning. At first Kennedy, bought as a bustling centre-forward, looked like another fairly expensive flop, but in time he proved to be one of the real stars of the '70s, after Bob Paisley reinvented him as a left-midfielder. Blessed with strength and stamina, as well as a cultured left foot, Kennedy scored 72 goals in just shy of 400 games for the Reds. He was sold in January 1982 for £160,000, at the age of 30; unbeknown to anyone at the time, Parkinson's Disease had started to ravage his body and had already began affecting his game; without which he may have lasted even longer at Anfield. But as it stands, he is deservedly recognised as one of the club's true legends.

Player	Quality	0.01pg	IN	OUT	VALUE	Ap	Details	
Ray Clemence	9.70	6.65	-1.6	10	**24.75**	665	18k 1967	£0.3m @33
Kevin Keegan	9.50	3.23	-1.5	10	**21.23**	323	£33k 1971	£500k 1977**
Emlyn Hughes*	9.70	6.65	-5.7	10	**20.65**	665	£65k 1967	£90k @32 '79
Steve Heighway	8.90	4.75	0	6	**19.65**	475	Free	Rel. @34
Ron Yeats	9.20	4.54	-2.2	6	**17.54**	454	£22k 1961	Rel. @34
Gordon Milne*	8.13	2.82	-2.9	9	**17.05**	282	£16k 1960	30k '67 @30
Peter Thompson	8.44	4.16	-3.2	6.5	**15.90**	416	£37k 1963	£18k @31 '74
Ian St John	9.10	4.25	-3.75	6	**15.60**	425	£37.5k 1961	Rel. '71 @33
Ray Kennedy*	9.10	3.93	-5.1	6.2	**14.13**	393	£180k 1974	£160k @30
Larry Lloyd	7.63	2.18	-3	7	**13.81**	218	£50k 1969	£245.5k 1974
Jimmy Case	8.50	2.69	-0.02	1.8	**12.97**	269	£500 1973	£265k 1981
Willie Stevenson	7.25	2.41	-1.7	4.2	**12.16**	241	£20k 1962	£48k 1967
Shankly Average 6.90			**-2.92**		**10.74**			
John Toshack	8.70	2.47	-5.5	4	**9.67**	247	£110k 1970	Free @29 '78
Geoff Strong	7.33	2.01	-3.5	3	**8.84**	201	£40k 1964	£29.5k@32 '70
Alf Arrowsmith	6.20	0.56	-0.2	1.7	**8.26**	56	£1.2k 1960	£25k 1968
Alec Lindsay	8.11	2.48	-4	1.4	**7.99**	248	£67k 1969	£25k @29 '77
All Managers' Average					**7.92**			
Peter Cormack	7.80	1.78	-4.9	2.8	**7.48**	178	£110k 1972	£50k @30 '76
James Furnell	5.67	0.28	-1.6	1.3	**5.65**	28	£18k 1962	£15k 1963
Kevin Lewis*	6.04	0.82	-3.2	1.2	**4.86**	82	£13k 1960	£18k 1963
Alun Evans	6.88	1.11	-6.7	3.2	**4.49**	111	£100k 1968	£72k 1972
Tony Hateley	6.25	0.56	-8.3	5.3	**3.81**	56	£96k 1967	£80k 1968
Peter Wall	4.20	0.42	-2.6	1.5	**3.52**	42	£26k '66 Sw.	£30k 1970
Robert Thomson	3.80	0.08	-0.6	0.2	**3.48**	8	£7k 1962	£3k 1965
Alan Waddle	3.75	0.2	-1.8	1.3	**3.45**	22	£40k 1973	£45k 1977
Trevor Storton	3.60	0.12	-1.1	0.5	**3.12**	12	£25k 1972	£18k 1974
Phil Chisnall	3.75	0.09	-2.2	1	**2.64**	9	£25k 1964	£12k 1967
Jack Whitham	4.83	0.18	-2.9	0	**2.11**	18	£57k 1970	Rel. 1974
David Wilson	1.00	0.1	-2	0.5	**-0.40**	1	£20k 1967	£4k 1968

Key: *Quality 0-10; pg = 0.01 per game; IN = fee paid relative to transfer record, 5 being 50%, 10 being 100%, figure expressed as negative, with weighting added to players over 28; OUT = fee player sold for/current transfer value/longevity in first-team, expressed as positive; FGV = future game value;* **VALUE** *= Value For Money; Ap = Appearances; Details lists cost and year, plus sale or retirement information. Inexpensive and youth signings who never featured for first team and reserve keepers excluded. * Club record fee ** English record fee*

Transfer Masterstroke

Ian St John? Ron Yeats? Ray Clemence? Emlyn Hughes? Steve Heighway? Ray Kennedy? A case can be made for all of the aforementioned when it comes to Shankly's best signing. But given the cost, where he was found, the impact he made, and how far he progressed — not to mention the fee he eventually left for — it has to be Kevin Keegan. Recommended to Shankly by Andy Beattie, a former colleague at Preston, Keegan was playing at lowly Scunthorpe United. Shankly sent chief scout Geoff Twentyman to check him out. Twentyman liked what he saw, and wrote up a positive report on the player. Incredibly, Shankly never even went to watch Keegan; as soon as Preston bid £25,000 he knew it was time to make a move. In May 1971 Liverpool agreed to pay £33,000 for the youngster, who had recently turned 20. Keegan was taken to the FA Cup Final against Arsenal that month, purely as a spectator; Shankly was instantly impressed with how hard Keegan took defeat — he'd only been at the club a matter of days and already he was taking it personally. Having impressed in the reserves, he made his first team debut in August 1971, starting against Nottingham Forest; within twelve minutes he'd scored the game's opening goal. He went on to score exactly 100 goals in his 323 games for the Reds. An English record transfer fee of £500,000 saw him move to Hamburg in 1977.

Expensive Folly

Alun Evans appeared to have it all when he signed for Liverpool in 1968 at the age of 19. He cost a massive £110,000 — an English record for a teenager — and started off brightly, scoring on his debut against Leicester City, a game Liverpool won 4-0, with all the goals scored in the opening 12 minutes. Evans scored six more times in a total of 33 league appearances that season. But he didn't maintain that promising start, and was never the same player after being attacked with a broken glass in a nightclub in 1971, an incident that left him facially scarred.

A year later Aston Villa paid Liverpool £72,000 for Evans, who was still only 23. Never a total failure at Anfield — he scored 33 goals in 111 appearances — he failed to reach the heights expected of him, and given transfer fee inflation, was sold for a significant loss.

One Who Got Away

Shankly's first thought when it came to strengthening Liverpool was to go back to Huddersfield for his teenage prodigy, Denis Law. The striker, about to turn 20, was not only out of Liverpool's price range but was also destined for a First Division club — not one languishing in the second tier of English football. Shankly enquired, but the Reds would only have been able to stretch to £20,000; a couple of months later, Law was sold to Manchester City for £55,000, a new English transfer record.

Another early target was the Leeds United defender, Jack Charlton. The tall centre-back — the younger brother of England and Manchester United starlet Bobby — was a tough, no-nonsense character with an eye for goal. (While Bobby made his name as a goalscorer, Jack registered almost 100 league goals, virtually half the total of his more illustrious and attack-minded sibling.) Shankly made two approaches for Charlton, and on the second occasion he felt he could get his man following Leeds' relegation; but the Liverpool board would not meet the asking price, refusing to go above £18,000, when the fee quoted was almost double that. Five years later Charlton, who remained at Leeds for his entire playing career, became an England international and was part of the World Cup-winning side. Fortunately, Shankly had by that time found an imposing centre-back in the form of the 'colossal' Ron Yeats.

Brian Clough, who eventually moved from Middlesborough to Sunderland for £45,000, was a striker Shankly was extremely keen on landing in his first year at Liverpool. Unfortunately Clough, whose career statistics were quite staggering — 197 goals in 213 league games for Boro — was well beyond Shankly's budget. Clough went on to score 54 goals in 61 games for Sunderland, but his career was effectively ended at the age of 27 when he ruptured his cruciate ligament; his return, aged 29, lasted just three games. Had he joined Liverpool, that particular collision would not have taken place; and had he avoided a similar injury, he wouldn't have taken up management at such a young age. And had he not been an established manager by the age of 30, it's unlikely he would have been making life tough for Bob Paisley's Liverpool a decade and a half later. So stumping up £45,000 might have been a ridiculously good bit of business! Of course, neither party could have any great regrets, given the way history panned out for both Liverpool and Clough.

In March 1967 Shankly was desperate to land Preston's Howard Kendall. Instead, Kendall was sold to Everton for £80,000 — the Deepdale club were keen to not sell a third talent to the Reds following on from Peter Thompson and Gordon Milne. Shortly after, Shankly inquired about Francis Lee, a slightly rotund 23-year-old forward at Bolton. "I recommended Francis Lee to Bill in my first week at the club," explained Geoff Twentyman. "I'd seen him play and thought, here's a great one for the future." Two months later, in October, he was sold to Manchester City for £60,000, where his reputation grew, along with his waistline. By the start of the '70s, Shankly had his heart set on Peter Osgood, the Chelsea striker. He offered £100,000, and when it was rejected, returned with a massive offer of £150,000. Again he was waved away, and Shankly left it at that. Four years later Osgood, then aged 27, joined Southampton for £275,000.

Frank Worthington was another major missed target, this time in the most comical of circumstances. Worthington, a 23-year-old maverick talent making waves at Shankly's old club Huddersfield, was all set to move to Anfield for £150,000 — a fee that would have made him the third most expensive striker in Britain. With the deal agreed, Liverpool had to wait to complete the formalities due to Worthington's presence on an England U23 trip. Peter Robinson met Worthington at Heathrow and took him to a nearby hotel to meet Shankly. Worthington liked what he heard, and agreed terms. The next day, back at Anfield, the contract was signed. All that remained was the medical — which he promptly failed due to high blood pressure. Worthington was known to like the high life, and was already developing a reputation as a womaniser. But his father had recently died, and it had been a stressful time for the young man. Shankly, concerned for the player's well-being, sent Worthington on a week's holiday to Majorca, to rest and reduce his stress levels. Despite dizzy spells and passing out in his hotel room while in Spain, rather than rest, Worthington was out enjoying the night life. Upon his return, Shankly could barely believe it: Worthington's blood pressure was even higher. Worthington promptly moved to Leicester City, but lacked focus throughout the rest of his career. Hindsight suggests he wasn't what Liverpool needed, as the Reds prospered without a player who was failing to live up to his enormous potential, but maybe Liverpool could have given him the discipline he needed.

Celtic's attacking midfielder Lou Macari, 24, was another one of those deals that was struck, only to fall through at the 11th hour. A £200,000 move had been agreed with the Scottish giants in January 1973, and Macari was invited down to Anfield, where he was guest of honour for an FA Cup game. However, he dallied over signing, and Manchester United came in and offered him more money. He promptly signed for them, and four months later they were relegated — while Liverpool won the league. "He couldn't play anyway. I only wanted him for the reserve team," Shankly told his players.

But there was one far more special player, who, like Macari, had Celtic connections but slipped through Shankly's grasp: one Kenneth Mathieson Dalglish. It was 1966, and Dalglish was a 15-year-old schoolboy arriving at Anfield for a trial. He played one game, for the B team against Southport Reserves in the Lancashire League. Liverpool won 1-0, but no further interest was expressed by the club. Years later, when Shankly saw the youngster play for Celtic, for whom he'd signed in 1967, he was livid, blaming his own club's scouts for letting such a great player slip through the net. He claimed he had no idea the player had been at Liverpool for a trial. But in his autobiography, Dalglish claimed that Shankly and Reuben Bennett had given him a lift back to the YMCA where he was staying after the match. Thankfully, Bob Paisley went out to remedy the situation eleven years later, but for an English record transfer fee. It cost a small fortune, but it all worked out fine in the end.

Budget — Historical Context

Manchester United obviously had to rebuild after the Munich air crash in February 1958, so it's a little unfair to be too critical of their spending during Shankly's early years. Of course, in the same period, Liverpool's team also needed rebuilding, albeit for very different reasons. Of the eight who perished on the German runway, six — Duncan Edwards, Tommy Taylor, Liam Whelan, Eddie Colman, Roger Byrne and David Pegg — were key players, while Jackie Blanchflower survived but never played again. Immediately after the crash, Matt Busby bought Ernie Taylor (£8,000), Stan Crowther (£18,000) and Albert Quixall (£45,000), but several important players, including Bobby Charlton, Bill Foulkes, Harry Gregg and Dennis Viollet were still part of the team, having survived the disaster. Johnny Giles made his debut in the immediate aftermath.

Between December 1959, when Shankly took charge of Liverpool, and 1964, when the Reds were crowned Champions, United signed the following players: Maurice Setters (£30,000), Tony Dunne (£5,000), Noel Cantwell (£29,500), David Herd (£35,000), Denis Law (£115,000), Pat Crerand (£56,000), Graham Moore (£35,000), John Connelly (£60,000) and Pat Dunne (£10,500) — a total of £376,000. In that same period, Liverpool paid out £196,750 — just over half as much. However, the United team that won the 1968 European Cup was comprised largely of home-grown talents; shorn of injured record-signing Denis Law, it cost on average only 10% of the English transfer record. As happened at a number of clubs over the following decades, success came not at the time of spending big, but a few years after, when promising young players came through the ranks.

The Leeds United that overtook Liverpool in the late '60s was another comprised mostly of youth team graduates. Of the team that won the 1970 FA Cup, Gary Sprake, Paul Madeley, Terry Cooper, Billy Bremner, Jack Charlton, Norman Hunter, Peter Lorimer and Eddie Gray all started out at the club. Leeds had paid £37,500 for Manchester United's Johnny Giles in 1963, and towards the end of the decade their two strikers — Mick Jones and Allan Clarke — had cost a whopping £100,000 and £165,000 respectively. But the average was still only 21.4% of the English record — even though they themselves set that high-water mark in 1968 when snaffling 'Sniffer' Clarke.

The Liverpool side that beat Leeds in the 1965 FA Cup Final, and which was behind the league successes either side — Lawrence, Lawler, Byrne, Strong, Yeats, Stevenson, Callaghan, Hunt, St. John, Smith and Thompson — averaged out at just 13% of the English record.

RECORD

League Championships: 1963-64, 1965-66, 1972-73
FA Cup: 1965, 1974.
UEFA Cup 1973.
Division Two Championship: 1961-62.

	P	W	D	L	F	A	%
Overall	**783**	**407**	**198**	**178**	**1307**	**766**	**51.98%**
League	609	319	152	138	1034	622	52.38%
FA Cup	75	40	22	13	103	50	53.33%
League Cup	30	13	9	8	51	35	43.33%
Europe	65	34	13	18	114	54	52.31%

CONCLUSION

Whether or not Shankly was the best Liverpool manager will always be open to debate and conjecture. But there can be no doubting that he was the *most important*. It's like the first goal in a 3-0 victory — it needs to be scored before the others can follow. The second adds breathing space, and the third kills off the opposition's hope of a recovery. But the game is shaped by that first goal.

Or, to use an obvious metaphor, a house cannot be built until firm foundations are laid. If subsequent managers added extra storeys and extensions, they nonetheless all relied on the strength that underpinned it all. And that entire base was courtesy of the work undertaken by Shankly, as he changed the entire culture of the club.

Following his shock retirement in 1974, Shankly felt somewhat ostracised by the club. In later years he had to buy tickets to away games, and claims he wasn't treated with the respect he felt he deserved. A testimonial took place in 1975, and that netted him £25,000 as 40,000 fans flocked to Anfield to say their thanks. In many ways the club was moving on, just as it did when players left. But it clearly hurt the man who had done so much to rouse the sleeping giant. Six weeks after retiring he knew he'd made a terrible mistake; but by then the club was moving on without him. He asked John Smith if he could return, after his short break had left him feeling refreshed — not to mention lost, without the daily routine — but it was now Bob Paisley's team. He loved football with an incredible passion, and missed it terribly. "If there wasn't football at Liverpool he'd go to Everton," said Tommy Smith. "If there wasn't football at Everton he'd go to Manchester. If there wasn't football at Manchester he'd go to Newcastle. If there was nothing on he'd go to the local park and watch two kids kicking a ball. If there were no games on he'd organise one."

Shankly's death, in September 1981, was felt deeply on Merseyside. Aged 68, and having looked after himself fastidiously, he succumbed to a serious heart attack, while in hospital recovering from a minor one. The news reduced Paisley, Fagan and Moran to tears, and training was cancelled. Across the city, flags flew at half-mast. It was as if royalty had passed away. He loved Liverpool, and the fans he made so happy for so long, loved him in return.

Perhaps it's best to use the great man's own words to sum up his time at the club. "What I achieved at Anfield," he once said, "I did for those fans. Together we turned Liverpool into one huge family, something alive and vibrant and warm and successful."

"Of course I didn't take my wife to see Rochdale as an anniversary present, it was her birthday. Would I have got married in the football season? Anyway, it was Rochdale reserves."

BILL SHANKLY

1974 - 1983

BOB PAISLEY

"One of the things I keep reminding players is that when you're in a fog, you must stick together. Then you don't get lost. If there's a secret about Liverpool, that's it."

BOB PAISLEY

INTRODUCTION

In debates about who is the greatest-ever manager in British football, there is often a grave omission. Names routinely mentioned are those of Bill Shankly, Jock Stein, Brian Clough, Matt Busby and Alex Ferguson. In years to come, perhaps Arsène Wenger will warrant inclusion. But too often the name of the most successful is absent: Bob Paisley, a man who won three European Cups and, in the year after his retirement, his successor, Joe Fagan, with what was pretty much still Paisley's team, won a fourth. In nine years, Paisley also won the league six times — fewer than Alex Ferguson, but at a far more prolific rate. Tommy Docherty, the former Chelsea and Manchester United manager, once said: "It annoys me when they talk about the great managers and he never gets a mention. He was the best of the lot."

The problem in terms of perception is that Paisley inherited a team riding the crest of a wave. Also, unlike Clough, who'd succeeded at Derby, and Ferguson, who made his name at Aberdeen, Paisley hadn't had success at another club first, so couldn't point to that experience. And unlike pretty much every name mentioned, Paisley didn't build up a club from a position of relative failure. Of course, he was still an integral part of the initial Liverpool revolution. And while he didn't build Liverpool up from scratch, he definitely took a team he'd already helped fashion to a whole new level.

Then there was the fact that he didn't talk a good game — not to the press, at least. He didn't have the bullish bravado of Shankly, nor the style and swagger of a man like Malcolm Allison, whose style masked a lack of great substance. It says a lot about the man that Paisley turned up to sign Mark Lawrenson in 1981 dressed in cardigan and slippers.

Situation Inherited

Bob Paisley was a reluctant manager, telling his players that he only took the job under duress, and that it would only be a temporary appointment. He had grown used to Shankly threatening to walk away, but never doing so. So when the Scot actually did, the shock was immense. Peter Robinson said it was definitely "crisis time when Bill left. It was a bombshell and Bob was very reluctant to take the position."

When Shankly did finally walk away, Paisley was left wondering why his former boss chose that moment to quit. Did he have doubts about rebuilding his side yet again, as older players like Tommy Smith, Chris Lawler and Ian Callaghan reached the latter stages of their careers? Or was it that he wanted to go out at the top? On the face of it there was no logical reason in relation to the team itself; it was clearly in great shape and on the rise. And only two players, Lawler and Callaghan, were in their 30s.

Shankly told Smith and Robinson that he wanted Paisley to have the job, and Paisley wanted Shankly to keep the job — the best position in football at the time, and incredibly, like a hot potato, neither man wanted it, albeit for very different reasons. Shankly, now 60, was tired, and in need of a break from the routine after over 40 years in the game; Paisley, meanwhile, didn't see himself as a natural leader or someone who, like the silver-tongued Scot, could liase effortlessly with the media. And at 55, Paisley was hardly a young man.

Having reluctantly agreed to take the job, Paisley wanted to quit some weeks later, albeit without his resignation becoming public knowledge. He was being hounded by two journalists, who were fiercely critical of him, and was finding the extra administration work that went with the role a struggle. What Peter Robinson saw as the club's 'inner cabinet' — John Smith, Tom Saunders and Robinson himself — came together to persuade him to reconsider. Robinson dealt with the pressmen and Saunders was asked to take care of the admin.

As assistant manager to Bill Shankly, Paisley had a direct involvement in the signing and development of the players he would end up inheriting in 1974. While not the greatest team in the Reds' history, the side was in good health when Shanks stepped down. After seven years without the league title, the club had landed its 8th championship in 1973 along with the UEFA Cup, and a year later, in Shanks' swan song, beat Newcastle 3-0 at Wembley to land only its 2nd FA Cup. That season Liverpool finished runners-up to Leeds, who ran up 62 points, with Shankly's men five points behind. But the strength of that team could be seen in the fact that no other side finished with more than 48 points, and indeed, 12 clubs had tallies in the 40s. After seven years without a trophy, this was a rebuilt team that was very much on the up when the changeover occurred.

The jewel in Paisley's inheritance was Kevin Keegan, who would go on to become double European Footballer of the Year at Hamburg after helping Liverpool to the club's first European Cup. Keegan would be the first cherished player the club would lose against its will, and as such, presented a challenge to Paisley that his predecessor hadn't faced. In 1976 Real Madrid had been willing to pay £650,000 for Keegan, but he wanted to stay one further year — an inspired decision, as it culminated in the league/European Cup double. The fee Hamburg handed over was £150,000 short of what the Spaniards had been willing to pay, but by then Liverpool had achieved something far more valuable. And £500,000 still represented an English record.

Other players of seriously notable calibre were also in the squad in the summer of 1974: Ray Clemence, Emlyn Hughes and Phil Thompson were extremely well-respected England internationals with a good few years ahead of them, while Ian Callaghan, Tommy Smith, John Toshack, Alec Lindsay, Steve Heighway, Chris Lawler and Peter Cormack were top-class club-level players and, in some cases, fine players on the international scene. Other members of the squad included future Boot Room boy and manager, Roy Evans, and the man who would coach under Graeme Souness, Phil Boersma. Ray Kennedy, signed for Liverpool on the day Shankly resigned, proved a fitting parting gift. It would take him a while to make his mark at Liverpool, but he was another important part of Paisley's inheritance.

Paisley, already doubted by many because of his nature, faced a baptism of fire. In the Charity Shield — a game for which he picked the team but had yet to be officially named manager — Kevin Keegan exchanged punches with Leeds United's Billy Bremner (in the days when 'raising your hands' meant lamping someone good and proper rather than a tender touch of the cheek) and both received red cards. The two men threw off their shirts as they walked off the pitch; in what now seems an incredibly harsh punishment (and even did in more conservative days, before footballers baring their pecs and abs was the norm), Keegan, on top of a three game ban for fighting, received a further *eight* game ban for removing his shirt and thus bringing the game into disrepute. It's a bit like a man on trial getting 15 years for murder and an additional 37 years for contempt of court. So not only was Paisley replacing the greatest manager in the club's history, he was hamstrung by the absence of its best player for the first two months of the season.

Players Inherited
Squad

Player	Quality	Age	Adj	Inheritance	Year	Age
Emlyn Hughes	9.70	0	0	9.70	1974	27
Ray Clemence	9.70	0	0	9.70	1974	26
Kevin Keegan	9.50	0	0	9.50	1974	23
Ray Kennedy	9.10	0	0	9.10	1974	23
Phil Thompson	9.07	0	0	9.07	1974	20
Steve Heighway	8.90	0	0	8.90	1974	26.5
John Toshack	8.70	0	0	8.70	1974	25
Jimmy Case	8.50	0	0	8.50	1974	20
Alec Lindsay	8.11	0	0	8.11	1974	26
Larry Lloyd	7.63	0	0	7.63	1974	25.5
Average	**8.00**			**7.25**		**27.1**
Brian Hall	7.18	0	0	7.18	1974	27.5
Tommy Smith	9.08	-2	0	7.08	1974	29
Peter Cormack	7.80	-1	0	6.80	1974	28
Ian Callaghan	9.08	-5	2	6.08	1974	32
Phil Boersma	5.99	0	0	5.99	1974	25
Chris Lawler	8.64	-4.5	0	4.14	1974	31.5
Alan Waddle	3.75	0	0	3.75	1974	20
Trevor Storton	3.60	0	0	3.60	1974	24.5

First XI

Player	Quality	Age	Adj	Inheritance	Year	Age
Ray Clemence	9.70	0	0	9.70	1974	26
Alec Lindsay	8.11	0	0	8.11	1974	26
Emlyn Hughes	9.70	0	0	9.70	1974	27
Phil Thompson	9.07	0	0	9.07	1974	20
Tommy Smith	9.08	-2	0	7.08	1974	29
Brian Hall	7.18	0	0	7.18	1974	27.5
Peter Cormack	7.80	-1	0	6.80	1974	28
Steve Heighway	8.90	0	0	8.90	1974	26.5
Ian Callaghan	9.08	-5	2	6.08	1974	32
John Toshack	8.70	0	0	8.70	1974	25
Kevin Keegan	9.50	0	0	9.50	1974	23
Average	**8.80**			**8.26**		**26.4**

Key: *Quality 0-10; Age = -1 point for every year from 28 onwards, eg -4 for 31 year-old, and -1 point from 30 onwards for keepers, eg -4 for 33 year-old; Adj = adjustments for players either exceptionally fit/unfit for their age, or soon to leave; Inheritance = total out of 10. Excludes players not part of first team picture.*

State of Club

John Smith (later to be knighted for his services to football) had only recently taken charge of Liverpool. Appointed in 1973, the man known as the 'dapper chairman' was a major influence on the club over the next 17 years, until his retirement in 1990. His 17 seasons coincided with eleven league titles and four European Cups.

Despite his general excellence, Smith did incur Paisley's wrath early on in their relationship as chairman/manager. Smith had just spoken to the local press about the current playing staff and potential transfer targets, and Paisley was furious. He made it perfectly clear that any further such disclosures would lead to his swift resignation. Smith apologised, and an important marker had been laid down by the new manager.

Peter Robinson, who would later be the chief executive and vice chairman, was the club's general secretary. Robinson would go on to make his name as one of the game's great administrators; it may seem like a contradiction in terms, as fans only really remember players and managers, but Robinson achieved an almost legendary status among those men who facilitate what happens on the pitch without themselves ever getting close to it. It's clear that you need vision not just on the pitch but behind the scenes, and the partnership of Robinson and Smith was the Dalglish/Rush of the administration world.

Assistance/Backroom Staff

Continuity was the watchword when Paisley was appointed manager in 1974. Nothing really changed behind the scenes; there was just a natural evolution. Paisley had played a large part in what Shankly had done, so he wasn't going to dismantle it on the spot.

Joe Fagan became assistant-manager, and Reuben Bennett remained as part of the Boot Room until the late '70s. Following Ronnie Moran's appointment onto the coaching staff on a full-time basis in 1968, Bennett's role changed from head of training, with him now working under the broad title of 'special duties'. One of Shankly's final acts as Liverpool manager was to advise the 25-year-old Roy Evans to consider a future in coaching. Bob Paisley was also keen on the idea. He told Evans that although he was steady enough, he was never going to be a regular in the first team — and as such, he should look to the future and concentrate on coaching. Evans was reluctant to hang up his boots, as would be the case for most players in their mid-20s. Indeed, almost all, when faced with the same situation, would have sought to continue playing in the lower divisions. But clearly Evans had something about him in the way he thought about the game, and decided it was more prudent to join the Boot Room. And it was a decision that was justified, as he played an important role behind the scenes for the next 20 years, and then enjoyed four seasons as the club's manager.

Tom Saunders continued to spy for Liverpool in Europe, making dossiers on unknown opponents from across the region, as well as working as the club's youth development officer. Saunders brought Frank Skelly into the Liverpool set-up in 1973, to work as a scout; Skelly discovered Bruce Grobbelaar, who played for Crewe Alexandra, while on loan from Vancouver Whitecaps. But Geoff Twentyman, the chief scout, was perhaps the most important person at the club after the manager. Paisley's trust in Twentyman was implicit. Paisley agreed to pay £300,000 — a lot of money at the time — for scrawny Welsh teenager Ian Rush, without having ever seen the striker play; just as Shankly had never watched Kevin Keegan. Twentyman was the scout with the golden touch, and that continued throughout Paisley's tenure. He discovered Phil Neal at Northampton Town and Alan Hansen at Partick Thistle — although the latter was a player who had once been on a four-day trial with the Reds as a 15-year-old. At that time, Hansen was more interested in golf, although he'd come to see football as his future career. Upon Twentyman's recommendation in 1977, he was finally brought to the club.

Management Style

Paisley was man of few words, and those he did utter were invariably mumbled and garbled. Thingamajiggy, whajamacallit, gubbins and doins. The players nicknamed him 'Dougie Doins', such was his inability to remember the names of opposition players or to speak particularly coherently.

If at times he struggled to choose the right words, he did at least carefully consider what his intended meaning was. In the build up to games, he was famed for giving the opposition what he called a 'bit of toffee' — the act of flattering them, so that they perhaps had an inflated opinion of themselves. As opposed to denigration, it gave them nothing to rail against. 'Toffee' was designed to encourage complacency, not a thirst for revenge. The most famous instance was a young and up-and-coming Gordon Strachan, who'd been playing very well for Aberdeen, who Liverpool were due to meet in the European Cup. Paisley praised him to the hilt. The danger is always that it can inspire such an opponent; but, as planned, the player wilted under the attention, perhaps even believing his own hype.

Not noted as a motivator, Paisley was clever enough to get the best out of his men. His treatment of the young Ian Rush highlights how he goaded a player to respond positively. Rush had played a handful of games, but had yet to score. "All you ever want to do is to lay the ball off all the time. You're afraid to take responsibility on your own shoulders," Paisley told him. Rush grew irritated. He barked back that he thought it was about retaining possession at Liverpool. "Your trouble is that you're frightened to think for yourself," Paisley told him. "As a centre forward, your main job in the team is to score goals. But you haven't scored a single goal for us yet. That's why you're not playing." He told Rush that he needed to adopt a more selfish attitude, at the right time and place — with the place being the penalty area and the time when the ball was at his feet. The row continued, until Rush, arguing back that he could score goals, yelled at Paisley "You can stick your club!" before storming out of his office, convinced he'd just put himself on the transfer list. Just as the door was closing, Paisley said, "We bought you to score goals for us. Why don't you go out there and prove you can do that?"

From a tense situation, with a promising young striker wanting out of the club, Paisley had kept his cool and, rather than consigning the angry young man to a swift exit, had set a fire burning within. If Rush really wanted to leave, he could, but Paisley waited to see a positive reaction first. It proved instant: Rush scored six goals in his next five reserve games, and as a late sub against Finnish part-timers Oulun Palloseura he finally registered his first Liverpool goal: a simple tap-in, but it was a start. Rush began the next match, against Exeter in the League Cup, and scored two more, deciding that even in the company of world-class stars he was going to be selfish if the situation dictated. Having scored three goals against inferior opposition, Rush was retained in the starting line-up against Leeds, and this time responded with his first league goals: a brace, fired past John Lukic, the keeper who would be in Arsenal's goal when they won the league title at Anfield eight years later. Rush, who had set his heart on a move to Crystal Palace following his row with the manager, was now a fully-fledged top-flight goalscorer. And from that moment, he never looked back. The wily old manager had roused the wiry young striker into releasing his full fury on First Division defences. For a man not noted as a motivator, it was a canny piece of work.

Unique Methods

One of the greatest lessons Paisley learned was as Shankly's assistant in the Scot's final season in charge; a lesson that helped the Reds go on to conquer Europe. Red Star Belgrade had beaten the Reds 2-1 in Yugoslavia, but Shankly and Paisley were obviously confident going into the second leg with Chris Lawler's away goal in the bag. However, despite Lawler scoring again, Liverpool were beaten 2-1 for the second time, as the Yugoslavs sat back and counter-attacked. Shankly praised Red Star's ability, but said Liverpool fans would never pay to watch football like it. However, privately it prompted the Boot Room into a stern look at how football was changing. The more patient continental approach seemed the way forward. Also, after a decade with Tommy Smith and Ron Yeats as brutish stoppers, and with Larry Lloyd a like-for-like replacement, the Boot Room concluded that the position needed someone more technically adept, able to bring the ball out of defence and start attacks, rather than just repel them. Circumstance intervened. With Lloyd injured, Phil Thompson, originally a midfielder, moved back to fill in. Smith moved to right-back and Emlyn Hughes partnered Thompson at the heart of the defence. Partly by design, partly by fortune, the new formula was hit upon.

Shankly later explained the change that took place from 1973 onwards. "We realised at Liverpool that you can't score a goal every time you get the ball. And we learned this from Europe, from the Latin people. When they play the ball from the back they play in little groups. The pattern of the opposition changes as they change. This leaves room for players like Ray Kennedy and Terry McDermott, who both played for Liverpool after I left, to sneak in for the final pass. So it's cat and mouse for a while waiting for an opening to appear before the final ball is let loose. It's simple and it's effective ... It's also taken the spectators time to adjust to it." For his part, Paisley noted that "We realised it was no use winning the ball if you finished up on your backside. The top Europeans showed us how to break out of defence effectively. The pace of their movement was dictated by their first pass. We had to learn how to be patient like that and think about the next two or three moves when we had the ball."

The European experiences of the 1960s certainly helped form the way the club treated continental football. "Travel, and its effects, is the most underrated part of the game," Paisley recalled. "When English clubs first competed in Europe they went on their holidays. They were excited about going to exotic places and used to spend almost all week away. We cut it down to spending as little time as possible in the country — as late as we could get in and as soon as we could get out. That was our philosophy. We'd train until the last possible moment at home before starting our journey, because what training we did abroad was only going to be a light session. We'd take our own water, too. That's not to say the water was tampered with abroad. But it is different and you never know how people react. Different water can cause stomach upsets, for instance."

Strengths

Ray Clemence offered a particularly apposite analysis of what made Paisley such a good manager. "For me," Clemence said, "he was a better coach than motivator of men, but a shrewd judge of a player and very strong tactically." Despite this, Paisley never saw himself as a tactician. "I didn't talk tactics because I wasn't taught tactics. I was merely advised on certain things about my game."

Having spent so long around football, and then worked with an innovator like Shankly, not to mention the other Boot Room boys who pooled their knowledge, Paisley had great wisdom. He just had a deep understanding of the game, and all its component parts. "He could assess all positions," Clemence said, "even my speciality of goalkeeping."

It wasn't that tactics were distrusted, but the modern terminology and jargon certainly was. "There are people who can talk me under the table about football," Paisley once said, "but if they had to explain what they are talking about they would be under it." While the Reds rarely set up specifically to counter the opposition (although European away games were treated differently to those at Anfield), that did not mean in-game changes weren't made. Paisley was tactically astute, but there was little tampering with a system ahead of games. The coaches adapted to the circumstances as the play unfolded — shifted players around if need be, or made a substitution — but the first instinct was to go with their natural game. And a big part of Paisley's great tactical brilliance was knowing which players were needed, and where they would fit into the team. Get that right, and the tactics are more able to dictate themselves.

There can be no greater tactic in football than finding intelligent, gifted and adaptable players who can think for themselves, and forming a harmonious blend in a team. It obviates some of the need for clever thinking on a game-to-game basis; that took place with the overall masterplan. Phil Neal never had to worry if he wanted to go on an overlap; someone would have the nous to cover him. Neal was told that if he joined an attack, to stay with it. He was now a forward, until the move broke down. If Paisley had been fielding a 'fancy Dan' right-winger who didn't track back, then the team would be in trouble; but that wasn't the Liverpool way. Such a player wouldn't be in the team to start with.

While Paisley rarely changed a winning team, he did alter the formation — at least in his early years. Having bought Kenny Dalglish to replace Kevin Keegan, he explained how that changed: "Because of the difference between them, there was a change in Liverpool's style when we signed Kenny. With his subtlety, a 4-4-2 formation with the accent on passing was clearly our most effective line-up, whereas in the past we had often employed 4-3-3 as well."

Paisley understood about the flow of a game, and in an age when only one substitute was allowed, he was loathe to use it lightly. He told David Fairclough that he preferred to use him as a sub, because his pace and direct running could help turn a game in Liverpool's favour. But if the Reds were holding onto a slender lead, Paisley was rarely tempted to make changes. "I'd really rather have someone limping around, as long as he isn't doing damage to himself," he said, "because if you bring on some young sub, he just raises the tempo of the game, running around like a blue-arsed fly, and then all of a sudden the whole flow of your game can disappear, and you can finish up losing it."

Ray Kennedy stands out as the player who benefited most from Paisley's wisdom, and whose tactical realignment gave the Reds a new dimension. Kennedy, bought by Shankly as a burly centre-forward, replaced Toshack as Kevin Keegan's strike partner at the start of Paisley's first season, and he did well enough. But the manager then moved the former Arsenal man a little deeper, to play behind the more established strike pairing. Kennedy again showed some quality, but it was only the following season that he nailed down a role in the side — on the left of midfield. Clearly Kennedy had the skills necessary for the role — excellent control, an eye for a pass, and the ability to score goals — but given his size and previous role, it still wasn't an obvious move to make. But it worked to perfection; Kennedy was reborn.

While tactics have always been part of football, there were arguably fewer variations back in the '70s and '80s. Formations were most likely to be 4-4-2, although in the case of Liverpool, the role of Dalglish between midfield and attack might have been described as 4-4-1-1 in today's game. It's fair to say that football has evolved tactically since the days of Shankly and Paisley; that's only natural, as all sports develop over time. But the progression of ideas and methodologies has clearly been accelerated by the advances in technology. Television has accelarated the proliferation of systems by which comparisons can be made, while computer software has enabled managers to look into all aspects of the playing style of both their own personnel and that of the opposition. There was less information readily available to hand in the '60s and '70s. One problem Paisley faced was that, due to the Reds' success, everyone could see how they played; but checking out the opposition wasn't as easy in return. John Neal, the Chelsea boss, observed: "It's strange really, but every manager in the land can recite precisely how Liverpool play because they see them so often on television. But how many managers know how to beat them?" In turn, scouting the opposition, particularly in Europe, was taken very seriously at Liverpool. Before the European Cup Final of 1977, Tom Saunders watched Borussia Mönchengladbach in person on no less than six occasions.

The greatest strength of Bob Paisley, though, had to be his ability to sign the right players for his team, allied to an excellent sense of when to let existing players go. Not only were his signings on balance the best of any Liverpool manager, but he never kept a player past his sell-by date. Unlike Shankly, Paisley was ruthless when it came to letting older players go. He didn't enjoy the process, but he didn't let any sentimentality cloud his judgement.

Weaknesses

Paisley's weakness, if he had one, was his inability to communicate particularly clearly. Dealing with the media was fraught, and even his own players were sometimes left scratching their heads. In 1977, England striker David Johnson, who'd cost a club record £200,000 a year earlier, went public about his frustration with Paisley. "The manager and myself, for some unknown reason, have never really been able to communicate and so a feeling of unrest has affected me." But it seems churlish to pick up on Paisley's failure with words. His record proves that more often than not he got his message across to the team, and that was the main thing.

Historical Context — Strength of Rivals and League
When Bob Paisley took charge, Leeds United had been the club's greatest rival, having just pipped the Reds for the league title in Shankly's last season. But while the Yorkshire club struggled after replacing their legendary manager (Don Revie), Liverpool moved from strength to strength after replacing theirs. In what seems almost unthinkable now, Manchester United were relegated that eventful summer in 1974, although they'd finish 3rd in the top division two seasons later. At that time it wasn't unheard of for promoted teams to take their momentum into the First Division, as Nottingham Forest showed in 1978 by winning the league as a newly promoted side. Manchester United's new-found momentum quickly faded, and although they beat Liverpool in the 1977 FA Cup Final, it would not be until 1980 that they made any kind of serious title challenge, finishing two points behind Paisley's men. Two third-placed finishes in 1982 and 1983, both times considerably off the pace, was as close as they would come to challenging Paisley's domination. Ron Atkinson succeeded Dave Sexton in 1981, after the latter had been in charge at Old Trafford for four years. Sexton had previously been the manager of QPR, where he had come within a whisker of landing the league crown. The west Londoners found themselves top after playing their final game of the 1975/76 season, but Liverpool's late win over Wolverhampton Wanderers pushed Rangers down to second, and Paisley had the first of his six league titles.

With Revie taking charge of England in the summer of 1974, Jimmy Armfield, these days a respected pundit on BBC radio, led Leeds to the European Cup Final in his first season, suffering a 2-0 defeat to Bayern Munich. Assisted by Don Howe, who later found greater fame after returning to Arsenal, Armfield was responsible for rebuilding Don Revie's ageing side, and under his stewardship Leeds never finished outside of the top ten. The Elland Road club qualified for the UEFA cup, and reached FA and League Cup semi-finals, but were never a serious threat to Paisley's Reds.

In 1981 Aston Villa emerged as a force, albeit temporarily, winning the league under Ron Saunders, followed 12 months later by the European Cup (with Tony Barton now in charge following Saunders' resignation), before the Midlanders fell out of the picture. Ipswich, managed by Bobby Robson since 1969, were also fully established as a strong side by the end of the

'70s. They gave Liverpool a fairly strong run for their money in 1982, but finished four points behind the champions. Robson had taken perennial strugglers Ipswich to 4th in 1973, and in the following nine seasons, the Portman Road outfit finished lower than 6th only once, in 1978 — when a 1–0 victory over Arsenal landed them the FA Cup. Ipswich finished 3rd in 1977 and 1980, and were runners-up to Aston Villa in 1981, in what was Liverpool's worst league campaign under Paisley, when the Reds finished 5th. It was however a season in which Liverpool won both the European and League Cup, and Ipswich landed the UEFA Cup. When Bobby Robson took charge of England in 1982 the Suffolk club quickly fell away into mediocrity, posing no threat to the Liverpool manager during his swan song. In Paisley's final season, Watford, with a youthful John Barnes raiding down their left wing, emerged under Graham Taylor, finishing 2nd in their first season in the top flight, albeit 11 points adrift of the Reds.

Bête Noire

It's fairly clear that Brian Clough was the only major thorn in Paisley's side during his time as Liverpool manager. Derby County, previously managed by Clough but now led by Dave Mackay, won the title in Paisley's first season, two points ahead of Liverpool in 2nd. Clough, after a stint at Brighton, moved to Leeds in 1974, but lasted only 44 days. However, by the start of 1976, he pitched up at Nottingham Forest, and a great rivalry with Bob Paisley was set in motion. In 1977, when Liverpool won their first European Cup, Nottingham Forest were Second Division Champions. A year later, they were supplanting Paisley's side as Champions of England. A year after that, they usurped the Reds as European Champions — beating Liverpool in the 1st round of the competition — and retained the trophy a year later. But in a tit-for-tat exchange, Paisley, whose side had regained the league title from the Midlands club, then took back possession of the European Cup too. Forest remained a top-half team for the remainder of Paisley's career, but never rivalled the Reds again. However, Clough, who had experienced a hostile rivalry with Don Revie, had nothing but respect for Paisley: "He's broken this silly myth that nice guys don't win anything. He's one of the nicest guys you could meet in any industry or any walk of life — and he's a winner."

Pedigree/Previous Experience

Untested as a manager beyond the environs of the reserves' Central League, it's fair to say that Paisley's pedigree was seriously questioned. He seemed the archetypal no.2, a willing assistant but someone who didn't exude natural leadership skills. It is all the more amazing to think that the man who won six league titles and three European Cups only managed for those nine years. He started at the top, and went out at the top.

Defining Moment

Paisley greatest challenge presented itself off the pitch — or rather, on the *training* pitches. What could be more of a test for Paisely than seeing his great friend and predecessor, Bill Shankly, turning up at training during his first season in charge?

Paisley was the club's new manager. But becoming 'boss' was his greatest challenge. Shankly, appearing at Melwood, was being called 'boss' by the players, even though he was no longer in charge. Shankly's presence, while far from malevolent, undermined Paisley. A newspaper article, in which Paisley was horribly misquoted as saying that *he* had run the show even during Shankly's time, cut deep into the Scot's heart. He should have known that his former assistant would never say such a thing, and even though Bob, who was blameless, apologised, the damage was done. Shankly never turned up at Melwood again. In time both men acknowledged it was the right decision, but the circumstances behind it were unfortunate.

Crowning Glory

If there was one season that Bob Paisley will be most remembered for, it is 1976/77, when he took Liverpool to within a whisker of English football's first ever treble, and won the country only its second European Cup. With the league title wrapped up, Manchester United awaited in the FA Cup Final, and Borussia Mönchengladbach would be the opposition in Rome for the European Cup Final.

Defeat against United at Wembley — 2-1, with all three goals scored in a five minute spell at the start of the second half — was a double-edged sword. While it was hard to take, Paisley felt victory might have sated a little of the hunger ahead of something truly unique. Two other sides had already achieved the domestic double of league and FA Cup, but none had ever won the league and the European Cup in the same year; indeed, until that point, United were the country's sole victors, in 1968. The Liverpool manager regretted his selection at Wembley, opting to leave out Ian Callaghan and play three forwards. His thinking was affected by a strange decision by the FA. Should the game go to a replay, it would be held in late June — a quite ludicrous date. After an especially long and hard season, that was the last thing his players needed, and he tried to win the game outright on the Saturday. But again he saw a benefit to his selection: Callaghan, at 35, might not have been fresh for the game four days later. Although Callaghan was approaching retirement, it shows an awareness of the limits that playing games in quick succession place on a player. In previous seasons, Bill Shankly had rested an entire team ahead of cup finals. Getting it wrong at Wembley allowed Paisley the chance to get it right in Rome.

The journey back to Liverpool after the FA Cup Final took place by train, and is seen as a key factor in the victory four days later. The players' mood was understandably low, and a two-hour delay did nothing help their spirits. The events that followed would now be frowned upon as incredibly unprofessional: the players drank wine to help them unwind, and a food fight then broke out, with even the players' wives embroiled in the mêlée. It started when Steve Heighway began throwing sugar. Before long a group of depressed players were enjoying themselves with abandon, and a defiance arose. Songs started being sung. An even stronger sense of togetherness was engendered in a railway carriage, in highly unusual preparations for the biggest game in the club's history.

Paisley explained: "People who sit in the stand perhaps don't realise the extra pressure exerted by the emotional side of the game. It's not easy to cope with and it's quite possible to become drunk on four ounces of wine gums! But I knew as I left Lime Street and headed for home that the players' attitude was right. They knew they still had a job to do."

That night Paisley picked his team: the same one that ended the game against United. John Toshack was injured, but Paisley kept him in the squad to disrupt German planning; he knew they were terrified of his aerial presence, following the UEFA Cup Final four years earlier, and he wanted them to think the Welsh striker would be playing; another example of Paisley's canniness.

Typical of Paisley's pre-match talks, he did not focus on the opposition. Phil Neal recalled that the main thing the manager discussed was how the previous time he'd been in Rome was on the back of a tank, liberating the city at the end of World War II. It wasn't that the opposition were taken lightly, or their strengths hadn't been assessed; as mentioned earlier, Tom Saunders had seen them in the flesh six times. But that was not something to worry the players with. Relaxed, they gave what Paisley described as the best performance in the club's history. Terry McDermott gave the Reds the lead in the 28th minute, shortly after Ray Clemence had failed to hold a shot from Rainer Bonhof, only to see it come back off the post. Allan Simonsen equalised for the Germans in the 51st minute, and a little over ten minutes later, Clemence was faced with Uli Stielike bearing down on his goal, one-on-one. But Clemence won the dual, with what he rates as his most important save for the club. Then Tommy Smith, playing his 600th game, rose high to head home a Steve Heighway corner. With the game nearing its conclusion, Kevin Keegan, on 100 goals for the club, was upended in the area as he looked certain to score his 101st, and Phil Neal calmly (outwardly, at least) despatched the spot-kick. Paisley leapt up from the bench and waved his arms in triumph; unusual for a man who usually kept his emotions in check. But he had earned his delirious celebration.

Hundreds of Liverpool fans — out of the 27,000 who'd made the journey to Rome — crashed the victory banquet. Paisley, however, sat quiet and stone-cold sober as he took in the events. "I like a drink and, in common with most people, I enjoy celebrating a great victory," he recalled. "This, though, was different. It was no ordinary triumph. The buffet at the banquet was magnificent enough to have fed my regiment throughout the war, with enough champagne to have sunk Noah's Ark. But I wanted to remain sober. I was drinking it all in — the atmosphere, the sense of pride, of achievement, of joy and reward for ten months' hard labour. I wanted to savour every moment."

Legacy

Has there ever been a better set of players handed on by a retiring manager — not just at Liverpool, but anywhere in England? Most sane men wouldn't think of walking away from a team that contained Dalglish, Souness, Rush, Whelan, Hansen, Neal, Lawrenson and Nicol. But Paisley was a not young man when he took charge, and almost a decade later, approaching his mid-60s, he was entitled to put his feet up. He went out in precisely the right way — at the top, with his team English champions for the second successive season. Such was his legacy, the spine of his team would enable two successive managers to win league titles and, within twelve months, another European Cup.

TRANSFERS

Transfers In

Few Liverpool managers have made as good a first signing as Paisley did with Phil Neal; and certainly none have proved to have been as successful in terms of trophies won. Neal was the sole presence on the pitch in all four of the club's European Cup successes of the era, and was even present for the fifth final, lost to Juventus in 1985.

A clever overlapping right-back whom Paisley described as a "natural player who understood the game", Neal had scored an impressive 27 times in 187 games for Fourth Division Northampton by the age of 23. Liverpool stepped in with a £60,000 bid with Neal set to join Aldershot. It was a big step-up in quality, and initially he spent life in the reserves, like so many of Liverpool's signings. Then, out of the blue, he was hoisted from the reserve squad, for whom he was about to play at Anfield, and told to report to

Goodison Park, where the senior team were about to face Everton. Neal, thinking he was there to sample the atmosphere, was told to get changed — he was playing. And so began a career that spanned 650 games and amassed 60 goals. While many of his goals were penalties, including in the 1977 European Cup Final, he also popped up with important strikes having raided down the wing, not least Liverpool's goal against Roma in the European Cup Final seven years later.

Paisley's second signing was Terry McDermott, who had impressed for Newcastle against the Reds some months earlier in the FA Cup Final, for £170,000. The combined fees for Neal and McDermott came more-or-less entirely from the sale of Larry Lloyd, with the big centre-back asking to leave upon losing his place in the team. Lloyd moved to Bristol City for £240,000 and Liverpool reinvested wisely. McDermott, a skilful midfielder with boundless energy, had an eye for goal — often spectacular ones at that — and would later become the country's Footballer of the Year. In his 329 appearances he bagged an impressive 81 goals, before being sold back to Newcastle in 1982, at the age of 30, for £100,000.

Next, Joey Jones signed for £110,000 from Wrexham, at the age of 20. He only spent three years at the club, scoring three times in 78 league games at left-back, before he returned to Wrexham for £210,000, following the arrival of Alan Kennedy. In his fairly brief stint on Merseyside, Jones became a massive cult hero for his incredible commitment. He was immortalised in the famous banner unfurled by Kopites at the 1977 European Cup Final which read "Joey Ate The Frogs Legs, Made The Swiss Roll, Now He's Munching Gladbach".

England striker David Johnson arrived from Ipswich in August 1976 for a new club record, £200,000. Johnson would do well at Liverpool, without ever quite reaching the heights of some of the legendary strikers before or since. He scored 78 goals in six years, playing 210 games, but the emergence of Ian Rush hastened his disappearance from the first team picture. A former Everton striker, Johnson returned to Goodison Park at the age of 30, but scored only five times in 50 games.

While Paisley rarely got it wrong in the transfer market, the year between 1977 and 1978 was his golden period. Excluding Steve Ogrizovic, brought from Chesterfield for £70,000 as back-up to Ray Clemence and who went on to be an excellent top-level keeper with Coventry, Paisley struck a quite stunning hat-trick of signings. Alan Hansen, Kenny Dalglish and Graeme Souness represented the kind of quality acquisitions that, by rights, should be spread out across a lifetime in the game — if a manager is both incredibly wise and especially lucky. And yet they were all procured within seven months of one another. It's doubtful that any club in the history of English football has made three such crucial signings in such a short space of time. The trio of

Scots are all now Liverpool legends; about as good as you're going to get in defence, midfield and attack.

Hansen was the first to arrive, with the 21-year-old signed from Partick Thistle for £100,000 in May '77. Relatively unknown outside of Scotland, Hansen would go on to represent Liverpool for the next 13 years, playing 620 times, and eventually captain the team. Tall, elegant, and composed, Hansen was one of those defenders who opt to stay on their feet rather than dive recklessly into tackles. When he partnered Phil Thompson, the Reds' central defence looked more like an L.S. Lowry painting of stick-men. Crucially, the two had character and ability. Mark Lawrenson, who later partnered Hansen, was only slightly more muscular, but Gary Gillespie's intermittent appearances got the weight-ratio right back down again. Clearly Paisley had hit upon a type when deciding that the days of pure stoppers were gone, and in their stead came mobile, thoughtful and lean defenders who were comfortable on the ball. And in that regard, Hansen was the apotheosis. Even now, he is the benchmark for stylish centre-backs anywhere in England. Bob Paisley was in no doubt about his quality. "Alan Hansen is the defender with the pedigree of an international striker. He is quite simply the most skilful centre-half I have ever seen in the British game. He is a joy to watch. Alan has always been an excellent footballer, a beautifully balanced player who carries the ball with control and grace. He has a very measured, long stride and is much faster than he looks. I can't think of more than a couple of players who could beat him over 100 metres. He has both the ability and the patience to launch attacks from deep positions."

Next up, in August 1977, was Kenny Dalglish, signed from Celtic for £440,000. But more on 'King Kenny' later. As 1978 began, Paisley moved into the market once more, strengthening the midfield — or rather, signing an entire midfield rolled into one player — in the form of Greame Souness, purchased on 10th January. The combative (to put it mildly) Scot joined from Middlesbrough for £352,000, aged 24. Only Steven Gerrard, with his increased athleticism and more prolific goal rate, can arguably eclipse Souness as the Reds' most complete midfield General. But while Gerrard possesses gifts Souness lacked, the fiery Scot was the more fearful and imposing character. Souness was an absolute bully when it came to subduing and subjugating the opposition, and a commanding influence on his own team. He played 359 times for the Reds, scoring 55 goals. With the treble of 1984 completed, Souness packed his bags for Italy. He played for two years at Sampdoria, before returning to Scotland as player/manager of Rangers.

Kevin Sheedy, another midfielder who excelled in the '80s, was signed from Hereford for £80,000 in 1978, in yet one more great piece of talent-spotting by Paisley and his scouts. However, the Ireland international was that rare exception: the player released by Liverpool to go on to not only do better on an individual basis, but to rival the success of those still at Anfield. To make matters worse, it was with Everton. Sheedy, who arrived at Liverpool aged 18 and was sold at 22, scored more than 100 goals for the Toffees in over 400 appearances; for the Reds his tally read two goals in just three starts and two substitute appearances. It shows that even very good players can fail if their path to the first team is blocked by even better players, while some individuals improve beyond recognition as they mature.

At £330,000, Alan Kennedy was very expensive for a full-back in 1978; it's hardly a position worthy of many big-money deals. The previous season had seen Jones, Smith and Hansen deployed at left-back at some stage, so as a position it was proving problematic. Full of energy and character as well as a willingness to get forward, Kennedy, signed from Newcastle United at the age of 23, was hardly one of the game's aesthetes, goalscorers or playmakers who usually warrant such a price tag (only a fraction short of what Souness had cost, which itself was the highest transaction involving two English clubs). And yet he more than repaid his hefty fee, scoring 20 times — including some crucial goals — in 359 games over the next seven years. In 1981 and 1984 he scored the goals that clinched the European Cup: the first a finish in the 81st minute to beat Real Madrid 1-0, as he burst through on goal from a throw-in, and the second the decisive penalty against Roma in the shootout.

In May 1979 Paisley once again tapped the Scottish market when buying Frank McGarvey from St Mirren for £300,000. The striker, aged 23, never settled at Anfield and left after just 10 months. With Ian Rush signed to fill the gap of promising young striker, McGarvey moved to Celtic for a small profit. McGarvey played 245 times for Celtic over the next five years, scoring 113 times.

Another relative failure was Israeli defender Avi Cohen, bought from Maccabi Tel Aviv for a reasonably hefty £200,000. In his two-and-a-half years at the club the left-back only played 23 times, scoring just once — having already netted an own goal in the same game. However, it was a league-title decider — against Aston Villa at Anfield, in 1980 — and his strike at the right end put the Reds 2-1 up, and on the way to a 4-1 victory. In November 1981 he returned to Maccabi Tel Aviv, for half the original fee. Alan Hansen said he was arguably the most talented foreign player he played with, but the Israeli didn't adapt well to English football.

The 1979/80 season saw the arrival of two more future superstars, albeit either side of another relative failure. The one who didn't work out was Richard Money; Paisley couldn't resist some puns on the value of the investment and the player's surname, but in truth Money offered little more than cover after arriving from Fulham at the end of the '79/80 season. Bought for £50,000, he moved to Luton in 1982 for twice that amount. The first of the two major successes acquired in that campaign was Ronnie Whelan, an Irish teenager brought in for nothing from Home Farm at the start of the season. It would take Whelan a couple of years to make the breakthrough, but once he did he made a big impact, initially on the left of midfield when replacing Ray Kennedy and then, in later years, as the holding central midfielder. In almost 500 games Whelan netted a total of 73 times, including a memorable double to defeat Spurs in the 1982 League Cup Final and a superb winner a year later to overcome Manchester United to win the same competition.

Next came Ian Rush, bought from Chester in May 1980 for £300,000. The 18-year-old had just made his debut for Wales, but like Whelan it took him time to break through at Liverpool. Once he did, it was the start of a record-breaking career with the club, split over two periods. Rush spent 15 of the next 16 years at Anfield, scoring a club-record 346 goals in 660 games. He also holds the all-time record for most FA Cup Final goals (five); is the joint record League Cup goalscorer with 49 goals, shared with Sir Geoff Hurst; was the first player to pick up five League Cup winners medals; and still holds the record as top Merseyside derby goalscorer with 25 goals for Liverpool against Everton. Not bad for a player who, when his sale to Juventus and repurchase is taken into consideration, left the club *up £100,000* on his transfers.

In March 1981 Paisley moved to secure the signing of 23-year-old Bruce Grobbelaar from Vancouver Whitecaps for £250,000. When Ray Clemence sought a new challenge that summer, the South African began an eleven-year stint as the club's undisputed no.1. Prone to both eccentricity and error, he was a remarkably agile shot-stopper, and, as a former soldier, a tough character. With Clemence now at Spurs, Grobbelaar kept his place in goal from his Liverpool debut on August 29th 1981, through to August 16th 1986, playing 310 consecutive matches. It was a figure he would double in his remaining eight years at the club, leaving for Southampton after 628 appearances.

Paisley then broke the club record fee twice in succession, although the fees involved were still some way short of what those rival clubs were paying on their major deals. Australian Craig Johnston was the first, signing from Middlesbrough for £650,000 in April 1981. Just 20, Johnston was an upbeat, lively character with boundless energy on and off the pitch, but as such slightly difficult to handle. He infuriated and delighted the crowd, and his managers, in equal measure. In 1988, after 271 games and 40 goals, he quit, aged just 27, to be with his sister in Australia, who was seriously ill. On balance he was a very good player for Liverpool, if not one of the all-time greats. In 1991 Graeme Souness looked at bringing him back to the club, as it still held his registration, but it didn't work out, and Johnston went on to invent the Predator football boot.

In August 1981 Paisley finally got hold of Mark Lawrenson, having attempted to do so four years earlier. Lawrenson, a cultured centre-back who could also play in midfield, cost £900,000 from Brighton. He would go on to form arguably the greatest centre-back partnership the club has seen — and there is some stiff competition — when he played alongside Alan Hansen. Lawrenson scored 18 goals in his 356 games for the Reds, but a serious Achilles tendon injury in 1987 led to his premature retirement a year later.

In October 1981 Paisley continued his run of inspired signings when he agreed to pay Ayr United £300,000 for Steve Nicol. Originally a right-back, he could not displace Phil Neal, and made his breakthrough on the right of midfield during the 1983/84 season. That campaign ended with him missing a penalty in the Reds' successful European Cup Final shootout. His versatility was recognised in 1988/89, when he won the Footballer of the Year award after playing in six different positions that season. In the previous campaign he'd scored seven goals in his first seven games — from right-back, including an incredible hat-trick from open play away at Newcastle. After just over a decade in the first team, and 46 goals in 468 games, Nicol, by then a centre-back, was released to Notts County.

Less inspired was the June 1982 signing of John McGregor, a centre-back from Queens Park. Only 19, and signed for nothing, it was no great gamble, and the Scot failed to make it into the first team. A lot more was expected of striker David Hodgson, who moved from Middlesbrough for £450,000 in August. But he was to prove another disappointment. Two reserve goalkeepers then followed: Bob Wardle, who later had to retire following an eye injury, and Bob Bolder, picked up from Sheffield Wednesday in 1983 for £125,000. Neither man featured for the first team, due to Grobbelaar's remarkable run of over 300 consecutive games.

Paisley's final signing was that of Jim Beglin from Shamrock Rovers, in May 1983, for £20,000. Still not 20, the player had been due to join Arsenal when the deal fell through. Liverpool moved in, and secured the player initially on a month's loan; but ten days into it a permanent deal was struck. Having made his debut in November 1984 at left-midfield, Beglin was increasingly part of the first team picture over the next 18 months, before being given regular games in the left-back slot by Kenny Dalglish as a replacement for Alan Kennedy. After just 98 games, Beglin's Liverpool career was curtailed by a seriously broken leg at the age of 23. He played briefly for Leeds and Blackburn, but it was clear he was no longer the same player.

Player	Quality	0.01pg	IN	OUT	FGV	VALUE	Ap	Details
Alan Hansen	9.59	6.2	-2	8		**21.79**	620	£100k 1977 Ret. '91 @36
Ian Rush (1)	9.71	3.31	-2	10		**21.02**	331	£300k 1980 £3.2m 1987**
Phil Neal	9.01	6.5	-1.9	7		**20.61**	650	£66k 1974 Rel. @34
Ronnie Whelan	8.61	4.93	0	7		**20.54**	493	Free 1979 Rel. @33
Bruce Grobbelaar	8.29	6.28	-1.7	7		**19.87**	628	£250k 1981 Rel. @37
Steve Nicol	8.53	4.68	-2	7		**18.21**	468	£300k 1981 Rel. 1994 @33
Kenny Dalglish**	10	5.15	-10	10	2	**17.15**	515	£440k 1977 Retired
Graeme Souness	9.68	3.59	-8	10		**15.27**	359	£352k 1978 £650k'84 @31
Average	**7.6**		**-3.53**			**12.16**		
Terry McDermott	8.53	3.29	-5	5.3		**12.12**	329	£175k 1974 £100k'81 @31
Mark Lawrenson*	9.00	3.56	-6	4	1	**11.56**	356	£900k 1981 Ret. inj. '88
Joey Jones	6.76	1	-2.1	4.5		**10.16**	100	£110k 1975 £200k 1978
Jim Beglin	6.71	0.83	-0.1	0	2	**9.44**	83	£20k 1983 Retired @27
Alan Kennedy	7.94	3.59	-7.5	5.3		**9.33**	359	£330k 1978 £100k'85 @31
All Managers' Average						**7.92**		
Craig Johnston*	7.33	2.71	-4.3	0	1	**6.74**	271	£650k 1981 Retired @27
David Johnson	7.06	2.13	-5.7	1.3		**4.79**	213	£200k 1976 £100k'81 @31
Avi Cohen	4.82	0.24	-1.7	0.6		**3.96**	24	£200k 1979 £100k 1981
David Hodgson	5.06	0.49	-3	0.8		**3.35**	49	£450k 1982 £125k 1984
Kevin Sheedy	3.88	0.05	-1.8	0.6		**2.73**	5	£80k 1978 £100k 1982
Richard Money	3.94	0.17	-2.3	0.7		**2.51**	17	£50k 1980 £100k 1982

Key: *See page 51.*

Transfer Masterstroke

Without a shadow of a doubt Bob Paisley's transfer masterstroke has to be Kenny Dalglish — quite simply the best player ever to represent the club. Dalglish wasn't cheap: £440,000, an English record in 1977, although still £60,000 less than the club had just received that summer from Hamburg for Kevin Keegan. Having sealed the deal, Paisley said to Peter Robinson "We'd better get out of Glasgow before they realise what they've done."

Other signings are in close contention, though. While no player eclipsed Dalglish in terms of quality, others were bought for far less, represented the club far longer, and won lots more medals. The £100,000 spent on Alan Hansen was a case of daylight robbery — the best value for money out of all Paisley's signings. Ian Rush, Ronnie Whelan and Steve Nicol were all taken from relative obscurity to form the backbone of 1980s Liverpool FC; indeed they were all valuable players in Dalglish's own time as manager. Graeme Souness was another inspired signing who offered excellent value for money. But despite his British-record fee, none can eclipse Dalglish; a player who made everything come together on the pitch. "I just hoped that after the trials and tribulations of my early years in management, someone up high would smile on me and guide my hand," Paisley recalled. "My plea was answered when we got Kenny Dalglish.

What a player, what a great professional!"

Dalglish's time north of the border brought incredible success. Five Scottish Championships, four Scottish Cup-winners' medals, one Scottish League Cup-winners' medal and a hugely impressive haul of 167 goals for a striker who was so much more than just a finisher. It seems crazy now to think that plenty of people doubted the wisdom of the signing, and wondered whether or not he could hack it south of the border. But it's easy to forget how influential Kevin Keegan had become by 1977, and how irreplaceable he seemed. Dalglish not only made a seamless transition, but he actually improved the team. However, Paisley, a long-time admirer of the Scot, had wanted both players in the same team. He felt great players could always play together, and he appreciated their contrasting styles. "Kevin's ability to run with the ball would have been complemented by Kenny's outstanding ability as a purveyor of it, his liking for people being around him enabling him to capitalise on his great vision. Kevin injected a racy tempo with his mobility whereas Kenny stroked the ball around." Dalglish was someone who read what team-mates and opponents did, whereas Keegan reacted to them.

Dalglish was handed Keegan's no.7 shirt, so comparisons were inescapable. But he got off to a great start, scoring after just seven minutes on his league debut away at Middlesbrough, and then again on his home debut against Newcastle. In his debut season he notched 30 goals, including the winner in the 1978 European Cup Final at Wembley, as the Reds retained the trophy.

So was Dalglish better than Keegan? Tommy Smith, who played with them both, has no doubts, saying "Dalglish was the better player. His talent was heaven-sent." And Paisley was also in no doubt: "Of all the players I have played alongside, managed and coached in more than 40 years at Anfield, he is the most talented." When Liverpool met Hamburg in the 1977 European Super Cup, Liverpool thrashed Keegan's new team 6-0, with Dalglish the star of the show. The ghost of Keegan had been lain to rest.

Paisley's Liverpool went on to dominate English football for the remainder of his days in charge, with Dalglish the fulcrum for the attacking play. In 1979 they regained their league title with a record number of points — 68, under the old two points for a win system. They were undefeated at home, and conceded just 16 goals in 42 games. Dalglish scored 25 goals that season and was voted Footballer of the Year. Paisley's Liverpool retained the Championship in 1980, won the League Cup three years in a row between 1981 and 1983, and won the second of what would end up being three consecutive titles in 1983. With Dalglish in the team, the Reds also won two more European Cups. Dalglish was in his pomp, and became Footballer of the Year for the second time in 1983.

Expensive Folly

Considering that by 1982 several top-flight managers had flops on their hands who cost as much as £1.5m, Paisley's failure with David Hodgson, bought for £450,000, is therefore easy to put into perspective. Not quite 22, Hodgson was a young pace merchant who lacked that extra something special to flourish at Liverpool. He started well, scoring four times in his first six games, but only scored six more in his remaining 43 appearances. Two years after his arrival he was sold to Sunderland for just over a quarter of the fee originally paid.

Frank McGarvey, who, relatively speaking, cost more than Hodgson when he was signed for £300,000 in 1979, would be another obvious candidate, particularly as the Scot never even played a first team game. But within a year Liverpool had sold him for £325,000. As such, he can almost be considered a non-signing.

One Who Got Away

Not many players dared refuse Liverpool by the time Paisley was in charge. The club had the money to go for all of its main targets — in contrast to early life under Shankly, and in more recent years — and Liverpool had by then reached the pinnacle of the European game. When Kevin Keegan left for pastures new, Liverpool were linked with Arsenal's Liam Brady and Birmingham's Trevor Francis. However, Brady, while respected, was not on Paisley's radar. Francis, meanwhile, was seen as too injury prone; Paisley felt it was crucial that players could be called upon all season long. And anyway, he'd already lined up a replacement: Kenny Dalglish.

One player the club did fail to land was Mark Lawrenson — initially at least. Although he was finally signed in 1981, the Reds had bid £75,000 four years earlier, when the stylish Preston centre-back was only 19. At the time Lawrenson moved to Brighton, whose manager Alan Müllery outbid Paisley with an offer of £112,000. After four years on the south coast it cost Liverpool a club record £900,000 to bring him back to the north-west. Even then, Liverpool almost missed out; Müllery had agreed to sell him to Manchester United. Fortunately for Paisley, the club's hierarchy were at the same time agreeing to sell him to Liverpool.

Joe Jordan, the tough Scottish centre-forward, admitted he had turned down Liverpool in 1978, opting instead to move to Manchester United for £350,000, a record transfer between English clubs. A few days later Paisley moved to sign Graeme Souness, for £2,000 more. Jordan would be the one left with regrets, while Souness and Paisley instead collected medals.

Budget — Historical Context

Once Manchester United were promoted back to the top flight in 1975, they continued to spend heavily to try and regain top billing in English football. The side that beat Liverpool in the 1977 FA Cup Final (including the substitute) cost on average almost one-third of the English transfer record: 30.7%. Liverpool's twelve men, by comparison, cost only a quarter of the record: 24.6%. Come forward six years, to the 1983 League Cup Final, and United's team, though much changed, was still at an almost identical percentage of the record fee. However, Paisley's side, with the addition of Dalglish, Souness and Lawrenson in particular, now cost 36.1%.

In between, United, who were runners-up to Arsenal in the FA Cup in 1979 and in the league to Liverpool in 1980, fielded a more expensive side; the team that lost to Arsenal at Wembley in 1979 averaged at 40% of the English record. Bryan Robson, the English transfer record holder between 1981 and 1987, was absent from the 1983 League Cup Final, significantly reducing the average cost as they lost 2-1 to Paisley's men, while in 1980 United had signed Nottingham Forest's Garry Birtles for £1.25m. Also in the side in the early part of the decade were Ray Wilkins, signed from Chelsea for £800,000 in 1980, and Gordon McQueen, who broke the English transfer record in 1978 with his £495,000 move from Leeds. Lou Macari and Frank Stapleton were another two expensive players still in the ranks.

But apart from 1980 and a couple of cup finals three years either side, United were not the main rivals to Paisley's Liverpool. That honour belonged to Nottingham Forest. Unlike United, Forest were initially lacking in big-money signings. The team that won the 1979 European Cup cost just over 20% of the English record. It included Larry Lloyd, sold by Paisley for £240,000 in 1974 but who, two years later, was picked up by the Midlands club for just a quarter of that figure. In goal, Peter Shilton had cost £270,000 in 1977, a month after Paisley's capture of Dalglish set a new record at £440,000. Otherwise it was mostly bargains and home-grown talents, with one exception: Trevor Francis, the country's first million-pound footballer, who arrived at the start of 1979. By contrast, Garry Birtles cost Clough just £2,000 in 1976.

One team who spent extremely big at the start of Paisley's reign was Everton. Burly striker Bob Latchford set the new English record, at £350,000 in 1974, at a point when Everton were on the up; the Toffees had ended 7th in the table after three bottom-half finishes. Midfielder Martin Dobson cost £300,000 that same summer — a new record for a cash deal (Latchford's move involved player swaps, and was valued at £50,000 more). The 1974 signings moved towards the million mark with Jim Pearson, a striker who cost £100,000. Everton finished 4th the next season, just three points off Derby County and two points behind Liverpool. In 1976 Everton signed two players for a combined £400,000, one of whom was the talented Duncan McKenzie; a year later they bought Dave Thomas from QPR for £200,000 and goalkeeper George Wood from Blackpool for £140,000. John Bailey, a left-back who cost £300,000, was added in 1979. Billy Bingham, and Gordon Lee, who took over in 1977, both spent lavishly, but Everton finished 11th and 9th in 1976 and 1977 respectively. They did reach the League Cup Final in 1977, only to be beaten by Aston Villa, and lost to the Reds in the FA Cup semi-final when McKenzie had a goal disallowed for handball (a decision Evertonians are still bitter about). A couple of bright seasons followed, with 3rd and 4th-placed finishes, but they were miles off the pace both times, and then they finished 19th in the 22-team league a year later. Everton eventually did come good in the mid-'80s; by then, however, Bob Paisley had retired.

RECORD
League Championship: '75-76, '76-77, '78-79, '79-80, '81-82, '82-83. European Cup: 1977, 1978, 1981. League Cups: 1981, 1982, 1983. UEFA Cup 1976.

	P	W	D	L	F	A	%
Overall	**535**	**307**	**132**	**96**	**955**	**406**	**57.38%**
League	378	212	99	67	648	294	56.08%
FA Cup	36	20	7	9	62	27	55.56%
League Cup	53	32	13	8	98	31	60.38%
Europe	61	39	11	11	140	49	63.93%
Other	7	4	2	1	7	5	57.14%

CONCLUSION
Whether or not Bob Paisley is Liverpool's greatest manager, he is certainly the man who lifted the club to its zenith. Indeed, in terms of achievements in relation to time spent in the job, he cannot be bettered in English football. Alex Ferguson has since exceeded his number of league titles and, along with Brian Clough, come close to matching Paisley's three European Cup triumphs. But Ferguson, at the time of writing, has been in the job for two-and-a-half times as long. The only way Paisley can be overlooked for the top spot in the pantheon is on account of inheriting a successful side to start with. Modest to a fault,

he credited his predecessor. "Bill Shankly set such a high standard," he said. "Liverpool have been geared to this sort of thing for 15 years. I have just helped things along."

However, with the work he put in behind the scenes, particularly his tactical acumen and how he offered a crucial counterpoint to Shankly's abrasive edge, Paisley was heavily responsible for Liverpool rising out of the old Second Division in the first place. Allied to the incredible success he achieved once he'd taken full control of the team, you have testimony to a quite remarkable football man, who died in 1996, at the age of 77, after Alzheimer's Disease had cruelly claimed his remarkable set of memories.

Ron Aktinson, a rival manager at West Bromich Albion and Manchester United, perhaps coined the greatest summation of the man: "If Bob Paisley had been on the continent or in America, in whatever capacity or field he worked, and achieved what he achieved, I think he'd be rated higher than the President, the Lord Mayor, the King or the Queen or whatever."

"I go by records and Bob Paisley is the No 1 manager ever!"

ALAN HANSEN

1983 - 1985

JOE FAGAN

*"You may have found me mean and thirsty in my search
for trophies, but the bad news is the man who is taking my
place is hungrier than me. Fagan's the name and I don't
think he'll need any help from the Artful Dodger!"*

BOB PAISLEY ON JOE FAGAN

INTRODUCTION

Joe Fagan is almost certainly the hardest Liverpool manager to judge,
given the briefness of his tenure, the superb side he inherited and
the unique success that followed. How many managers can say that
their career as a boss lasted only two years, and that they reached the
European Cup Final both times? Or that, in their debut season, they
won an unprecedented treble that included a European Cup secured in
the city of the opposition?

Fagan didn't have to build a team, let alone rebuild one, and yet he
oversaw the most successful season in the history of the club — an historic
treble every bit as notable as Alex Ferguson's 15 years later. While both
managers won the league title and the European Cup, the third trophy
in Fagan's case was the lesser-ranked League Cup to Ferguson's FA Cup.
But the League Cup was no easy stroll in the 1980s, while having to play
a strong Everton side in the final made it an even tougher ask, given the
sharp derby edge. The fact that every single leg went to a replay (one,
against Fulham, going to a second) meant that the Reds played 13 games

to win the trophy; by contrast, in 2003, it took the Reds only six. In the days before rotation, such a gruelling season must have taken its toll.

Liverpool didn't exactly romp to the league title, but in the circumstances, with so many games in other competitions, it was understandable. Graeme Souness brilliantly summed up why they were justifiable winners: "By our standards we didn't deserve to win the league this year. But by everyone else's standards, we did."

Situation Inherited

Following in the footsteps of one legend is tough enough, but having to succeed two is almost unheard of in football. In his favour, Fagan was a crucial part of the process that had been oiling the machinery for so long. The club still took a lot of managing, but it took a clever man to know that change for change's sake — in order to put his stamp on the club — was not necessary. Like Paisley, Fagan was a man of little ego, and he let the club be about the team, and the football on the pitch, and not about enhancing his own image and asserting himself unnecessarily.

Players Inherited

Squad

Player	Quality	Age	Adj	Inheritance	Year	Age
Ian Rush (1)	9.71	0	0	9.71	1983	21.5
Mark Lawrenson	9.00	0	0	9.00	1983	26
Alan Hansen	9.59	-1	0	8.59	1983	28
Steve Nicol	8.53	0	0	8.53	1983	22.5
Ronnie Whelan	8.41	0	0	8.41	1983	22
Bruce Grobbelaar	8.29	0	0	8.29	1983	26
Sammy Lee	7.64	0	0	7.64	1983	24
Average	**8.46**			**7.46**		**26.3**
David Fairclough	7.36	0	0	7.36	1983	26
Kenny Dalglish	10	-5	2	7.00	1983	32
Jim Beglin	6.71	0	0	6.71	1983	20
Graeme Souness	9.68	-3	0	6.68	1983	30
Alan Kennedy	7.94	-2	0	5.94	1983	29
David Hodgson	5.06	0	0	5.06	1985	23
Phil Neal	9.01	-5	1	5.01	1983	32

First XI

Player	Quality	Age	Adj	Inheritance	Year	Age
Bruce Grobbelaar	8.29	0	0	8.29	1983	26
Alan Kennedy	7.94	-2	0	5.94	1983	29
Mark Lawrenson*	9.00	0	0	9.00	1983	26
Alan Hansen	9.59	-1	0	8.59	1983	28
Phil Neal	9.01	-5	1	5.01	1983	32
Steve Nicol	8.53	0	0	8.53	1983	22.5
Graeme Souness	9.68	-3	0	6.68	1983	30

Sammy Lee	7.64	0	0	**7.64**	1983	24
Ronnie Whelan	8.41	0	0	**8.41**	1983	22
Kenny Dalglish**	10	-5	3	**8.00**	1983	32
Ian Rush (1)	9.71	0	0	**9.71**	1983	21.5
Average	**8.89**			**7.80**		**26.6**

Key: *Quality 0-10; Age = -1 point for every year from 28 onwards, eg -4 for 31 year-old, and -1 point from 30 onwards for keepers, eg -4 for 33 year-old; Adj = adjustments for players either exceptionally fit/unfit for their age, or soon to leave; Inheritance = total out of 10. Excludes players not part of first team picture.*

The squad Fagan inherited was easily the strongest of all those covered in this book — an average *Quality* rating of 8.44, and an *Inheritance* rating of 7.44.

The same applies to the First XI, which scored 8.86 for *Quality*. However, the *Inheritance* rating was 7.76, a fair way behind the team Paisley took charge of in 1974. The 1983 vintage was a team at the peak of its potential, but one that would need rebuilding before too long. The two most important players — Dalglish and Souness — were reaching the end of their most effective days as Liverpool players. Also, the two full-backs were now in their 30s.

State of Club

By 1983, Liverpool were one of Europe's elite; three European Cups in the previous six years, and a couple of UEFA Cups shortly before that. A succession of league titles helped confirm that the club was being expertly run in every single aspect. Success was breeding more success. Continuity and stability were key: the majority of the coaching staff had been in place for years, if not decades; John Smith and Peter Robinson were well established as the club's main men away from the football; and even the club's chief scout and youth development officer had been in place since the mid-to-late '60s.

"I didn't expect to get the job," Fagan said, "but I'm very pleased to accept it. In this game you don't expect anything at all, you just work at your own job." He would later give his reasons for accepting. "I took the job because I was in a rut when they offered it to me. Ronnie Moran and Roy Evans were doing the training and I was just helping Bob, putting in my two penneth-worth." But he knew the challenge that faced him. "I suppose if I really thought about what I have to prove, I'd be climbing up the wall."

Assistance/Backroom Staff

Joe Fagan became the last of the original Boot Room boys to assume the mantle of club leader. Reuben Bennett had retired in the late '70s, but Ronnie Moran was still an important part of the set-up, as was Roy Evans, still only in his mid-30s. Despite his age, Fagan was the natural choice, but Moran, aged 49, would have been in the club's considerations. "People have been asking me for years if I ever had any ambitions to be the manager," Moran explained, "but it wasn't like that here. Bob never thought he'd become boss until Shanks retired, Joe never thought about it until Bob went, and I certainly never thought about it. We were all happy to do whatever we were asked to do." Moran would never be asked to perform the ultimate job, beyond on a caretaker basis, but spent another 15 years at the club in senior coaching roles.

With Fagan running the first team, Chris Lawler was brought back to the club as reserve team manager. He also helped with scouting missions and was part of the daily coaching staff on the pitches at Melwood.

Management Style

Lugubrious in appearance but not character, Joe Fagan, a tall ex-centre-back born in Liverpool, was a lively, likeable character who could be stern when necessary. Having joined the club a year before Shankly's appointment, he might have worried for his future, but the new manager kept the coaching team together. Shankly knew Fagan well — years earlier, when managing Grimsby, he'd tried to sign the player, who spent most of his career at Manchester City.

Fagan was certainly questioned during his brief tenure. If he felt he'd answered his critics by winning an unprecedented treble in 1984, the start to the following season would prove a rude awakening. Graeme Souness was gone, and Ian Rush wasn't fit to play until October. By the time the striker returned, Liverpool were sitting 20th in the 22-team division. Had Fagan's success been down to the team Paisley bequeathed him? Liverpool recovered, finishing 2nd in May and reaching the European Cup Final for a the second consecutive year, but it was to prove a disappointing campaign.

"When we did slip up," Ian Rush said, "he could be vicious, and he used to get far angrier than I ever saw Bob Paisley. And Fagan wasn't bothered by reputations, either. Dalglish and Souness would be blasted in the dressing room just as much as the youngest player." Rush also recalled an incident in 1984 when, having overcome the brutal tactics of Dynamo Bucharest to reach the European Cup Final, Fagan entered the dressing room as if something was seriously amiss. He was crestfallen. He moved slowly to the centre of the room, and the celebrating squad fell quiet. Having got the players' attention, Fagan then burst into a jig of delight.

Just like his predecessor, the role initially proved difficult. "The first couple of weeks were a bit rough because my mind was racing everywhere," he said, "yet I seemed to be doing nothing. I was frightened to death I would end up like Bob after his first season in charge, without a trophy." But he was a popular choice with the players, and had their full backing, as Mark Lawrenson attested: "The biggest tribute I could pay to him would be when he got the job I think every single man in the first team squad was desperate for him to be successful."

Fagan's style was simple and straightforward. "I'm not one for the *bon mots* like Bob or the abrasive quips like Shanks," he once said. "What I have to offer is one word — honesty. I couldn't be devious if I tried." Jim Beglin, the young Irish left-back who made his debut under Fagan, said of him: "He was just a very genuine, nice man. He was a very humble, down to earth person. He had a lovely way about him and was very gentlemanly. Underneath that soft exterior, there was also a hardened professionalism. Joe had authority and when strong words were needed, Joe could produce them."

As well as being prepared to lay down the law when required, he was not afraid to make tough decisions. He dropped Kenny Dalglish for the first time in the player's career. "The only parts of the job which I disliked were press conferences and dropping players," he said after his retirement. "But I dropped them just the same, even Kenny Dalglish! What a daft devil I was!"

Somewhat controversially, three weeks before the biggest game of his career, Fagan took the players to Israel for a week's holiday. The league season had ended, and the wait for the European Cup Final was something that the manager feared would play heavy on the players' minds. The Italian press were disbelieving at what they saw as totally unprofessional behaviour, but as with the incident on the train ahead of the previous final the Reds had contested in Rome, the tension needed to be broken; as in 1977, the result was the same: a relaxed performance that led to victory. Gary Gillespie, an unused substitute when Liverpool completed the treble on May 30th, explained the manager's thinking behind breaking up the three-week wait with a change of scenery that allowed the players to let their hair down: "It's a long time to dwell on things, and be at home. All you do is monotonous day-to-day training. So it was suggested that we went to Israel for the week, and it was a real blowout, a real blast, with just one game. It was all about camaraderie. We knew we had business to attend to, but that was three weeks down the line. We trained hard when we came back, and the rest is history."

Unique Methods

Having been a key factor in establishing the Reds' style of play over the years, Fagan's ideas had already been thoroughly incorporated into the club's ethos. For decades, training sessions had been fastidiously documented, with players' form and fitness monitored, routines outlined, as well as the weather conditions duly noted. These daily journals, kept in the Boot Room, became a crucial reference point, with Shankly, Paisley and then Fagan referring to them to discover how problems from the past had been overcome. Kenny Dalglish described the Boot Room as "a university for football. It was a bunch of intelligent guys discussing football." As such, Joe Fagan was a key professor.

Between 1983 and 1985 there would be a team meeting on a Friday morning before training, when the side for the next day would be announced. Some mention would be made of the opposition strengths, but more in passing than anything else. In so many ways he was simply perpetuating the methods he'd originally helped develop.

Fagan once said "Our methods are so easy, sometimes players don't understand them at first." Jan Molby was just one example of a new player who found the simplicity surprising. Used to the Ajax way of playing, he approached Fagan 40 minutes before his debut against Norwich. "What do you want me to do?" he asked. "Listen," the manager replied, "we've signed you because you're a good player, just go and show us what a good player you are, whatever you want to do."

Another example of the simplicity could be seen in Fagan's instructions to his players. "We tell our defenders to be pessimistic, always anticipating a mistake which might give an opponent a scoring opportunity. And we tell our forwards to be optimists, always expecting that the ball knocked in will get through to them in a scoring position." It was pure common sense.

Strengths

Like Bob Paisley, Joe Fagan had been working closely with the team long before becoming manager, so he knew that continuity was the key. While radical change is almost always necessary sooner or later, Fagan recognised that this was not yet the case at Liverpool. Above all else, Fagan had the ability to impart his considerable wisdom. He was, like Paisley, an incredibly knowledgeable football man who was able to get the best out of his players, and to inspire their loyalty. These are key strengths. It's no good knowing a lot about the game but continually rubbing players up the wrong way, and failing to get them to play for you, either from mishandling them or through lack of respect. Equally, it's no good being likeable if the players will take advantage; the steel has to be there too, in order to be successful. Fagan had a perfect balance of straightforward honesty, unquestionable authority and football acumen. There was nothing remarkable about him — he didn't have the incredible motivational skills of Shankly, and perhaps lacked the really sharp tactical mind of Paisley, but he had a little bit of everything needed to prosper.

Weaknesses
It could be argued that Joe Fagan's record in the transfer market wasn't quite good enough. But with such a talented squad, there wasn't an immediate sense that change was required. Given his brief stay in the job, long-term planning didn't affect him too deeply.

However, one major blow Fagan did receive was his captain's decision to move to Italy at the end of the manager's first season. "When Souness left for Sampdoria," Michael Robinson noted, "it was as if we'd lost three players." With Souness gone and Dalglish's effectiveness starting to wane, neither player was adequately replaced. But then again, players of such quality are not easily discovered. If they were not such rarities, their names wouldn't be mentioned in such awed tones decades later.

Finally, there was the issue of the manager's own age; already 62 when he took charge, he was never going to be a long-term appointment. While he was awarded the job on merit, there was an element of a 'stop gap' nature to the decision.

Historical Context — Strength of Rivals and League
By 1983, Manchester United were experiencing something of a revival under Ron Atkinson, the flamboyant Liverpool-born manager who had done so well with West Brom in the late '70s. But United were proving more of a cup team; in the league, they finished 4th in both of Joe Fagan's seasons, without ever posing a serious threat. When Fagan took charge, it was only three years since Nottingham Forest completed back-to-back European Cup triumphs, and only 12 months after Aston Villa, following on from the Reds' winning their third European crown since 1977, had garnered England's sixth success in six seasons. English football was clearly very strong at the time, with Villa finishing down in 6th the season they conquered Europe, as, domestically, others leapfrogged them.

When Liverpool won the 1984 title, Southampton, under the guidance of Lawrie McMenemy, were the surprise runners-up. The Saints had been boosted by the arrival of Kevin Keegan in 1980; his capture helped raise the profile of McMenemy's outfit. Four years later, Southampton finished with 77 points, three behind Liverpool, even though Keegan had by that time moved to Newcastle. Another England star, Peter Shilton, had arrived at The Dell, while a future Liverpool star, Mark Wright, aged 21 at the time, was about to win his first England cap on account of his impressive performances with the south coast club. Nottingham Forest, still managed by Brian Clough but without both Shilton and Trevor Francis, were no longer the force of a few years earlier, but they finished 3rd, a further three points behind Southampton.

A year later, and both Southampton and Forest had fallen outside the top four, with Spurs moving up to third. But it was Everton who won the league in 1985, thirteen points ahead of Liverpool, who were runners-up with 77 points. It was the fourth year running that the Reds' league total diminished, which, while far from conclusive (given that three of the seasons ended with a league title), was perhaps indicative of a deterioration. The Reds had won the league in 1982 with 87 points, and again a year later, with 82. The third successive title, achieved with Fagan as the new manager, came courtesy of an 80-point haul. Within four years, Liverpool had registered a ten point loss.

Bête Noire
Fagan wasn't in charge long enough to stir any great rivalries into action. But with Howard Kendall awakening Everton from their slumber, Liverpool's successes and failures would be directly affected by their neighbours. Everton were defeated in the 1984 League Cup Final after a replay, courtesy of Graeme Souness' long-range winner. A year later, Liverpool finished 2nd in the league, 13 points behind their local rivals. In the '80s, Liverpool was clearly the premier city of English football — the city won seven consecutive titles between 1982 and 1988.

Pedigree/Previous Experience
Unlike Bob Paisley, Joe Fagan at least had some previous managerial experience beyond Liverpool's reserves — albeit 25 years before he took charge at Anfield. Fagan started out as player-manager at Nelson FC in the Lancashire Combination, and led the club to championship titles in 1950 and 1952. Nelson narrowly missed out on re-election to the Football League, and so in 1954 Fagan moved to manage Rochdale. Clearly it was vital experience gained by the young man, but these were low-key appointments well away from the top end of the game, and a million miles away from the pressures and expectations at Anfield.

Defining Moment
Three months before the 1985 European Cup Final in Brussels, Fagan, at the time of his 64th birthday, had announced to members of the club's hierarchy that he was contemplating retirement. He was tired, and the job had taken its toll. He would make a final decision at the end of the season, but it was widely accepted that he would be stepping down. In a Brussels hotel room, on the eve of that ill-fated game, Sir

John Smith called a board meeting. The directors were informed that Fagan would be retiring after the game the following day, and that Kenny Dalglish would be taking over.

It is a great pity that Fagan, with the chance to bow out at the top, suffered a fate far worse than he could have expected. In his mind, as the plane touched down in Belgium, defeat would have been the worst conceivable outcome. But to lose in amongst the far more significant *loss* of 39 opposing fans turned the whole experience about as sour as it could possibly get.

Crowning Glory

In 1984, with the League Cup in the bag, and the league title sewn up, all that remained in order to complete an historic treble was the small matter of playing AS Roma in their own stadium for the European Cup.

Phil Neal gave the Reds the lead, following up at the far post to prod home an early goal. Liverpool were looking fairly solid, although Roma had already forced Grobbelaar into one meaningful save. Then, just before half-time, Roma broke through when Pruzzo headed home Conti's cross. The game finished 1-1 after extra-time, and a penalty shootout beckoned. Fagan was calm, thanking the players for their efforts and commending their performance. Perhaps he was also resigned to failure, with the first-team having been beaten 5-0 by the youth team in a practice shootout a few days earlier. It didn't get any better when Steve Nicol blasted the opening attempt wildly over the bar. Di Bartolemi scored from Roma's opening kick, and the result was starting to look a formality. But then Grobbelaar intervened. The Zimbabwean became a legend that night, in what was the highlight of his career. "The biggest memory I have is the 1984 European Cup Final against Roma," he said, "and my 'spaghetti legs' routine during the penalty shootout that won us the trophy. People said I was being disrespectful to their players, but I was just testing their concentration under pressure. I guess they failed that test."

Conti was the first to succumb to the keeper's antics; Grobbelaar wobbled his legs on the goalline, and the Italian missed. Souness and Neal scored from their kicks, and Righetti kept his nerve for Roma, making the score 2-2 after three attempts each. Rush put Liverpool ahead with an unconvincing strike, but the keeper had gone the wrong way. Grazoli became the second of the Italian team's players to fall foul of Grobbelaar's distracting movements, blazing his effort over the bar. After four attempts each, the Reds were leading 3-2, and next up was Alan Kennedy with the chance to win the cup. Although he'd scored the winner in the 1981 final, his record with penalties was not impressive; he'd only taken two, in pre-season, and missed both. These misses could be interpreted in two ways: he was either someone who needed the big occasion to force him to focus, or he was a hopeless penalty taker who, if unable to score in meaningless games, stood no chance in what would have been the biggest moment of most footballers' careers. Fears of the latter were eased when he strode up and sent the ball past a wrong-footed Tancredi, into the top corner. It was the cue for delirious celebrations as Kennedy hopped with glee and the other players raced about the pitch with demented fervour.

Legacy

Like a man entrusted with the keys to a vintage Aston Martin, Joe Fagan helped keep things ticking over during his two years in charge, without attempting to modify and modernise. He didn't add any outstanding players, perhaps with the exception of Jan Molby, but he introduced plenty of good ones who were capable of doing a job for the first team. Liverpool would win the double in Dalglish's first season, so there still wasn't much wrong with the squad, but a lack of really top-class additions between 1983 and 1985 left Dalglish with quite a bit of work to do in the transfer market in order to take the club forward.

TRANSFERS

Transfers In

Joe Fagan's first signing was Gary Gillespie, a graceful Scottish centre-back in the Alan Hansen mould, who cost £325,000 from Coventry City. Quite remarkably, Gillespie had captained Falkirk at the age of 17. He then spent six years at Highfield Road, impressing Arsenal enough to make a move, but Liverpool stepped in to secure the services of the 23-year-old. He had his work cut out dislodging either Hansen or Lawrenson, and played only once in his debut season, but between 1986 and 1988 managed almost 100 games, with Lawrenson moved to full-back. In total, Gillespie played 214 games and scored 16 goals, before moving to Celtic for £925,000 — a phenomenal fee for a player who was 31.

Less successful was Michael Robinson, the 25-year-old Brighton striker who cost £200,000 in August 1983. While never totally convincing on an individual basis, his debut season was the club's greatest in terms of success. He featured 42 times on the way to the treble success, including a substitute appearance in the European Cup Final, and scored 12 times. Mark Lawrenson, who played with Robinson at Preston and Brighton, as well as for Ireland, before the two were united for a third time at club level, said "The nicest thing about

Michael was that he knew his own limitations. He would tell you himself that he didn't have a good touch for a big man and he was predominantly one-footed. But he was strong. He was very powerful and would chase everything. When the chips were down he would give you absolutely everything." Robinson himself said: "I've never known a shirt to weigh so heavy. I felt silly playing for Liverpool. I thought all my team-mates were far better." His limitations grew more obvious in his second season, and halfway through 1984/85 Robinson was sold to QPR for £100,000, having scored 13 goals in 52 games.

John Wark, purchased in March 1984 at the age of 26, was another signing who wasn't seen as a total success, although the Scottish attacking midfielder left fours years later with a very impressive statistical record. Having cost £450,000 from Ipswich, he scored 42 goals in 92 starts and a further 16 substitute appearances. His first full season saw him finish as top scorer, with 27 goals, although a series of niggling injuries followed by a broken leg limited his effectiveness from his second season onwards, and as a result his reputation as a top Liverpool player was never quite secured. Wark eventually returned to Ipswich for £100,000 at the start of 1988, having been a peripheral figure in Dalglish's rebuilt squad.

Another talented individual who didn't quite reach the heights expected, and who had also found himself out of the first team picture by 1988, was Paul Walsh. Outstanding in training, he never quite translated his ability into matches on a regular basis. Not yet 22 in May 1984 when he moved to Anfield, the diminutive striker cost £700,000 from Luton. It appeared Fagan had got a bargain, fighting off competition from Manchester United for the PFA Young Player of the Year. A clever player with bags of skill, Walsh scored 13 goals in 32 matches in his first season, but it was his 18 goals in 25 matches during the double season that showed his true potential. Ruptured ligaments ended his run in the side, and he'd only score six more goals for the club before his sale to Spurs for £500,000 in February 1988, after 112 games.

Jan Molby, signed from Ajax for £200,000 in August 1984, was seen by many as Graeme Souness' replacement. Having been brought to Liverpool on a ten day trial, the 21-year-old quickly impressed and a permanent deal was struck. But it wasn't clear when the Dane would be ready for the first team, or just what his was role would be, and so three months down the line Fagan moved to buy someone who was a bit more in the Souness mould. Signed in November 1984, Kevin MacDonald started slowly but eventually began to fulfil his promise, albeit under Fagan's successor. The tall, rangy midfielder cost £400,000 from Leicester City. Kenny Dalglish was very appreciative of his qualities: "A real work-horse for us in the middle of the pitch," he said. "Got about the pitch well, won the ball and gave it, kept everything simple. Never tired and did a really good job. Hugely underrated." A serious broken leg sustained in 1986 kept him out for almost two years, and he was never the same player again. He was released after 64 games, having scored five goals.

In January 1985, Fagan agreed a £250,000 deal for Oldham's teenage hopeful, Wayne Harrison. The youngster never played a game for the Reds, and at times must have wondered if he had run over a litter of black cats without realising, so horrific was his luck.

Player	Quality	0.01pg	IN	OUT	FGV	VALUE	Ap	Details
Jan Molby	8.59	2.92	-1.3		4	**14.21**	292	£200k 1984 Rel 1996
Gary Gillespie	7.29	2.14	-2.2		6.4	**13.63**	214	£325k 1983 £925k '91 @31
Average	**6.93**		**-2.53**			**8.25**		
All Managers' Average						**7.92**		
John Wark	7.06	1.08	-3		1.1	**6.24**	108	£450k 1984 £100k Jan '88 @31
Paul Walsh	6.76	1.12	-4.7		2.6	**5.78**	112	£700k 1984 £500k Feb '88
Michael Robinson	5.94	0.52	-1.3		0.6	**5.76**	52	£200k 1983 £100k 1984
Kevin MacDonald	5.94	0.64	-2.7		0	**3.88**	64	£400k 1984 Rel. 1989
Wayne Harrison	*-*	*0*	*-1.7*		*-*	*1.7*	*-*	*0*	*£250k 1985 Ret. 1992*

Key: *See page 51.*

Transfer Masterstroke

Rather than sign anyone astonishing — 8.59 was the highest rating for *Quality*, and none played 300 games — Fagan made several good signings who all, bar the teenager Wayne Harrison, contributed something to the Liverpool cause, with each receiving at least one league winner's medal. But there was one player who at times came close to being another world-class star: Jan Molby. While in later years Molby (and his belly) would stand out for all the wrong reasons, in the mid-'80s he was a sublime midfield General, whose passing skills helped open up countless opposition defences, while his long-range strikes and über-cool penalties helped him rack up 21 goals in all competitions in his second season. Possibly due to a period of adaptation, and the pressure of having to replace Graeme Souness, Molby struggled in his first season at the club, and it was only when Fagan was replaced by Dalglish that the Dane came into his own. "Jan was a very, very talented player," Dalglish said, "with a great knowledge and appreciation of how to play football." His finest moment in a Liverpool shirt came in a home League Cup match against Manchester United in November 1985. He dispossessed Norman Whiteside near the halfway line and strode past three United players before unleashing a long-range rocket that flew into the top corner like an Exocet. A TV strike denied the rest of the world the chance to witness what many still believe to be the greatest-ever Anfield goal.

Molby was a crucial part of the double-winning team of 1985/86, although this would be his finest season in a Liverpool shirt; never again did he reach such heights in a further decade at the club. Alan Hansen, who sung Molby's praises as a midfield playmaker who, unusually, could also dominate in the air, was particularly impressed with how he could also fill in at centre-back and sweeper without looking out of position. Injuries, and an inability to control his weight, resulted in a less-effective Molby over subsequent campaigns, while a three-month spell in prison in 1988 for a driving offence didn't help matters. Having played 34 league games in 1986/87, scoring 12 goals, he only managed to feature in 37 over the next three years.

While he never lost his skill and vision, Molby's lack of mobility became an increasing problem. He endured a revival of sorts in the early '90s, and shone in the 1992 FA Cup Final victory over Sunderland, but there will always be a sense of unfulfilled potential. Molby's Liverpool career was ended by Roy Evans in 1996, after 12 years but only 292 appearances; contrast this with Phil Neal's 650 in eleven seasons. In total Molby scored 62 goals, 42 of which were from penalties — with only three spot-kicks missed, resulting in an exceptional conversion rate of 93%.

Expensive Folly

Wayne Harrison, signed for £250,000 from Oldham Athletic in January 1985, was the world's most expensive teenager at the time. He is unquestionably the costliest mistake made by Joe Fagan. It wasn't so much that Harrison — aged just 17 — was a bad player, just that incredibly bad luck ended his career at Liverpool before it ever got started.

Signing Harrison was without doubt a gamble; the striker had played just two league games, and those were in the second tier of English football. He was allowed to stay with Oldham for the remainder of the '84/85 season, and he played a further three times for the Lancashire club. By the time he arrived at Liverpool, Fagan had retired; Kenny Dalglish duly received a promising player to blood in the reserves. But it was *blood loss* that was to prove the initial problem; having made good progress, and been on the fringes of the first team, the youngster, in a freak accident, fell through the glass panel of a greenhouse. On account of an ambulance strike, Harrison had to wait a long time for Army medics to arrive. He was lucky to escape with his life, but his experiences with hospitals and operations were far from over. Over the next few years he endured a series of serious injuries. Each time he fought back, and got himself back into contention. But then, during the last reserve game of the season against Bradford City in May 1990, he collided with the goalkeeper. The collision shattered the cruciate ligaments in his knee. Again he fought to try and make a recovery, but it was futile. In 1992, after 23 football-related operations, and seven years after arriving at Anfield, he was forced to accept that, aged 24, he had to retire, never having played a first-team game for the Reds. He remains the perfect example of how a player — and indeed, the manager who signs him and those who subsequently inherit him — needs luck as well as talent. Harrison had a bucket-load of the latter, but precious little of the former.

One Who Got Away

In the summer of 1983, Liverpool were close to signing rising Danish star, Michael Laudrup. Reports suggested that the 19-year-old was due to sign, but the deal fell through when the club looked to make it a four-year contract, whereas the striker, represented by his father Finn, only wanted to sign for three years. Laudrup instead moved to Juventus, although it would take him two years to actually play for the club. The rule that limited the number of overseas players to just two meant that Laudrup had to go on loan to Lazio for two seasons, with French maestro Michel Platini and Polish striker Zbigniew Boniek the two established foreign stars. In the process, Liverpool lost out on one of the truly outstanding players of the mid-to-late '80s and early '90s. He could have been the perfect long-term replacement for Kenny Dalglish, but it wasn't to be.

Budget — Historical Context

In 1985, when Everton overtook Liverpool, they did so with a relatively inexpensive team. Having spent big in the previous decade, only to flop, they now relied on products of their youth system, along with a handful of bargain signings — including Kevin Sheedy, who'd cost just £100,000 from the Reds in 1982. Only Adrian Heath, who cost £700,000 in 1982 (46%), was vaguely expensive. On average, the team — Neville Southall, Gary Stevens, Kevin Ratcliffe, Derek Mountfield, Peter Reid, Trevor Steven, Paul Bracewell, Kevin Sheedy, Adrian Heath, Andy Gray and Graeme Sharp — cost just 11% of the English transfer record. By contrast, the Liverpool side of the time was just over 30%.

The Manchester United team that beat Everton 1-0 in the 1985 FA Cup Final — Gary Bailey, John Gidman, Arthur Albiston, Norman Whiteside, Paul McGrath, Kevin Moran, Bryan Robson, Gordon Strachan, Mark Hughes, Frank Stapleton and Jesper Olsen — cost 25.5% of the English record.

RECORD

League Championship 1983/84.
European Cup 1984
League Cup 1984

	P	W	D	L	F	A	%
Overall	**131**	**70**	**37**	**24**	**225**	**97**	**53.44%**
League	84	44	25	15	141	67	52.38%
FA Cup	9	5	2	2	23	7	55.56%
League Cup	16	8	7	1	27	9	50.00%
Europe	19	13	3	3	34	10	68.42%
Other	3	0	0	3	0	4	0.00%

CONCLUSION

It's a sad legacy of an ill-fated European Cup Final that the enduring image of Joe Fagan is one of a broken man at Speke airport, clutching his face as tears stream down his cheeks. Having spent 27 years at the club, he was bowing out at the worst possible moment. His retirement, which lasted until his death in July 2001 at the age of 80, was tarnished by the awful conclusion to a wonderful career at the club.

While he is generally not regarded in the same bracket as Shankly and Paisley, Fagan topped them both in terms of achievements in a single season. For that, he will always be fondly remembered. Whether or not Fagan was a true great, he oversaw the club's *greatest season*, and was a European Champion. For that, he will remain something of a legend.

"What I have to offer is one word — honesty.
I couldn't be devious if I tried."

JOE FAGAN

"Few great players make the transition into management. The reason is that great players are normally like soloists in an orchestra. They perform alone and tend to look down on teammates with lesser ability. That was never Kenny Dalglish. He was like a conductor. He brought other players into play. He understood that not everyone was blessed with the greatest of skill. He had patience both as a player and as a manager."

BOB PAISLEY

1985 - 1991
KENNY DALGLISH

INTRODUCTION

It's certainly far harder to judge where Kenny Dalglish fits in at the top end of the Liverpool management table than it is to judge him as a player. As the latter, he was simply the best — the King. No argument. His six years as manager were also full of success, and in the middle of his reign, the football was resplendent, and at times breathtaking — almost certainly the most aesthetically pleasing seen in the club's history. But his tenure didn't quite reach the heights of Paisley's, and he hadn't had to build the club up like Shankly. Meanwhile, his six years marked the club's exact exile from Europe, which removed one area of comparis, particularly with the man who had brought him to the club in 1977 and who dominated on the continent.

While Liverpool fans were not exclusively to blame for the European ban — firstly, because the fans of other British clubs had caused plenty of trouble themselves in order to sully the reputation of English supporters, and secondly because the deaths of 39 Italians at Heysel came when a creaking old wall collapsed amid *two* fighting nations — they did contribute to the dark ages of English football. By this point the best players had already started to move abroad — most notably, technical players like Graeme Souness, Liam Brady, Ray Wilkins, Trevor

Francis (and, er, Luther Blissett), with Chris Waddle and Glenn Hoddle to follow — and the imports into England, bar the odd exception, were not of a similar quality. It meant that the top division was not at its strongest just a handful of years after the country's clubs had dominated European competition. Even so, Dalglish's job was to beat what was put in front of him, and it was not his fault that trips to Rome and Madrid were no longer on the agenda, and places like Plough Lane, Wimbledon, were.

The other question mark over Dalglish is the situation he bequeathed his successor. The Hillsborough disaster in 1989, in which 96 lives were lost, effectively marked the end of the great league-winning dynasty. One more title was bagged, in 1990, but Dalglish was feeling the strain. The team his successor inherited was ageing badly.

Situation Inherited

The day before the final at Heysel, Sir John Smith announced to the club's directors that he'd appointed Kenny Dalglish as the new manager, following Joe Fagan's retirement. To some it came as a massive shock, although a year earlier Graeme Souness had told a Scottish journalist that he expected Dalglish to be the club's next boss. With Fagan the third, and final, remaining member of the original 1959 Boot Room to take the role, it would have to be someone from the next generation. All eyes were on Ronnie Moran, the most senior coach, with Roy Evans, still in his 30s, a less likely option. Chris Lawler was seen as having an outside chance, and from within the playing staff, Phil Neal was a strong candidate. But Dalglish was the man Smith wanted.

Liverpool were still the envy of England, but the situation at the club was far less rosy: Dalglish took the reigns in the immediate aftermath of the Heysel tragedy, when a shellshocked Joe Fagan, hoping to retire with a wonderful win, found his last game to be the stuff of nightmares. Quality was still very much in abundance on the playing staff in 1985. Graeme Souness had moved to Sampdoria in 1984, but otherwise all the key players from the phenomenal treble-winning side were in place — including, of course, Dalglish himself. The player-manager aside, the squad included key men such as Alan Hansen, Ian Rush, Ronnie Whelan, Mark Lawrenson, Steve Nicol and Bruce Grobbelaar, plus Jan Molby, a player who hadn't quite found his form in his debut season as Souness' replacement, and who had struggled to hold down a place in the team, but who would go on to net 21 goals in Dalglish's first campaign as manager. One player who presented Dalglish with a problem was Phil Neal, the club captain, who was upset at being passed over for the manager's role. In an act of pettiness, he refused to call Dalglish 'boss'. Before the subject had been raised, Neal told the press he didn't have a future at Anfield; as a result he was stripped of the captaincy. He quickly took a move to manage Bolton.

Due to the post-Heysel exile, Dalglish is the only manager covered in this book not to take his team into Europe. The ban affected all clubs, and while Liverpool were seen as being to blame, the supporters of other clubs had played their part. A year earlier, also in Brussels, a Tottenham fan was shot dead and a further 200 held by police following a riot before the UEFA Cup Final against Anderlecht; the same year England fans had caused almost £1m of damage in Paris following defeat to France. To further highlight the trouble of the times, in 1986 five people were stabbed in a riot between 150 Everton, Manchester United and West Ham supporters on a cross-channel ferry, which was severely damaged and forced to return to England. But the rest of the English clubs returned to European competition in 1990, with Liverpool, who would have qualified for the European Cup, having to wait an extra year. By this time Dalglish had resigned and Graeme Souness was in charge. Europe was back on the fixture list, but alas the Liverpool of old had withered away in the interim.

Players Inherited Squad

Player	Quality	Age	Adj	Inheritance	Year	Age
Ian Rush (1)	9.71	0	0	9.71	1985	23.5
Ronnie Whelan	8.61	0	0	8.61	1985	24
Alan Hansen	9.59	-3	2	8.59	1985	30
Jan Molby	8.59	0	0	8.59	1985	22
Steve Nicol	8.53	0	0	8.53	1985	24.5
Bruce Grobbelaar	8.29	0	0	8.29	1985	28
Mark Lawrenson	9.00	-1	0	8.00	1985	28
Sammy Lee	7.64	0	0	7.64	1985	26
Craig Johnston	7.33	0	0	7.33	1985	25
Gary Gillespie	7.29	0	0	7.29	1985	25
Average	**8.11**			**7.05**		**26.6**
Paul Walsh	6.76	0	0	6.76	1985	22.5
Jim Beglin	6.71	0	0	6.71	1985	22
John Wark	7.06	-1	0	6.06	1985	28
Kenny Dalglish	10	-7	3	6.00	1985	34
Kevin MacDonald	5.94	0	0	5.94	1985	24.5
Alan Kennedy	7.94	-4	0	3.94	1985	31
Phil Neal	8.94	-7	0	1.94	1985	34

First XI

Player	Quality	Age	Adj	Inheritance	Year	Age
Bruce Grobbelaar	8.29	0	0	8.29	1985	28
Alan Kennedy	7.94	-4	0	3.94	1985	31
Phil Neal	8.94	-7	0	1.94	1985	34
Alan Hansen	9.59	-3	2	8.59	1985	30
Mark Lawrenson*	9.00	-1	0	8.00	1985	28
Steve Nicol	8.53	0	0	8.53	1985	24.5

Jan Molby	8.59	0	0	**8.59**	1985	22
Ronnie Whelan	8.61	0	0	**8.61**	1985	24
Craig Johnston	7.33	0	0	**7.33**	1985	25
Kenny Dalglish	10	-7	3	**6.00**	1985	34
Ian Rush (1)	9.71	0	0	**9.71**	1985	23.5
Average	**8.77**			**7.23**		**27.6**

Key: Quality 0-10; Age = -1 point for every year from 28 onwards, eg -4 for 31 year-old, and -1 point from 30 onwards for keepers, eg -4 for 33 year-old; Adj = adjustments for players either exceptionally fit/unfit for their age, or soon to leave; Inheritance = total out of 10. Excludes players not part of first team picture.

In terms of *Quality*, the First XI, fresh from back-to-back European Cup finals, was still incredibly strong in 1985. But Phil Neal and Alan Kennedy were in the twilight of their careers, so replacements were needed. As a result of Neal moving to Bolton, Steve Nicol was moved to right-back. In Jim Beglin, Dalglish already had a player capable of filling the left-back slot, and before too long he was in the team, while Gary Ablett would emerge in 1986. Alan Hansen had turned 30, but was an especially good reader of the game. And of course, there was Dalglish himself, who had now turned 34. These age adjustments weaken the First XI *Inheritance* rating to an average of 7.23, a full point lower than the side Paisley inherited, and half a point lower than the side Paisley left for Fagan. So it was still a great side on paper, but some key players were beginning to edge over the hill.

While players like Paul Walsh, Kevin MacDonald and Jim Beglin were in the squad and ready to either fill in for, or replace, the older members of the side, none was at quite the same standard as his predecessor. In Dalglish's first season, Hansen remarked to the manager that this was the worst Liverpool side he'd played in. Within a few months the Reds would land the league and FA Cup double. Even so, it was clear that some serious work in the transfer market would be needed before too long.

State of Club
Sir John Smith and Peter Robinson — two of the game's sharpest administrators — were still running the show. Smith had phoned Dalglish prior to the team leaving for Belgium for the 1985 European Cup Final, and asked if he and Robinson could come visit him at home. "I said aye, that was all right," Dalglish recalled. "Then they told me what it was about, and I said they could still come."

Towards the end of Dalglish's tenure, Noel White replaced Sir John Smith as chairman. Smith had been spending an increasing amount of time with Sport England, of which he was also chairman, as well as with his own business. It would be alongside White that Dalglish would sit and announce his resignation to the world in 1991.

Assistance/Backroom Staff

In 1985, Ronnie Moran and Roy Evans, like the floodlights, were still permanent fixtures at Anfield. Chris Lawler, appointed by Joe Fagan, was still in place as reserve team coach — although he would soon be departing in acrimonious circumstances.

Perhaps the key involvement for Dalglish should have been that of Bob Paisley as an advisor — which is akin to having Leonardo Da Vinci on hand to teach you how to paint. Dalglish had stipulated that Paisley's assistance would be vital if he were to take the role, and the club was able to persuade the great man out of retirement, on a two-year contract. But as it transpired, Dalglish would not need much help from his former boss.

A year into his reign, and with the 1985/86 double freshly under his belt, Dalglish began to make a number of serious changes to the back-room staff. With Tom Saunders retiring at the age of 64, Steve Heighway took over as youth development officer. Saunders would later return to the club after being elected to the board of directors in 1993, and assist future managers in their administration tasks, until his death in 2001.

Also in the summer of 1986, Dalglish appointed Phil Thompson onto the coaching staff. Thompson had been training at Melwood twice a week; the former Liverpool captain had moved to Sheffield United two years earlier, but was now finding himself out of the first team picture. Interestingly, Thompson was offered the role of managing the reserves in conjunction with also playing for the second string — a slightly strange offer seeing as Thompson, now in his 30s, had been considered not good enough for Liverpool in 1984, and now the same was felt at Sheffield United. It can only have been to offer support and guidance on the pitch, in the way Ronnie Moran had between 1966 and 1968. Thompson had been appointed a couple of weeks before Lawler was told his services were no longer required. That conversation only came about after Lawler, wondering why he hadn't received his bonus when the other coaching staff had, went to see Dalglish. Naturally, it came as a massive shock to Lawler, and given that he hadn't done anything *specific* wrong — no serious failings, no misdemeanours — he did not take it well. But Dalglish was reshaping the club, and the first sacking of a member of the Boot Room was not something he would shy away from in order to maintain his vision, even if he didn't handle the situation particularly well. While he'd been successful with the reserves, Dalglish saw Lawler as too quiet, not forceful enough. The same could never be said of Thompson; in fact, he'd often be charged with being the opposite.

If sacking Lawler was a shock, then replacing Geoff Twentyman, the club's chief scout, with another ex-captain, Ron Yeats, was an even more stunning move. Yeats, who also took on Saunders' role of scouting missions to assess the opposition, had no prior scouting experience, and was replacing arguably the best man in the business. Twentyman and Saunders had been two of the club's great unsung heroes after two decades' sterling service, with Twentyman in particular responsible for bringing some of the club's greatest names to Anfield.

Saunders, meanwhile, had brought through some talented locals, like Phil Thompson and Sammy Lee. If anything, in his first twelve years Steve Heighway would surpass the work of Saunders, and unearth the best batch of home-grown talent the club had ever seen. By contrast, Yeats had little chance of matching the incredible feats of Twentyman, and, after one more summer of astute dealing, the next 12 years would see a change in quality of the players recruited to Anfield.

Shortly before his departure, Twentyman recommended two more players: Peter Beardsley of Newcastle and John Barnes of Watford. A year later Dalglish would sign both. By that time Twentyman was a year into working for Graeme Souness at Rangers. Beardsley and Barnes would be the last great signings made by Dalglish, and only one more enduring talent arrived at Anfield in the next four years — Ray Houghon, snapped up later in 1987. Whether or not it was down to the managers — after all, a scout can only *recommend* players and leave the decision to sign to the man in charge — it is damning to note that, with the exception of Jamie Redknapp and Rob Jones, the players signed by the club prior to the arrival of Gérard Houllier were mediocre at best; not all were necessarily mediocre in terms of ability or what they had shown at their previous clubs, but for one reason or another none shone as expected when wearing the red of Liverpool.

Was that down to Yeats? It's hard to say. He was heavily involved in the spotting of Sami Hyypia, and Didi Hamann was also signed in 1999, so he can point to later successes. But Liverpool weren't finding great hidden talents in the way they had with Twentyman as the club's eyes and ears.

Management Style

Upon Dalglish's appointment, Graeme Souness explained that his good friend had an ingredient vital for success: he scared people with a growl, and sometimes with even just a look. As well as being respected as a player, Dalglish was a strong character who could command respect as a man. He was no soft touch, as his former team-mates would discover.

As a neighbour, Mark Lawrenson had shared a lift to training with Dalglish for a number of years, but once the Scot became manager the relationship changed overnight. Lawrenson, struggling with injury, had agreed to coach at a summer soccer school in Dublin on the opening day of pre-season training in 1985, and was instantly rebuked. The centre-back felt firmly put in his place, and accepted Dalglish's punishment.

While possessing more of a sense of humour than his dour image portrays, Dalglish had a poor relationship with the press. Terse, taciturn, and at times just plain rude, he did not play the media game. The result was that journalists became more critical, and less likely to give him the benefit of the doubt before putting the boot in. While his approach was understandable — the press can be difficult for a manager to deal with, as well as having their own agenda — rubbing them up the wrong way just increases the criticism, which ramps up the pressure. It may lead to a siege mentality that can inspire success, but it can also foster a sense of negativity around a club.

Ironically, Dalglish would later be called upon by the media to offer his views on the club, and appear on TV as a match summariser. To his eternal credit, he tries to see things from the perspective of the manager, and refuses to land the low blows so common from a number of other ex-players.

Unique Methods

In a precursor to rotation, Dalglish liked to be flexible with his line-ups. He was trying to be unpredictable, rather than protect legs for a long campaign, although that may have been in his thinking too. He didn't go in for the wholesale changes seen from all big clubs in the modern era, just one or two from game to game. At times there would be a settled side for a run of matches, but never in the manner of the past. He liked to omit Peter Beardsley against the more physical teams like Wimbledon and Arsenal, while Jan Molby would be shifted from a standard midfield role to playing behind the front two (Ian Rush, and either the manager himself or Paul Walsh), and then converted to sweeping behind the back four. In time Beardsley found himself sitting out more and more games, and his selection — or lack of — became a hot topic. It wasn't always apparent why he was omitted — the forward was left out even when he was the top scorer in the country. The Geordie started to feel victimised, although he later admitted that he came to understand it was not personal, but tactical. The manager claimed that the player had a stress fracture during his final months in charge, which partly explained some of the omissions. Dalglish also felt that Beardsley needed to be more ruthless as a finisher, and it's something the player himself agreed with. In and out of the side, Beardsley's confidence started to crumble — but Dalglish was merely trying to pick the right team to win each game.

Dalglish also refrained from naming the team until shortly before kick-off; a method, like rotation, employed by Rafa Benítez. The players weren't always happy with it, but it did serve to guarantee that no-one could ease off in the build-up to a game, and complacency couldn't easily set in. Ronnie Moran, a member of the 'old school', felt the new development was a brilliant move — there was a lot more intensity in training, with 16 strong possibilities fighting to be in the next line-up.

But of course, no method in football is fail-safe, and every philosophy involves weighing the pros against the cons. Dalglish was heavily criticised for his inconsistency of selection whenever the team lost, or hit a sticky patch of form, but his record over his six years in charge is testimony to the wisdom of his methods. Dalglish has by far the best win percentage out of all the club's managers in the last 50 years, in both the league and across all competitions. Given that Alan Hansen felt the 1986 team was the worst Liverpool side he'd played in, and that many felt that the 1990 team wasn't vintage either, that suggests Dalglish was doing something very right indeed.

Strengths

Initially, identifying and signing good players was Dalglish's key attribute. And in many ways it needed to be. Not only were some of the players he inherited edging over the hill, and his star striker eyeing a move abroad, but some cruel injuries would rob him of a number of key players.

Kevin MacDonald, a key component in the double-winning team, was finally starting to look capable of growing into an inspirational midfielder when, in September 1986, he broke his leg; he would return to playing 18 months later, but the injury had taken its toll and he was not the same player. Jim Beglin, emerging as a fine young left-back, suffered the same fate: a broken leg in the same season; unlike MacDonald, he wouldn't return to the first team even for a few token appearances. John Wark was another who broke his leg in 1986. Steve Nicol missed the whole of the second half of 1986/87, although returned to full health for the following season. But Mark Lawrenson was seriously injured at the back-end of Dalglish's second season, with the defender approaching his 30th birthday. The Achilles tear ended Lawrenson's career.

The biggest of all the departures in Dalglish's time was when, in 1986, Ian Rush announced that he would be joining Juventus, effective from the summer of 1987. The deal, valued at £3.2m, was the most expensive in British football history. While a surprise in many respects — unlike Kevin Keegan a decade earlier, Rush did not seem the kind of extrovert personality naturally suited to such a move — there was an inevitability about the best British players leaving for the continent during the 1980s. In 1984 Rush had been lured by the lira on offer by Napoli — who offered Rush a £1m signing-on fee, aside from his wages, and were prepared to pay Liverpool £4.5m — but no deal was struck. However, with the Reds excluded from European competition, the club could not hang onto its prized asset. Dalglish, still a relative rookie, had to deal with something particularly rare: Liverpool as a selling club. He wanted Rush to stay, and told him that while the club were happy to cash in if he was set on a move, they were equally happy to retain his services. He also told Rush that the club wouldn't object if he wanted to join Juventus, who had offered £3.2m, instead of Barcelona, who had bid £4.3m. Rush preferred Italy, which was seen as the world's best league, and turned his back on a country that would have more suited his style of play, and a club that had an English manager in Terry Venables, as well as a friend and compatriot, Mark Hughes, already in the team. It also meant that Dalglish didn't have as much money to reinvest in the team — but of course, by choosing a tough, defensive league, it ultimately made Rush returning to Liverpool more inevitable.

All the same, the money Juventus paid was enough to help Dalglish rebuild his side. His view to the club's finances was simple: "The people who come to watch us play, who love the team and regard it as part of their lives, would never appreciate Liverpool having a huge balance in the bank. They want every asset we possess to be wearing a red shirt and that's what I want, too."

Rush spent what was meant to be his swan-song season at Liverpool scoring goals in his customary fashion — notching 40 times — but it was a trophy-free year, with Everton crowned champions. With weird timing, the Reds also finally lost a game in which Rush had scored: the 1987 League Cup Final against Arsenal breaking the seven-year run, as the Gunners came back from a goal down to seal a 2-1 victory. The loss of the most potent striker the English game had seen for decades was a big psychological blow, but it was quickly offset by Dalglish's canny reinvestment of the fee. (Compare, for example, how Gérard Houllier wasted the money received for Robbie Fowler 14 years later.) Rush certainly wasn't missed. Even so, he made a welcome return for an extended encore 12 months later, having struggled to adapt to Italy both on and off the pitch.

With Rush gone, the manager himself more-or-less retired, and a number of injuries and retirements, Dalglish had to build a new Liverpool team — and he did so in some style. Not only did he match the domestic feats of the past, he did so with a more flamboyant style. The 1987/88 side didn't have as many tough characters and pure fire-and-blood winners as some of the sides fielded by Shankly, Paisley and Fagan, but it had some supreme individual ability and a quite breathtaking understanding. And all this was achieved with Lawrenson, the club's most mobile defender, on crutches after a failed comeback attempt and, before the season was out, moving into management at

Oxford United.

Another strong point was that Dalglish wasn't afraid of players confronting him, having the strength of character to discuss why a certain decision had been made. Ronnie Whelan went to the see the boss, unhappy at being left out of the 1988 FA Cup Final, and later said: "Kenny doesn't mind if you argue with him. But you can argue until the cows come home and you'll never win." Like a referee, a manager is unlikely to change his mind, but it takes a special skill to placate a disgruntled player and have him walk out of the office feeling that he is an important part of the set-up.

Weaknesses

While it was perfectly human of Dalglish to succumb to stress — and, given that there were some exceptional extenuating circumstances, it might seem churlish to describe doing so as a weakness — but ultimately he couldn't cope, and that has to be recognised. Football managers deal with the weight of expectations of thousands, and in Liverpool's case, millions of fans. There can be no doubting that it's an incredibly difficult job; those who survive in the management game are built of different stuff when it comes to handling the unique kinds of pressure. Many managers work very long days, and simply cannot switch off from their job. Thought processes become obsessions. Hair quickly turns grey.

Dalglish's tenure began as it would end — under great pressure and scrutiny. But initially he coped admirably. His first game, against Arsenal at Anfield, was played in front of the world's media as all eyes turned to the club after the death of 39 Juventus supporters. The pressure would ramp up over the years, not least after great success in his inaugural campaign; increasing already stellar expectations. Then there was the sublime football of 1987/88, which was impossible to maintain. The old Liverpool way would no longer be as acceptable — grinding out results would be frowned upon after the élan of that vintage season.

By the end, he was desperate to escape the goldfish bowl. "In the past I would make the decision, usually more right than wrong and move on without thinking. Now I agonised over everything," Dalglish explained. "The biggest problem was the pressure I was putting myself under in my desire to be successful." He was experiencing headaches, and a rash had covered his body, even spreading onto his face. Almost daily a doctor visited Anfield to give him injections. Meanwhile, at home he was edgy and irritable, and constantly barracking his children; something he found incredibly upsetting. Having been pretty much teetotal, he began drinking wine in order to be more relaxed around his family. He was not in a good way, physically and psychologically.

A breaking point had to come, and on February 21st 1991, sitting ashen-faced alongside Noel White, he publicly announced his resignation. "I just can't take it any more. I'm tired. The pressure is incredible. I can cope during the week but on match days I feel my head is exploding." He claims he'd reached the decision before the most recent match, but clearly that tipped him over the edge; it's one thing deciding to do something, another entirely to go through with it. That game was the 4-4 FA Cup draw with Everton — a match which had seen the Reds throw away the lead no less than *four* times, the third of which was in the dying moments of normal time, and the fourth at the end of extra-time. Originally, Dalglish had thought about resigning at the end of the 1989/90 season. He had originally told his wife Marina that he could only see himself in the job for five years, and as that milestone approached he was holding off signing a new contract. But he fought off his doubts and kept going. Without such a horrible game (from a management perspective) to endure, maybe he would have soldiered on yet longer, but it seems unlikely that the pressure would have abated. While Dalglish said that he knew beforehand that the match would be his last, there was an incident in the game that reinforced his belief. Sitting alongside Ronnie Moran with the Reds leading 4-3, Dalglish wanted to move Molby back to sweeper, to contain Tony Cottee, who was proving a handful. Moran suggested holding fire, and Dalglish acquiesced — but more out of a sense of indecision than agreement. When it came to making decisions, the old certainty had been replaced by doubts, and he felt weak-willed. Cottee equalised yet again, to make it 4-4, and Dalglish later noted that "the hesitation confirmed I was right to quit".

It wasn't just Dalglish wilting under the pressure at the time. Club captain Alan Hansen was also feeling the strain. "It makes me laugh when people talk about how confident I seemed on a football field because the reality is quite different. I suffered badly from pre-match nerves, and found it increasingly difficult to cope with the pressures of playing for a club like Liverpool." It had reached the point where nothing short of total success was expected, and even the fans had become blasé about the accumulation of silverware.

In terms of the football Liverpool played, at its peak the team resembled Dalglish the player: stylish, thoughtful and committed. But as time passed, as well as being defensive to the media, the manager's team selections were also growing increasingly cautious. The flair started to ebb out of Liverpool's game, and defenders were increasingly lining up in midfield. Was the desire to *hold on*, to *protect*, a legacy of the loss of life at Hillsborough, or just another example of a manager trying to minimise the stress by reducing the risks?

Dalglish's reasons for resigning were widely mocked in the media. Surely pressure is the preserve of the unemployed or the struggling nurse, and not that of a very wealthy man involved in sport, it was argued. While such observations are true to a degree, the manager of Liverpool Football Club carries the escapist hopes of the unemployed, the struggling nurse, and all manner of different people in society. He affects the mood of an entire city and increasingly, in this modern football age, millions of other tiny enclaves all over the world. It's a big burden to carry, as is being responsible for the livelihood of those the club employs. Dalglish had bonded even more closely with the fans following Hillsborough — they had become more personal to him, not just faces in a bustling crowd, but real people whose lives often revolved around the club — and he did not want to let them down. While Shankly's famous words were always meant to be tongue-in-cheek — football is of course *not* more important than life and death — it summed up the often illogical importance that people place on following their team. Football may not be more important than life or death, but it does add an incredible amount of value to the lives of those who pin their weekly hopes around a successful result. While Hillsborough, with the loss of 96 lives, including young boys and girls, put into perspective the relative irrelevance of winning or losing, paradoxically it also served to highlight the incredible importance of the club to its community.

And that's before the pressure a perfectionist, a winner, like Dalglish puts on himself. Football is not like golf, snooker, darts or tennis, where the athlete carries his own hopes. Team sports bring an added responsibility, as seen in how golfers wilt when it comes time to perform as a collective in the Ryder Cup.

Despite his decision, Dalglish harboured hopes of returning later that year. "If Liverpool had waited until the summer, and then asked me to go back as manager," he explained, "I would have gone back". But by April Graeme Souness had been appointed manager. The board had asked Dalglish repeatedly to reconsider his decision when he tendered his resignation, and even suggested that he take a break until the summer and return for the next season. But no, he was adamant that he was going that day, and going for good. So it was no surprise that the club moved on and began to look elsewhere.

Historical Context — Strength of Rivals and League

In the mid-to-late '80 — still a time when a number of teams felt they had a realistic chance of winning the title — Arsenal and Everton provided Liverpool's main opposition. George Graham's Gunners perhaps borrowed some of the methods of Shankly's Liverpool — not always the most aesthetically pleasing side in the country, but often the most determined and gritty. Arsenal had few of the exceptional individual talents that Shankly could call on, but they had a relentless strength and an obdurate defence.

Aston Villa provided the main threat in 1989/90. Perhaps it's indicative of the weakness of the league at that time that their two strikers were Ian Olney and Ian Ormondroyd. The pair scored a rather pathetic 22 league goals in their 144 games for Villa, and were not good enough to sustain careers in the top flight. David Platt's goals from midfield were the main threat, but this was not in any way, shape or form a great team. The exile from European football was taking its toll, and soon Platt would be joining the exodus of top British talent that had already diminished the quality of the top-flight; Platt moved to Italy for £5.5m, but by contrast, the record fee paid by an English club was just over half that amount. While it was proving hard for any club to lure top-quality foreign stars to England, the fact that Liverpool were thinking of bidding on Sunderland's Marco Gabbiadini and were trailing QPR's Roy Wegerle shows the dearth of available talent. So while the league had grown weak, there was also precious little talent to mine, as well as the lack of resources to compete with Italy and Spain. Without European football, it became harder to entice top players to the club.

As such, it's impossible to say that in the '80s, or indeed the preceding decades, it was easier or harder to manage than in the current day, where the best players from any part of the world can be lured to the *entire* Premiership. Now there's almost limitless choice. (But of course, that also makes scouting more complicated, given how far afield the search has expanded.) What is true is that, relative to their rivals, Liverpool were able to spend bigger in the late '80s than was possible 20 years later.

Manchester United were in a bit of a sorry state throughout the bulk of Dalglish's tenure, with the exception of one year when they finished 2nd. In 1987/88, as Liverpool blitzed their way to the title, United finished as runners-up with 81 points, perhaps indicative of the massive improvements they'd go on to make at the start of the next decade. Alex Ferguson's previous campaign — his first — had been fairly miserable, with United finishing 11th, but things would get much worse before they got decisively better. History now tells us that many of the elements were in place for United to topple Liverpool by 1989, but they would finish 11th again, and then 13th, five points above the relegation zone, before the long-term improvements would take hold. In Dalglish's final season United, fresh from winning the FA Cup, rose to 6th in the league and won the UEFA Cup-Winners' Cup. Their time was about to come, aided by Liverpool's demise.

Bête Noire
Howard Kendall at Everton was almost certainly the man whose success vexed Dalglish the most in the early part of his tenure. Dalglish wrested the title off Kendall in his first season, but a year later the Everton manager was back, to land the crown. But the threat of Kendall was seen off for good a year later. As such, George Graham probably dented Dalglish's hopes more than any other rival. It started with the League Cup Final of 1987, and culminated most famously at Anfield on May 26th 1989. Graham's Arsenal would also win the title in 1991, with their obstinacy contributing to the pressure Dalglish found himself under in his swan song season.

Pedigree/Previous Experience
Like Bob Paisley and Joe Fagan, Dalglish had no prior first-team management experience in the football league. However, at least his two illustrious predecessors had spent many years in the game *assisting* managers, as well as spending a number of years overseeing the reserves, while Fagan had managed at non-league level. Dalglish was a complete rookie, but he was clever enough to surround himself with people who knew the ropes, with Paisley on hand to offer assistance. In the end, he didn't seek out Paisley's advice that much. According to Ian Ross, the former Liverpool utility man, Paisley hadn't been consulted once during the first six months of the arrangement. Dalglish had learned a lot from Paisley, and had requested his knowledge be on tap, but when it came to it, Dalglish was proving to be very much his own man.

Subsequent Career
At Blackburn Rovers, bankrolled by steel magnate Jack Walker, Dalglish became only the third manager to lift the Championship with two different clubs — a feat previously achieved by Herbert Chapman and Brian Clough. Despite losing 2-1 at Anfield on the final day of the 1994/95 season, the Lancashire club were crowned champions when Manchester United failed to beat West Ham. It was just like old times, with Dalglish winning the title in front of the Kop and United crestfallen. Having achieved his aim, he surprised everyone by immediately moving to an 'upstairs' role as Director of Football; Blackburn promptly imploded. Next he moved to Newcastle, but his football was seen by fans as too defensive following on from Kevin Keegan's gung-ho attacking. When Dalglish took over, in January 1997, Newcastle were 4th in the table; they eventually finished 2nd, and went into the Champions League at Liverpool's expense, where they beat Barcelona 3-2. Proving his judgement in the transfer market was as strong as it had been in his early days at Liverpool and Blackburn, Dalglish signed crowd favourites Nolberto

Solano, Gary Speed and Shay Given, as well as future Liverpool star Dietmar Hamann. The manager also took the club to an FA Cup Final in 1998 — a rarity on Tyneside — but the Geordies finished 13th in the Premiership, with just 44 points. Two games into the following season, both of which were drawn, Dalglish was sacked. He then experienced a brief spell as Director of Football at his *alma mater*, but his partnership with rookie John Barnes saw Celtic struggle. With Barnes sacked mid-season, Dalglish saw out the campaign as caretaker, during which time the Bhoys beat Aberdeen 2-0 to win the Scottish League Cup. Shortly after, he was replaced by Martin O'Neill, and hasn't managed since.

Defining Moment

Unquestionably, the defining moment of Dalglish's reign came on April 15th 1989. Until then it had been a relatively straightforward job — it was just about managing a football team, albeit one with lofty expectations and intense pressure. But that fateful day at Hillsborough changed everything. Understandably, something fundamentally altered within Dalglish. For a while the job became about being a grief counsellor whilst also carrying his own sadness. Football was secondary. Indeed, it didn't even rank that highly — there was the aftermath of a disaster, and that was it. The game itself was the last thing on everyone's mind. Liverpool was a community in mourning.

The toll it took on the club might not have been instantly obvious. Once the football eventually resumed, the Reds came back strong to win a number of consecutive league games, only falling at the final hurdle against Arsenal (to Michael Thomas' last-gasp title-winner, in the 3,420th and final minute of the season), and then landed the FA Cup in Dalglish's second all-Merseyside final, in which Ian Rush repeated his double from three years earlier. The following year the Reds won their 18th league title, but it was after that point that the cracks began to appear for the manager. The end came in February 1991. Dalglish severed all ties with the club 14 years after first arriving.

Crowning Glory

Clearly, Dalglish took English football to a new level in 1987/88. Liverpool finished the season with 90 points, equalling Everton's record, despite playing two fewer games. The Reds won 26 games and lost just two, scoring 87 goals and conceding only 24. The success was achieved with Dalglish's 1987 signings weighing in heavily with goals. Aldridge scored 29, Barnes 18, Beardsley 17, and Houghton added a further seven — an incredible 71 goals from the new boys. To underline how much this was his team and not the work of his predecessors, Steve McMahon, Dalglish's first signing, added an impressive nine more goals from centre-midfield.

The stats do some justice to the brilliance of that season, but cannot tell the whole story: one of stunning interplay and darting movements off the ball; of defenders attacking and players interchanging across the pitch. The brilliance culminated in a 5-0 thrashing of 2nd-placed Nottingham Forest in April 1988. Michel Platini, European Footballer of the Year for three years running earlier that decade, had already described the 2-0 victory over Arsenal as a "European display". Now former England winger Tom Finney was saying that the football in the 5-0 victory over Nottingham Forest was the best he'd ever witnessed; even Brazil couldn't play so well at that pace, he said.

Legacy

Dalglish's legacy is the one slightly murky aspect of his spell as Liverpool manager. The squad he left for Graeme Souness was full of players who were past their best, some recent signings who were patently not good enough, and a smattering of youngsters who were not yet ready for the first team. If he hadn't resigned, Dalglish would have had a hell of a job on his hands sorting out the wheat from the chaff.

But while it would not reap rewards in time to benefit him, Dalglish's overhauling of the youth system was perhaps his greatest legacy. A club can only discover the blossoming talent that already exists in the area — or at least it could at the time, before permission was granted to cast a net further afield. Attracting exceptional kids like Steve McManaman and Robbie Fowler to the club was not a formality; both were Evertonians, for starters. The same was true of Michael Owen and Jamie Carragher a few years later. Before Steve Heighway took charge, very few players were making the grade through the Liverpool youth ranks; in the next 12 years, the club produced its best clutch of local talent. Perhaps it was all merely coincidental — the result of the cyclical nature of the emergence of home-grown players, and the random act of a future star just happening to be born in one part of the country and not another. Despite Heighway continuing to work in the same way after 1998, when Steven Gerrard broke through, only fairly mediocre players, with the exception of Wayne Rooney, emerged on Merseyside.

TRANSFERS

Transfers In

It's fair to separate Dalglish's signings into two categories: the great (1985-1988) and the not-so-great (1988-1991). It is not an exact categorisation; there are some exceptions. But on the whole, the purchases the Scot made in his first three years would wipe the floor in a six-a-side game with those made afterwards.

Dalglish's first signing, in 1985, set the tone for those initial impressive major acquisitions. Former Evertonian Steve McMahon was snapped up from Aston Villa for £350,000, and while he never quite reached Souness' imperious heights, he did go a long way to replacing the mixture of grit, good distribution and an eye for goal. The Scouser left the club six years later with 50 goals from 276 games, at a rate of one goal every 5.5 matches — impressive for a non-penalty taker.

In his first couple of years, Dalglish made a number of lower key, inexpensive signings; the kind of gambles that most managers make when bolstering a squad, and which inevitably end up as a very mixed bag. Mike Hooper was an able reserve goalkeeper, bought from Wrexham for £40,000 in October 1985 at the age of 21. Hooper lasted eight years at the club, eventually racking up 72 appearances, mostly at a time when Graeme Souness was trying to decide between the Bristolian, a young and erratic David James and an ageing Bruce Grobbelaar. Never good enough to stand a realistic hope of being the Reds' long-term regular custodian, Hooper was eventually sold to Newcastle in 1993 for 13 times what Dalglish had paid, making the signing a good bit of business.

Liverpool paid Sunderland £250,000 for Barry Venison's services on July 31st 1986 — a decent but unspectacular full-back. Venison would go on to play 110 league games for the club, and helped in winning the league titles of 1988 and 1990. As the defence around him deteriorated, with class replaced largely by mediocrity, he was more exposed; had he been fortunate enough to play alongside prime-years Hansen and Lawrenson, he might have flourished, but instead he stagnated and moved to Newcastle in 1992, being reborn as a holding midfielder and even managing to win two England caps. Another full-back, Steve Staunton, was spotted as a 17-year-old playing in Ireland for his home club of Dundalk, and was signed in September 1986 for a measly £20,000. The young left-back did well after making his debut in 1988, and even scored a hat-trick in a League Cup match — as a substitute! But he was sold three years later, by Souness, for 55 times what the club had paid; some mark-up on a canny bit of business by Dalglish.

Striker Alan Irvine arrived in November 1986 from Falkirk, costing £75,000, but he never managed to settle. John Durnin, who arrived from Waterloo Dock in 1983, became a professional in March 1986, but never made the grade, registering just one start and one further substitute appearance. Mike Marsh, another striker, was signed in August 1987 from Kirkby Town, making his debut two years later as a 19-year-old against Charlton Athletic. Neither tall nor quick, he was shunted around the pitch by Souness, under whom he briefly flourished. Marsh excelled in midfield against Genoa in the UEFA Cup in 1992, having scored a crucial goal from right-back against Auxerre in the winter in a thrilling, and necessary, 3-0 win. But he was never able to translate his excellent skill and technique, which won him admirers in training, into consistent top-level success.

Getting back to major signings, Dalglish's judgement in 1987 proved peerless — almost certainly the club's best-ever calendar year when it came to buying a number of players, edging out 1977 on account of the extra transfers involved. Inward-bound transfers in '87, funded largely through the pre-agreed sale of Ian Rush to Juventus, saw Dalglish create what could finally be called *his* team. By the autumn of 1987, with Rush and Souness overseas, Lawrenson injured, and Alan Kennedy and Phil Neal long gone, only Alan Hansen, Steve Nicol, Ronnie Whelan and Bruce Grobbelaar remained as key men from Joe Fagan's treble-winning side of 1984. And, of course, Dalglish himself had unofficially hung up his boots. Craig Johnston was also still in the squad, but became increasingly peripheral, and retired in 1988. Meanwhile, Fagan signings Jan Molby, John Wark and Paul Walsh were also mostly out of the first-team frame.

Dalglish started the year as he meant to go on: John Aldridge arrived in January for £750,000, with Rush's departure already predetermined for six months' time. The Scouser was a deceptive talent. He didn't look much of a footballer in terms of grace and style, and wasn't the quickest or tallest. He also had no discernible skill. But within the box he was lethal, and particularly good in the air. The return of Ian Rush a year later meant that Aldridge, after one more season, was surplus to requirements, and sold for £1m to Real Sociedad in 1989. He became the first non-Basque player ever signed by Sociedad, and was a big hit in San Sebastián, scoring 40 goals in just 63 appearances. Keeping Aldridge at Anfield would have meant another player in his 30s inherited by Souness, but the striker continued to bag goals at a prolific rate for years to come; he scored a staggering 138 times beyond the age of 33 at Tranmere, albeit in a division below the top flight, and his final career tally was an unbelievable 476 goals. Unlike Ian Rush, he was a penalty taker, and scored 17 (27% of his overall total) from the spot for the Reds; his only miss was in the 1988 FA Cup Final, and costly it proved. After 50 league goals for the Reds in 83 games, the club then made a profit on his sale. You can't ask for more from any signing than to score an abundance of goals that help win major honours, and to then make the club a profit further down the line.

Chelsea midfielder Nigel Spackman joined Liverpool in February for £400,000, and while he wasn't a resounding success, he proved much more than just a squad player, making 50 starts and 13 substitute appearances in his 24 months at the club. Solid, unfussy and unhurried, some of his best football came as the holding midfielder in Dalglish's free-flowing team of '87/88; the 'water carrier' to keep things ticking over as the more skilful individuals wreaked havoc.

Peter Beardsley, a little gem of a player, arrived in July for £1.9m from Newcastle, although it took him a few months to settle. Part of Beardsley's initial struggle was that he was simply overshadowed by Aldridge, who couldn't stop scoring, and Barnes, who was in sensational form. Perhaps the little Geordie was also suffering under the burden of being the most expensive footballer in Britain at the time. But by the start of 1988 'Beardo' really began to come into his own. He was a real twinkle-toes-type player, often skipping between two hefty defenders after his trademark shimmy — kind of like a dog cocking his leg whilst performing the Riverdance, he lifted his foot high and to the side, before lowering it to jink one way or the other.

Ray Houghton, purchased from Oxford in October for £825,000, was the final piece of the Dream Team jigsaw, and rounded off a great year in the transfer market. He slipped seamlessly into a side that went on to record a 29-game unbeaten start to the league season and progress to the FA Cup Final. Mobile, tenacious, busy, and not without skill, he was a hugely effective player who added a new dimension to the Reds' play, particularly with the way he switched wings with John Barnes in the fluid system. He scored 38 goals in 202 games for the Reds before he was sold to Aston Villa for £900,000 at the age of 30.

Ian Rush returned for £2.8m in 1988, just a year after departing for Italy. Never able to recapture the prolific form of his younger years, and with a lot to live up to as a returning legend, he was still a welcome addition to the team; had an unknown player achieved what he did between 1988 and 1996, he would have been considered a big success. With Aldridge gone, Rush came to the fore in 1989/90, scoring 26 goals in a season that saw the Reds land the title. In his second spell, Rush managed 90 league goals in 245 games — a fine tally, but nowhere near as impressive as his first seven years, during which scored 139 in 224 matches; of course, Rush also scored a staggering 117 cup goals for the club in his two spells. The diminished return was perhaps also due to an altered role once Robbie Fowler appeared on the scene in 1993, as well as the fact that the man who created most of Rush's goals in his first spell was now the team's manager. And of course, it encompassed the tail end of the Welshman's career, when the intelligence was getting sharper but the the trademark pace was a thing of the past. When any player arrives at a club, one thing that is hard to judge is the effect he has on those around him — how much he teaches them, directly or indirectly, and any influence on their attitude. In Fowler's case, he clearly owed a debt of gratitude to Rush, and while the teenage heir to the no.9 shirt was always destined for great things, the presence of the elder statesman undoubtedly helped him reach his potential.

Making far less headline news, centre-back Nicky Tanner, signed for £30,000 from Bristol Rovers in July 1988, managed 50 games for the Reds, mostly under Graeme Souness. Not the most graceful, Tanner was solid, both physically and in his play. Another defender, David Burrows, arrived in October 1988 from West Bromich Albion, the fee set at £550,000. It was money well spent — the value about right — with Burrows featuring in the 1990 title-winning side, and leaving for West Ham in 1993 for a profit after almost 200 appearances for the Reds.

Glenn Hysen arrived in 1989, when the high-profile signings weren't working out so well for Dalglish. Liverpool beat off competition from Manchester United, for whom the centre-back was about to sign from Italian side Fiorentina for £650,000. The silver-haired Swede was part of the league-winning side at Anfield in his first campaign, and often excelled, but never quite reached the heights Liverpool fans were accustomed to over the course of his career. It was a time when Kopites were used to Mark Lawrenson, who'd retired less than two years earlier, and Alan Hansen, who was entering his final season; as such, almost anyone would suffer by comparison. Hysen seemed to struggle more than most when it came to the difficulties the team experienced under Graeme Souness, although by that stage he was in his early 30s; as such, he only lasted until 1992, when he returned to Sweden. As it was, it would be a whole decade before Liverpool signed another totally successful centre-back, in the form of fellow Scandinavian Sami Hyypia.

Steve Harkness was also picked up for £75,000 in the summer of 1989, at the age of 17. Harkness made his debut two years later, at QPR, and served the club in a steady if unspectacular manner under both Graeme Souness and Roy Evans, and briefly under Gérard Houllier, who experimented with him as the holding midfielder. In his full decade at Liverpool Harkness managed to play 139 times, and is probably best remembered as one of Evans' three centre-backs in the 3-5-2 formation.

The biggest instant impact of any Dalglish signing was probably made by Ronny Rosenthal; John Barnes captured the imagination like no other new player arriving at Anfield, but not even he could affect the destination of the league title in his first few appearances. The Israeli's seven goals in eight games when on loan from Standard Liege helped the Reds secure the 1990 championship, but he failed to build on his surprise success once a permanent £1m deal was secured in the June of that year. Quick, strong and direct, Rosenthal was in truth a graceless bustler with a big heart who often bulldozed his way through defences and thumped shots at goal. An impact signing, 'Rocket Ronny' was also an impact player, making 57 substitute appearances, some 15 more than he gained through starts. In his next three-and-a-half years at the club,

Rosenthal only managed to double his total goals tally.

Attacking midfielder Don Hutchison was brought to the club from Hartlepool in November 1990 for £175,000, after Dalglish and his scouts saw the 18-year-old's potential in a video they received from the selling club's chairman, who was seeking to cash in on his team's League Cup escapades against Spurs. Hutchison made his debut in 1992, under Graeme Souness. Two years later Roy Evans opted to sell the player for a tidy profit, making him another successful Dalglish purchase in monetary terms, even if the Scottish international didn't really fulfil his potential at Anfield. Hutchison arrived a couple of months after the Reds had signed 21-year-old Irish striker Tony Cousins from Dundalk for £70,000. Cousins lasted two and a half years at Anfield but never played a game before being released.

If Ronny Rosenthal provided the biggest impact, David Speedie, having just turned 31 when he arrived for £650,000 in February 1991, was Dalglish's most left-field signing. Every manager seems to make at least one; the older player who's been around the block, and who has ability, but whose signing comes totally out of the blue. Gary McAllister was one such player signed by Gérard Houllier, while Rafa Benítez shocked the football world by bringing back Robbie Fowler five years after he'd been sold. Six goals in 12 games from Speedie, including two against Everton and one against Manchester United, seemed the start of a promising late-career stint at Anfield but Graeme Souness had other ideas. Speedie dropped down a division, to upcoming Blackburn Rovers, and by October was being managed by Dalglish once again; in 36 games *en route* to promotion, Speedie netted 23 times, only to be sold as soon as Rovers reached the newly-formed Premiership.

Having covered 'impact' and 'surprise', Jimmy Carter was Dalglish's most *baffling* signing; so ineffectual was he that the former US President of the same name, at the age of 66, might have done as good a job. What's more bizarre is that Liverpool managed to offload the ex-Millwall winger to their closest rivals at the time — George Graham's Arsenal — where he also flopped. The best thing that can be said about the signing of Carter is that the Reds got most of their money back.

Dalglish at least redeemed himself with his final signing: Jamie Redknapp, bought from Bournemouth for £350,000. Never destined to be one of the true greats like Souness and Gerrard, he was however a fine natural footballer with an ability to pass long and shoot from distance. As such, he was a very good Premiership player for a number of years and proved excellent value for money. Redknapp racked up 308 appearances for the club in just over a decade, a tally that, but for a series of injuries in his later years, would have been far greater. He scored 41 goals, before moving to Spurs in 2002.

Player	Quality	0.01pg	IN	OUT	FGV	VALUE	Ap	Details	
Steve McMahon	8.43	2.77	-2.3	6.2		**15.10**	277	£350k '85	£900k@30 '91
John Barnes	9.67	4.07	-6	7		**14.74**	407	£900k June '87	Rel. 1997 @34
Jamie Redknapp	7.41	3.08	-1.2	5	1	**14.29**	308	£350k 1991	Rel 2002
John Aldridge	8.89	1.04	-5	7.4		**12.33**	104	£750k 1987	£1m '91 @31
Ray Houghton	7.99	2.02	-4.3	6		**11.71**	202	£825k Oct '87	£900k@30 '92
Steve Staunton(1)	6.82	1	-0.1	3.8		**11.52**	100	£20k 1986	'91 for £1.1m
Mike Marsh	5.76	1.01	0	3.3		**10.07**	101	Free	£1.25m Sw.'93
David Burrows	5.94	1.93	-2	3.3		**9.17**	193	£550k 1988	£1.25m Sw.'93
Peter Beardsley**	8.75	1.75	-10	7.8		**8.30**	175	£1.9m Jul '87	£1m '91 @30
Average	**6.31**		**-2.96**			**8.19**			
Don Hutchison	5.12	0.6	-0.6	3		**8.12**	60	£175k 1990	£1.5m 1994
All Managers' Average						**7.92**			
Nigel Spackman	6.18	0.63	-2.7	3.8		**7.91**	63	£400k 1987	£500k'89 @29
Barry Venison	6.24	1.58	-1.3	0.7		**7.22**	158	£200k 1986	£250k 1992
Mike Hooper	5.06	0.73	-0.2	1.5		**7.09**	73	£40k 1985	£550k 1993
Ian Rush (2)**	8.76	3.29	-10	5		**7.05**	329	£2,700k 1988	Rel. @36
Steve Harkness	5.35	1.39	-0.3	0.5		**6.94**	139	£75k 1989	£750k 1999
Nick Tanner	3.88	0.59	-0.1	1		**5.37**	59	£20k 1988	Ret inj. '94
David Speedie	5.59	0.14	-4.6	3.2		**4.33**	14	£675k '91 @31	£450k @31
Ronny Rosenthal	6.18	0.97	-3.7	0.6		**4.05**	97	£1m 1990	£250k 1994
Alan Irvine	2.94	0.04	-0.3	0.5		**3.18**	4	£75k 1986	£100k 1987
Glenn Hysen	5.29	0.93	-4.4	0		**1.82**	93	£600k '89 @30	Rel. @33
Jimmy Carter	3.00	0.08	-3	1.7		**1.78**	8	£800k 1991	£500k 1991

Key: See page 51.

Transfer Masterstroke

John Barnes, signed for £900,000, was undoubtedly Dalglish's masterstroke. While Steve McMahon would prove to be the best signing in terms of *Value for Money*, Barnes was the player who made the difference; the player who took the team to the next level.

The fee wasn't cheap by 1987 terms (60% of the record), but was still less than half what the club would pay for Beardsley later that same summer. There were a lot of doubts about Barnes before his arrival; he was clearly talented, but could he hack it at a big club? The answer was an emphatic 'yes'. It also hadn't helped that he'd been holding out for a move to Italy. Arsenal had withdrawn their offer in a huff as a result, and Barnes almost had no alternative but to sign on the dotted line with Liverpool. With games rarely televised, and Anfield closed for repairs due to a collapsed sewer beneath the Kop, the buzz about Barnes had grown through his initial away performances. The home game with early league-leaders QPR, televised as the main highlights in the evening, showed what the fuss was about. The Reds won 4-0, demolishing QPR, who imploded like the Kop sewer. Barnes scored two goals — one brilliant, the other almost off the scale. The first saw him exchange passes with Ronnie Whelan before curling a shot into the top corner past a young David Seaman (who that day perfected his look of dejection, as later made famous by the efforts of Nayim and Ronaldinho). But Barnes' second goal was the stuff of genius. He won the ball on the halfway line, and strode purposely upfield. Faced with three defenders, including England internationals Terry Fenwick and Paul Parker, he jinked to his left and then, with balletic grace and a seemingly impossible shift of his weight from one side to the other, glided to his right. The finish itself was made to look simple, with the ball slid under the advancing Seaman, but again, it perhaps showed why Barnes was so devastating. Other skilful players might have looked to do a little extra, and, with a rush of adrenaline, showboated the finish with a dink or yet one more dummy or shimmy. The beauty of Barnes' skill was that he never did the unnecessary, never wasted time with the superfluous. It was a defining moment in the season; it scared the life out of every top division footballer watching the TV that night, and a new Liverpool side had officially come of age.

Having terrorised full-backs on the wings, Barnes would later be asked by Dalglish to use his talents to take centre-backs to task. Excellent in the air, his skill and strength served him well as a centre-forward, and in 1989/90 he scored 28 goals, making him the country's top scorer, just edging out Ian Rush on the last day of the season. He had an ability, if you will, 'to hold and give but do it at the right time'. When an Achilles tendon injury robbed Barnes of his pace, he was later reborn as a central midfielder under Roy Evans, just to outline how excellent technical ability can make a player adaptable. Barnes' time at Liverpool came to a close a decade after arriving. He played 407 times for the club and scored 108 goals.

Expensive Folly

Most of Dalglish's major signings worked to perfection: McMahon, Aldridge, Beardsley, Houghton, Barnes and the returning Rush (although at almost £3m he wasn't great *Value for Money*). But the £1m spent on Ronny Rosenthal — 37% of the English transfer record — was probably the greatest waste. Of course, after such an impressive loan period, when the Israeli had been so sensational in helping land the 1990 title, it would have been a brave man who didn't stump up the cash, but once a permanent move was finalised he proved to be somewhat of a flash in the pan. In many ways it was the most inspired loan move in the history of the club, but one of the least successful transfers.

Jimmy Carter, at £800,000, was not cheap either. Dalglish felt the player had a bit of everything — pace, technique and the ability to cross the ball — but that his problems were of a mental nature, in dealing with the expectations at such a big club. Dalglish, having worked closely with the player, will know that better than most. But when it came to match-days, the fans saw a player who looked patently out of his depth.

One Who Got Away

In 1985 Liverpool had hoped to sign Paul Allen, the 23-year-old West Ham midfielder who, in 1980, became the youngest-ever FA Cup finalist. Talks were held, but Allen opted to stay in London, with Spurs.

Michael Laudrup, the Danish maestro who had been at Juventus since 1983 (although loaned out to Lazio until after Juve beat Liverpool in the 1985 European Cup Final), was once again linked with a move to Liverpool. In 1987, with Ian Rush due to join him in Italy, the Dane said "I will stay with Juventus until 1989, and then I think I'll join Liverpool". But instead he ended up at Barcelona, where he won four *La Liga* titles in a row, and then moved to Real Madrid, to instantly win a fifth. In 1999 he was voted the Best Foreign Player in Spanish football over the previous 25-year period, to highlight just what a talent the Reds had missed out on.

Budget — Historical Context

Having spent big in the mid-to-late '70s, Everton would only find success once they reverted to the products of their youth system, supplemented by a number of cheap young players bought from unfashionable clubs. The twelve men involved in the 1986 FA Cup Final defeat to Liverpool — most of whom had won Everton their league first title in 15 years the previous season — had an average cost of just 13.6% of the English transfer record. Of that side (Bobby Mimms, Gary Stevens, Pat Van Den Hauwe, Kevin Ratcliffe, Derek Mountfield, Peter Reid, Trevor Steven, Gary Lineker, Graeme Sharp, Paul Bracewell, Kevin Sheedy, Adrian Heath), only Lineker and Heath cost over £500,000. While Liverpool were one of the few big clubs yet to spend a million, the average cost of their side — famous for not including one Englishman in the starting XI (Grobbelaar, Lawrenson, Beglin, Nicol, Whelan, Hansen, Dalglish, Johnston, Rush, Molby, MacDonald, and substitute McMahon) — was double that of their neighbours, at 28.7%.

Like Everton, Arsenal's success under George Graham in the later part of the '80s was also largely down to their youth system. Tony Adams, David O'Leary, Paul Davis, David Rocastle, Michael Thomas, Niall Quinn, Paul Merson, Kevin Campbell and Martin Hayes were all home-grown talents who played for the Gunners during Dalglish's time at Liverpool. Expensive marquee signings like Charlie Nicholas and Steve Williams gave way to a group of talented youngsters and, on the whole, bargain signings. David Seaman (£1.3 million, 1990), Andy Linighan (£1.25m, 1990) and Alan Smith (£850,000, 1987) were the exceptions, but otherwise Graham bought relatively cheaply: Nigel Winterburn (£350,000 in 1987), Lee Dixon (£400,000 in 1988), and Kevin Richardson (£200,000 1987) were three very successful examples, with the first two playing well over 1,000 games for the Gunners between them.

One club who were spending big at the time was Manchester United. Alex Ferguson had taken charge in 1986, and by 1989 he'd spent in excess of £13m on players, with precious little recouped through sales; by contrast, Liverpool's gross spend in that period was almost exactly half, and that included the sale and repurchase of Ian Rush. As had Dalglish, Ferguson bought back the club's star Welsh striker after an unhappy time abroad, although Mark Hughes had been sold by Ron Atkinson. The United team that won the 1990 FA Cup Final — the result that saved Ferguson's job, after his third bottom-half league finish in four seasons — was formed from a number of expensive signings. Only Lee Martin, the unexpected hero in the replay, did not involve a fairly significant transfer fee, and only Bryan Robson was not a Ferguson purchase. The side — Jim Leighton, Paul Ince, Lee Martin, Steve Bruce, Mike Phelan, Gary Pallister, Bryan Robson, Neil Webb, Brian McClair, Mark Hughes and Danny Wallace — had an incredible average cost in excess of 50% of the English transfer record. Ferguson eventually dug himself out of a hole, but did so with a massively expensive average spend that, in relation to the English transfer record, was identical to the Chelsea side that Liverpool beat in the 2007 Champions League semi-final. Ferguson's spending dropped dramatically over the next three years, but by then he had assembled the majority of the side that would go on to win the 1993 Premiership title, and end a 26-year wait to become champions; at which point he broke the English transfer record on Roy Keane.

RECORD
League Championship: 1985/86, 1987/88 and 1989/90.
FA Cup: 1986, 1989.

	P	W	D	L	F	A	%
Overall	307	187	78	42	617	259	60.91%
League	224	136	56	32	437	187	60.71%
FA Cup	38	23	12	3	79	31	60.53%
League Cup	31	19	6	6	72	29	61.29%
Other	14	9	4	1	29	12	64.29%

CONCLUSION

Kenny Dalglish's tenure ended as it started — in the wake of tragedy; his time in charge bookended by the deaths of 135 fans in failing stadia. As a manager he will be remembered for the beautiful football of 1987/88, and the double two years earlier. Three titles in five full seasons, plus two FA Cups, achieved with the best win-percentage of any Liverpool manager in modern history, highlights Dalglish's quality. He bought brilliantly at first, while overhauling the youth system. But criticism of his later purchases, and the possibility that the sacking of Geoff Twentymen contributed, cannot be escaped.

How sad, though, that the manager's greatest side could not test its mettle in Europe. The fact is that in 1987/88 Liverpool would only have been in the UEFA Cup anyway, but had they contested the European Cup they would have stood a good chance of winning it, with the moderate talents of PSV Eindhoven beating Benfica in the final. It would have been interesting to see how the Reds fared against the *Rossinieri*, with the great AC Milan of Gullit, Van Basten, Rijkaard, Baresi, Maldini, Donadoni and Costacurta winning the Italian league in 1988 and romping to the European title in 1989. But it wasn't to be.

Not many outsanding players make great managers, but for a time Dalglish was certainly as adept in the dugout as he was on the pitch; a fact borne out by his league triumph with Blackburn in 1995, before his career tailed off. And as a man he will be remembered for the grace and dignity with which he conducted himself in testing times at Anfield. Few people have given more to the Liverpool cause, and Dalglish will forever be a club hero.

"I may have left Liverpool but the city and club will always be part of me."

KENNY DALGLISH

1991 - 1994
GRAEME SOUNESS

" I'm sure he'll be the first to admit that he made mistakes at Liverpool. It was his first big job in England and perhaps he tried to change things too quickly. "

TERRY MCDERMOTT ON SOUNESS, 2005

INTRODUCTION

On paper it was the perfect appointment. A canny ex-Liverpool player (and a Scot, to boot) with exacting standards, and whose football education after leaving Anfield had continued in the rarified tactical arena of Italy, before enjoying success north of the border with Rangers — an experience through which, unlike the man he replaced in the Anfield hot seat, he gained several years of management know-how before taking the job. Four titles in five years at Rangers, where he ended an almost-unthinkable nine-year wait for the championship at Scotland's most successful club at the time, suggested that Souness had everything needed to pump life back into a side that had started to show the first signs of deterioration. How could it go wrong?

Unfortunately, it did just that. Rather than end a long wait for the title, as he had at Rangers, Souness' failure on a number of levels led to the start of an even longer period without a league title.

The Liverpool Graeme Souness returned to was clearly different from the one he had left seven years earlier. He inherited an ageing side heading for decline, but rather than arrest it, he hastened the fall from the summit like a mountain climber discarding his guide ropes in favour of overcooked spaghetti. He also clearly suffered some bad luck — a serious Achilles tendon injury sustained while representing England rid John Barnes, the best player at the club, of his pace, and he was a shadow of his former self in between 1991 and 1994, while the massively influential Alan Hansen had just retired. But Souness' failure in the transfer market, and his decision to insensitively sell a story to *The Sun* newspaper on the anniversary of the Hillsborough disaster, meant that he contributed to his own inevitable downfall.

The timing of Liverpool's partial demise could not have been worse. The new financial landscape of the Premiership opened up in 1992, when the First Division changed its name. Meanwhile, the Champions League — in which Liverpool would not compete for almost a decade — was another cash-cow that began in 1992, when the European Cup was rebranded and the structure slightly altered, introducing a group stage and allowing more than one team from each country to participate. While Manchester United won league titles and cashed in on their success with heavy merchandising, Liverpool were left standing.

Also, Souness himself was going through changes. In 1992 he underwent a triple heart by-pass, something that would lead to him questioning his own inner strength, as well as indirectly leading to an alienation of many of the fans in its aftermath.

Situation Inherited

There can be no doubt that Graeme Souness inherited an ageing side about to head rapidly over the hill. Alan Hansen retired at the same time as Kenny Dalglish quit; the ultra-composed centre-back's knees were already held together with sellotape and blu-tack. Ronnie Whelan turned 30 at the start of Souness' first full season, as did Steve McMahon, while Ian Rush reached that age six months into his reign, just a couple of months before Steve Nicol and then Ray Houghton also entered their fourth decade. Plenty were already in their 30s: Bruce Grobbelaar was 33 — a good age for a goalkeeper, but at a custodian's peak, so he wasn't going to get any better; Glenn Hysen was almost 32; David Speedie 31; Gary Gillespie was on the cusp of 31; and Peter Beardsley had recently turned 30. Ronny Rosenthal was almost 28, but his problem was more to with a lack of real top-level quality rather than age. Jan Molby was also about to turn 28, but lifestyle issues were clearly hindering the Dane from reaching peak fitness; at times he resembled a man experiencing a mid-life crisis.

Sprightly young footballers of sufficient quality were thin on the ground in 1991. There was Steve McManaman, with a handful of appearances to his name. The same applied to Mike Marsh and Nicky Tanner, although the latter — a chunky stopper — was never sprightly and hardly the sufficient quality either. Steve Harkness, Don Hutchison and Jamie Redknapp, signed by Dalglish, were all yet to make their debuts, but would feature in the first team within a year. Robbie Fowler was in the pipeline, but still two years away. Dominic Matteo was another who would come through the ranks in 1993.

One player who did have a lot of potential and time on his side was 22-year-old Steve Staunton, a versatile defender. Souness promptly sold him. He later admitted it was his one regret with regard to those shown the door, but explained that it was down to the ruling that limited sides in European competition to three foreigners, and an Irish lad was classed as just that. Staunton had some fine years at Aston Villa, but later returned to Liverpool when his best days were behind him.

The task Souness faced clearly involved culling some of the older players. But the problem was more about which players he sold, and those he chose to keep. He was right to retain Rush, who was lean and fit, as ever; despite being dropped by his former team-mate in 1992/93, Rush responded with the goals that dragged Liverpool out of the bottom half of the table, and he was still having a positive impact on the team in 1994/95, under Roy Evans. McMahon was possibly rightly moved on, seeing as he appeared to be a fading force and £900,000 was too good a fee to turn down. Speedie and Hysen were surplus to requirements, while Gillespie was 31, and as with McMahon, an offer of almost a million pounds was too good to refuse. And by purchasing David James in 1992, Souness was building for the future, something Grobbelaar did not represent.

But then it starts to get more confusing. In Souness' first full season, Ray Houghton had been excellent, making his way into the six-man shortlist for PFA Player of the Year. Souness promptly sold him. Houghton did well at Aston Villa, proving his time was not yet up. Even more baffling — the manager's dunder-stroke — was to sell Peter Beardsley ... and not only that, to sell him to *Everton*. It's always easy to say what might have been, but Beardsley and Rush could have continued their natural partnership for a few years to come; it wasn't where the problems lay. A teetotaller, Beardsley fastidiously looked after himself, and was still going strong in the Premiership six years later. He managed another 210 top division matches for Everton and Newcastle United, scoring a further 71 league goals after his Anfield exit; not to mention countless assists. Souness later claimed that Beardsley and McMahon were looking for guarantees of first-team football and improved deals, without which they hinted they would leave. While he felt these and other older players needed replacing, he admitted he should have waited a year, in order to source suitable replacements first. He said he acted impetuously, and that it was a major mistake.

It wasn't just the fact that Souness got rid of too many good players with plenty still to offer — Houghton, Staunton and Beardsley in particular — but it was that he bought far too many inferior players to replace them. The non-native European ruling meant that clubs needed to field home-grown players and limit overseas stars, but then how did Istvan Kozma fit in with this scenario when Beardsley didn't?

Players Inherited

Souness claimed that "there were not many great players" at the club in 1991. In fact, he said there was just one — John Barnes. In terms of *Quality* ratings, he was right — Barnes was the only player rated in the '9' category, but that was before taking into account the injury that almost instantly reduced his effectiveness by a couple of points. Souness admitted that Barnes was not the player he had hoped to find. Ian Rush was of course a truly great player over the course of his Liverpool career, but was proving less prolific in his second spell. While his all-round play had improved, he was not the world-class predator seen in his first stay. There were a lot of players rated between 8 and 9 in terms of *Quality*, but every single one was entering the final phase of his career, leaving a poor *Inheritance* value.

In terms of *Quality*, the Brains Trust rated the squad Dalglish bequeathed at a respectable average of 6.76. However, taking age into account, the squad rating drops to a very worrying 5.41 per player. The first XI has a *Quality* rating of 8.01 — which looks incredibly strong, and reflects the fact that the team were recent champions and challenging again in 1991 — but when the crucial age weighting is factored in, the *Inheritance* drops to an alarming 5.64. This was a team living on borrowed time.

The average age of the squad was 27, but more alarmingly, the average age of the strongest XI was 30. The imbalance in the squad can be seen by the fact that there were four young left-backs in Staunton, Burrows, Ablett and Harkness, but of course only one could play at a time; in central midfield and up front, however, all were approaching or already well into their 30s.

Squad

Player	Quality	Age	Adj	*Inheritance*	Year	Age
Robbie Fowler (1)	9.43	0	0	**9.43**	1991	16
Ian Rush (2)	8.76	-2.5	2	**8.26**	1991	29.5
Peter Beardsley	8.75	-3.5	3	**8.25**	1991	30.5
John Barnes	9.67	0	-2	**7.67**	1991	27.5
Jamie Redknapp	7.41	0	0	**7.41**	1991	18
Steve Staunton (1)	6.82	0	0	**6.82**	1991	22.5
Jan Molby	8.59	-1	-1	**6.59**	1991	28
Ray Houghton	7.99	-2.5	1	**6.49**	1991	29.5

Player	Quality	Age	Adj	Inheritance	Year	Age
Barry Venison	6.24	0	0	6.24	1991	27
Ronny Rosenthal	6.18	0	0	6.18	1991	27.5
Gary Ablett	6.15	0	0	6.15	1991	25.5
Steve Nicol	8.53	-2.5	0	6.03	1991	29.5
David Burrows	5.94	0	0	5.94	1991	22.5
Mike Marsh	5.76	0	0	5.76	1991	22
Ronnie Whelan	8.61	-3	0	5.61	1991	30
Average	**6.88**			**5.58**		**26.5**
Steve McMahon	8.43	-3	0	5.43	1991	30
Steve Harkness	5.35	0	0	5.35	1991	20
Don Hutchison	5.12	0	0	5.12	1991	20
Mike Hooper	5.06	0	0	5.06	1991	27
Nick Tanner	3.88	0	0	3.88	1991	26
Bruce Grobbelaar	8.29	-4.5	0	3.79	1991	33.5
Gary Gillespie	7.29	-4	0	3.29	1991	31
Jimmy Carter	3.00	0	0	3.00	1991	26
David Speedie	5.59	-4.5	0	1.09	1991	31.5
Glenn Hysen	5.29	-4.5	0	0.79	1991	32.5

First XI

Player	Quality	Age	Adj	Inheritance	Year	Age
Bruce Grobbelaar	8.29	-4.5	0	3.79	1991	33.5
Steve Staunton (1)	6.82	0	0	6.82	1991	22.5
Gary Gillespie	7.29	-4	0	3.29	1991	31
Glenn Hysen	5.29	-4.5	0	0.79	1991	32.5
Steve Nicol	8.53	-2.5	0	6.03	1991	29.5
John Barnes	9.67	0	-2	7.67	1991	27.5
Ray Houghton	7.99	-2.5	1	6.49	1991	29.5
Ronnie Whelan	8.61	-3	0	5.61	1991	30
Steve McMahon	8.43	-3	0	5.43	1991	30
Peter Beardsley	8.75	-3.5	3	8.25	1991	30.5
Ian Rush (2)	8.76	-2.5	2	8.26	1991	29.5
Average	**8.04**			**5.67**		**29.6**

Key: Quality 0-10; Age = -1 point for every year from 28 onwards, eg -4 for 31 year-old, and -1 point from 30 onwards for keepers, eg -4 for 33 year-old; Adj = adjustments for players either exceptionally fit/unfit for their age, or soon to leave; Inheritance = total out of 10. Excludes players not part of first team picture.

State of Club

When David Moores became chairman in September 1991, Souness counted him as a friend. Their relationship would be tested in the years to come, with Moores, a passionate Kopite, caught in the middle of a battle between the fans and the manager.

While Sir John Smith had retired, Peter Robinson was still a key man behind the scenes at Anfield. However, in Tony Ensor, Souness had an enemy on the Liverpool board. Hugely critical of Souness in board meetings, Ensor eventually gave Moores and his fellow directors an ultimatum: either Souness was sacked or he would walk. And so

Ensor was forced to resign. Despite this, Souness said he felt let down by Moores through the difficulties that haunted him during his tenure, expressing a desire to see the chairman publicly back him in the manner he did in private.

Assistance/Backroom Staff

Long-standing lieutenants Roy Evans and Ronnie Moran were still on the scene. While Moran showed no great desire to manage the team as he approached 60, Evans had his hopes set on the job. But he was passed over with the appointment of Souness. Evans was eventually promoted to assistant manager in 1993, to offer a counterpoint to the abrasive manager. In the same year, Tom Saunders was voted onto the board of directors, his role being to help Souness, and subsequently Roy Evans, with administration and general support.

Phil Boersma, a coach and physiotherapist, was appointed to the coaching staff as Souness' right-hand man, with Walter Smith, the key influence behind Souness' success north of the border, staying at Rangers to become manager. There was an injury crisis soon after Boersma's arrival, and a change of training methods did not reflect well on the new man. Boersma was resented by the other coaches, and given that men like Roy Evans and Ronnie Moran were not egotists, it suggests there was a reason for the unease.

But the big story surrounded Phil Thompson, the man Souness had replaced as Liverpool captain some years earlier. Thompson was in charge of the reserve side, but was proving a slightly difficult character. His severe criticisms of players had led to a fallout with Steve Heighway, whose youth team players were not keen on stepping up to the reserves because of the stick they feared receiving. While this was unwelcome, it was worked around. The big bust up came when, with Souness in hospital recovering from his heart operation, Liverpool had faced — and beaten — Manchester United at Anfield to deny Ferguson his first league title. Afterwards, in the time-honoured tradition that stretched back to the Boot Room's genesis, the opposition coaches (minus Ferguson in this instance) congregated to discuss the game. Gathered around the dirty kits and crates, Thompson launched an attack on Souness, to the amazement of all present.

In his autobiography, Thompson claims to have no memory of the incident — a claim that seems dubious. Roy Evans, who witnessed the outburst along with United no.2 Brian Kidd, saw it differently. "It was always drummed into us that you never badmouthed one of your own, certainly not to opponents. We all stuck together and that was the way it had always been, whether or not you agreed with every decision. Phil shouldn't have said what he did but there was no reasoning with him."

While Thompson almost certainly have had some valid criticisms about some of Souness' signings and methods, it was clearly not the time, the place or the people to be telling. Word spread via Kidd, who was as shocked as Evans at the outburst, to Archie Knox and onto Walter Smith. From there it quickly made it to the Liverpool manager. Once Liverpool had won the FA Cup a week later, Souness wasted no time in asking the board to sack Thompson. Evans tried to talk the manager out of it, but just as Thompson wouldn't be distracted from his outburst, Souness was not going to listen to any reasoning.

Clearly Souness was put in a very difficult position. For all the manager's faults, he had the right to expect loyalty from his staff. If only based on the Shankly's warning, delivered to his staff 33 years earlier, Thompson had to go: "I don't want anyone to carry stories about anyone else. If you come and tell me a story about someone else, whoever you're telling the story about won't go, the one who carries the story will go. I want everybody to be loyal to each other. We'll all get together and have that one big strength." Thompson wasn't telling tales to the manager, but criticising him behind his back. It's hard to see how Shankly would have approved.

Sammy Lee came in to replace Thompson. Like him, Lee would later take an extended break from the club (albeit of his own volition, in 2004) before returning for a second spell behind the scenes, and a third at the club in total.

Management Style
Authoritarian, dictatorial, and ruthless: words that have been used to describe Souness. In many ways he has mellowed since he took charge at Liverpool at the age of 38, but back then he was by his own admission arrogant and abrasive, and in too much of a hurry. He felt "the job was easy" when he pitched up, but before too long realised it was quite the opposite.

Rumours about squabbles in the dressing room between the players and Souness were rife, with Ian Rush famously telling a Sky Sports interviewer that "teacups being thrown" was nothing new. Jan Molby saw both sides of Souness. "Unlike some of the players, I didn't have a major problem with Souness," he said in his autobiography. "Some of the lads didn't like his managerial style, and it's true he had a very short fuse. He'd come in after games and have a real pop at us. He was one of those managers who wanted to win so badly. Like Kenny, he was pretty calm before games, but afterwards he just couldn't control it. In September 1993, we lost 3-2 to Wimbledon at Anfield in the Premiership. We really were pathetic. Souness was livid. After storming into the dressing room, he picked up a bottle of smelling salts and threw it at the mirror. It smashed into a thousand pieces. That was the worst I ever saw him after a game. He'd have a dig after most matches and then he'd go and sit down. But on a Monday morning, he was big enough to forget about what had happened."

Many of the senior players were not prepared for the hard line taken by the new boss, with the situation perhaps exacerbated by the fact that several — Rush, Nicol, Grobbelaar, Gillespie and Whelan — had once been teammates. This was different to Kenny Dalglish taking control directly from within, not least because of the different personalities involved.

Souness felt the senior players lacked passion, and were becoming increasingly concerned with money; certainly they didn't seem to share his overwhelming desire to win. Mark Wright and Dean Saunders had arrived on higher wages than experienced stars like Rush and Houghton, and the existing stars wanted to know why. "The Liverpool I left," explained Souness, "was all about the dressing room and how good this team of professionals were. When I went back there I found a dressing room of people who were only interested in what their next contract was about and how much they were going to earn."

But perhaps hypocritically, Souness had left Liverpool purely for the financial gain. "I am moving for the money. There is no use lying about it," he said at the time. Later, in his autobiography, he said that he never wanted to leave Liverpool — his wife needed to get out of the country for tax reasons; but then how different is that to the players he inherited having their own monetary concerns or desires?

Rush, in particular, had a rocky relationship with Souness, and would end up being dropped in the second half of the 1992/93 season; whether or not it was intended to have such an effect, it certainly fired up the legendary striker, who returned to the team to score the goals that led the Reds away from a dangerous flirtation with the relegation zone.

Consolation at this time could be taken from the fact that Souness had fully blooded several new prodigious young talents like Steve McManaman and Robbie Fowler, allowing them to play and develop in the first team, where they were desperate to be — as opposed to many of the other senior players, according to Souness. He had also wanted the senior players to lead the way and set the example to the younger pros, in the way he had been shown the ropes by Steve Heighway, Phil Neal and Ray Clemence, and how, a few years later, he, along with Kenny Dalglish, had passed on his experience to the younger lads. But now — and this is something backed up by Roy Evans — most of the senior players seemed more concerned with themselves. A sense of selfishness and complacency had started to evolve. In the '70s and early '80s, the tendency for players to let their hair down with a drink was balanced out by the senior pros having a strong sense of knowing when the time was right, and they were also prepared to put in that extra effort in training to compensate. But now there was less responsibility being taken by the players.

However, for all his disagreements with Rush, Souness later praised the striker's work with Robbie Fowler. Even before Fowler was in the first team, Rush was advising him in the finer arts of leading the line. While Rush wasn't receptive to a lot of Souness' ideas, at least he pleased the manager by taking an interest in the development of the next generation of stars.

Unique Methods

Graeme Souness tried to instigate change, and do what Alex Ferguson had done at United — namely remove complacency, stop excessive drinking, and rebuild an entire squad.

Making the break from the past seemed to be Souness' main aim. Tommy Smith was now writing for the *Echo*, but also hanging around in the Boot Room. Souness felt it wasn't right to allow a member of the press special access to the inner workings of the club, even if he was an ex-captain. Souness' explanation was that his players, who were being criticised by the 'Anfield Iron' in his column, would think that he condoned Smith's comments; as such, Smith was asked to stay away. The expulsion only served to make Smith a harsher critic: "He sees himself as a Messiah. But he is leading the club down the drain," he said of Souness. Smith probably felt his presence was harmless, but clearly Souness had a point.

Jan Molby explained some of the changes taking place from 1991: "Souness seemed determined to shake things up on the training ground. He wanted Liverpool to be run along the lines of Sampdoria, whom he'd joined in 1984, but found it hard to get his ideas across. The famous five-a-sides were left intact but we first noticed the difference in his initial pre-season in charge. We had been used to doing everything short and sharp at Liverpool, with runs taking a maximum of eight minutes. Under Souness, they suddenly lasted 45 minutes!"

Molby claimed that Ronnie Moran and Roy Evans were upset by the changes, particularly to the pre-season training routine, which had been in place since the days of Shankly. But there was also the problem that the new methods were not working. "We ended up with more injuries — most of them to the Achilles tendon — in the first three months of Souness's first full season than we'd ever had," Molby explained.

Another problem area was the change to the daily training routine. Ever since Shankly's desire to have the players feeling more familiar with Anfield, and also to enable a cooling down period after training, the players would meet at the stadium to get changed and then take a coach to Melwood, and everyone would return to the ground to eat lunch after the morning's session. Souness felt that it made sense to have everything in one place — as is the case today. Anfield was becoming busier, with a shop open, function rooms hired out and a museum planned, and it was no longer as practical to get the players in and out.

Ronnie Moran, in particular, was resistant to change. He was old-school, and understandably not keen on altering the methods that had brought so much success. For his part, Souness, while respecting Moran, regretted that he didn't push the issue harder with the coach; he didn't want to completely move away from the 'Liverpool way', but felt certain changes were important. History would prove that it needed an entire shift away from Boot Room personnel to move the club into the modern age. In 1998, Ronnie Moran retired, and shortly afterwards, Roy Evans resigned. That allowed Gérard Houllier to make the essential changes to diet and preparation. Where Souness had felt constrained by those around him, Houllier was given *carte blanche* to alter things as he saw fit. While Houllier ultimately failed for other reasons — poor purchasing later in his tenure and limited tactics — the increased professionalism would prove to be beneficial in Liverpool's resurgence as a successful cup team.

Souness was also blamed when the club knocked down the fabled Boot Room. The decision was made in order to expand the press room. Souness maintained that it was the club's decision, and it's easy to sympathise with his explanation that such moves "did not come within a manager's brief". But by that stage, he was being blamed for everything that was changing at Liverpool. As well as press and fan criticism, he was becoming increasingly unpopular with those inside the club. Looking back on his final days at Anfield, Souness said: "I daren't play in a five-a-side, because if I collapsed, no-one would give me the kiss of life."

Strengths

Souness was passionate, but probably to a fault. "No-one ever tried harder at Liverpool than Graeme," Roy Evans later admitted. "I've never seen anyone so distraught when we lost games as he was. Sometimes you would fear for him getting into his car after a game, he looked so bad. I think, and Graeme would acknowledge this now, that he was too impetuous, wanting to change too much too soon. He discarded too many of the more mature players far too early."

After his triple-bypass heart surgery, Souness wondered if he was made of the same stuff; instead of tough teak, he felt more like brittle balsa. After one defeat, against Ron Aktinson's Aston Villa — a game famous for Dean Saunders, recently sold to Villa, scoring twice and Ronny Rosenthal, unbelievably, hitting the bar from a central position having gone around the keeper — Souness admitted crying all the way home in the car, having been due to join Atkinson for a meal after the game. He felt on the edge of a nervous breakdown.

Souness was a hard taskmaster, but tried to let bygones be bygones; however, once players were upset it was hard to turn them around. Having fallen out with Ian Rush on a number of occasions, Souness still made the marksman club captain. For a man seen as stubborn he could admit his mistakes, as Jan Molby attested. In 1991 he had told Molby that he didn't feature in his plans, but was big enough to admit he'd made a mistake, and recalled the Dane to the team.

Having played in Italy, Souness was looking to bring a more continental approach to Anfield. In that sense it can be argued that he was ahead of his time. Rightly, he felt that the days of the team being handed fish and chips on the team bus after the game needed to be consigned to the past, and a move to a more athletically-propitious diet of pasta was implemented. Ian Rush, for one, didn't take kindly to being told he couldn't eat a steak three hours before a game; his argument was that it had served him well enough over the years. Souness' counter-argument may well have been that Rush would be *even sharper* on a diet more conducive to aerobic exercise — something rival teams were no doubt cottoning on to, which would have given opponents more running power. And Rush wasn't exactly scoring as he had been in the past, although his own Italian experience — shorter and less pleasant than Souness' — perhaps scarred him to continental methodology.

Souness was a disciplinarian, but it is hard for one man to take on an entire squad which has an entrenched mindset, as Roy Evans later discovered. There may be some receptive players, but if they are in the minority, it's a tough task. Ultimately, the best way to instil discipline is to change the personnel, although that's easier said than done. If a manager can root out the hardcore of those who cause problems or resist instruction and — the crucial part — buy players who already have the right temperament, to lead by example, then he can have the team follow his thinking. But both Souness and Evans exacerbated their problems by spending a lot of money on players with questionable characters.

Weaknesses

Given that his was a reign of relative failure at best, Souness' weaknesses have already been covered extensively. In terms of the football played, it's hard to know for sure what Souness' tactics were. Such were the myriad failings of his players, a clear style of play never really evolved. Jan Molby felt the problem lay with the manager trying to toughen up the team: "Under Souness, we had become a team known more for our aggressive approach than our footballing ability. He wanted hard men who could look after themselves because he felt Liverpool had become a soft touch.

But it just wasn't true. We had our bogey teams — like Wimbledon — but it had nothing to do with losing the physical battle."

But it's clear that Liverpool *had* become a soft touch in the early '90s; unfortunately, Souness was not buying players with his own footballing ability, mental toughness and leadership skills — just those who shared his aggressive streak. They were physically strong, but not as concerned as the manager with *winning*.

Historical Context — Strength of Rivals and League

When Souness took charge in April 1991, Arsenal were looking like becoming the dominant team. With the Reds having fallen away after the shock of Dalglish's departure, the Gunners were on their way to completing their second title success in three years. But Arsenal's time as a league force under George Graham had come to an end; they would win both domestic cups in 1993, and the Cup-Winners' Cup in 1994, but they never again hit the heights under the Scot in what had now become the Premiership.

Leeds then briefly emerged as a real threat under Howard Wilkinson. Boasting an impressive midfield — Gary Speed, David Batty, Gary McAllister and Gordon Strachan — they won the title in 1992, helped partly by the introduction of Eric Cantona in the second half of the season. But Leeds finished 17th a year later, and their bubble had burst.

It was in 1992 that Manchester United finally appeared to be getting their act together as a league force, after cup successes in the previous two seasons. They pushed Leeds hard to the title, but lost 2-0 at Anfield in a game in which Ian Rush finally scored against the great rivals.

By the time Souness resigned, his friend and predecessor in the Anfield hotseat had not only taken Blackburn into the Premiership but had them on course to finish second in 1994, a year before landing the title. Like Souness, Dalglish had spent big, but unlike Souness, he got his key signings spot-on. There was clearly less pressure at Blackburn, and Dalglish no doubt had a freer hand to do as he wished — as opposed to what Souness was finding at Liverpool. But whereas Souness showed an interest in Leeds' David Batty, Dalglish went out and got him. Whereas Souness looked at Tim Flowers, Dalglish signed him. And within a year of Souness breaking the bank to sign Dean Saunders, Dalglish had snapped up Alan Shearer.

Bête Noire

Souness seemed to be at odds with everybody during his time in charge — players, ex-players, the press and the fans — but there were no outstanding rivalries amongst his peers. Liverpool were not in contention for honours long enough, and that's when the feathers tend to fly in spats between managers. But Souness was the man in charge when Manchester United finally ended their 26-year title drought, and as such, Alex Ferguson only increased the pressure on the Liverpool manager.

Pedigree/Previous Experience

Souness' time at Glasgow Rangers suggested he had what it took to manage a big club with huge expectations. Rangers had not won the league for a decade, but Souness landed the title in his first season, and after missing out in year two, won the title in the next two campaigns, and Rangers would make it a hat-trick shortly after he defected to Anfield in April 1991.

Souness' success as Rangers was built on sound principles: recruit good players from the stronger English game, who would shine in the weaker Scottish league. Once at Liverpool he tried the reverse, and of course it was a far more fallible strategy. It was one thing taking a good English player like Mark Walters to Scotland, where he could take advantage of inferior defences, but bringing him back to England would be far more testing for the tricky winger. And as for Istvan Kozma, raiding Dunfermline for their best player was unlikely to lead to an unqualified success; it wasn't the best £300,000 (a few million in today's money) the club has ever spent. Souness was tempted because the Hungarian had tended to do quite well against his Rangers side. Kozma arrived in February 1992, and was released 17 months later, after less than ten appearances.

Subsequent Career

Since leaving Liverpool in January 1994, Souness has enjoyed a colourful and extremely mixed career, although it mostly involves failure. In 1995 he took charge of Turkish giants Galatasaray, and is best remembered for planting the club's flag in the centre-circle of bitter rivals Fenerbahçe's pitch in triumph after the Turkish Cup Final in 1996. He moved to Southampton later that same year, and did fairly well in terms of league performance, helping them escape relegation with a fraction more comfort than they had the season before he arrived. After resigning following disagreements with the new chairman, he moved to Torino, but was sacked after four months, having found the board's interference a hindrance. Next stop was Benfica, where he signed Steve Harkness and Michael Thomas from Liverpool, and fellow Brits Mark Pembridge, Dean Saunders and Brian Deane: not exactly the cream of the Premiership even when at their peak, which they certainly weren't. He was sacked after two unsuccessful seasons. Perhaps his best years as a manager outside of Rangers were at Blackburn, where he won promotion to the Premiership in his first season, landed the League Cup two years later, and ended 2002/03 with an excellent sixth-placed finish, just four points behind Liverpool. However, the bubble burst and they slipped to 15th a year later, to end the overachievement. In 2004 he moved to Newcastle, but as it had at Liverpool, his time at a big English club proved disastrous. Again his record in the transfer market was called into question, in particular the £18m spent on Jean-Alain Boumsong and Albert Luque, while the £17m for Michael Owen was subsequently seen as an unwise investment, with the former Liverpool striker playing just 14 times in his first two seasons at St James' Park. Souness was sacked in February 2006, with Newcastle 15th in the table.

Defining Moment

Clearly the defining moment of Souness' Liverpool stewardship was the heart bypass surgery which took place at the time of the FA Cup semi-final against Portsmouth in April 1992, and how he promptly sold his story to *The Sun*; as far as fans on Merseyside were concerned, it might as well have been his soul. It was bad enough that he sold an interview and pictures of himself kissing his girlfriend upon the operation's success to that particular newspaper — which is still reviled for its dishonest and deeply insulting reporting of the Hillsborough disaster, and remains boycotted on Merseyside — but to do so on the eve of the third anniversary of the tragedy was unfathomably crass. To make matters worse, the piece, which was due to appear on the 14th, ran a day later, on the 15th — the very anniversary of the loss of 96 lives. Although he apologised profusely at the time, Souness later admitted that he probably should have resigned. Any goodwill left from his playing days which had survived a turbulent first season in the league was wiped away by needless and selfish actions. It could be argued that he wasn't thinking straight, but it seems that he knew what he was doing.

For Souness himself, the defining moment in terms of knowing he had reached a dead end came on the afternoon of the FA Cup 3rd-round replay defeat by Bristol City in January 1994. City were staying in the same hotel that Liverpool used ahead of preparations for an Anfield game, and were in the suite next to Souness' room for a pre-match briefing. Russell Osman, the manager of the opposition, was giving his team talk, and Souness could hear every word. Every individual's weaknesses were correctly assessed. The damning statement that if you matched Liverpool for effort then the Reds would crumble was something that, painfully, the Liverpool manager knew was only too true. City did just that, and won 1-0.

Crowning Glory

There's only one highlight to the Souness era, and that is the 1992 FA Cup success. The run to the final pitted the Reds against only one top-level team, and the final was against Sunderland of Second Division, but even so, it was a welcome trophy at the end of the manager's first full season. Unfortunately, it would be the only one he would win at the club. The excellence of Jan Molby, spraying passes from the centre circle, and the tricky runs of Steve McManaman, suggested a healthy union between the old and the new; the same applied to Ian Rush and new signing Michael Thomas, who scored the game's only goals. But it was an illusion: the blend of youth and experience did not bear fruit as anticipated.

Legacy

As Roy Evans would discover, there was a lot of work to be done with the squad in the spring of 1994. Indeed, that's why Souness himself called it quits, realising the job was beyond him. Any new manager would have a fresh perspective and players willing to impress and fight for their places, now that the slate had been wiped clean, but in truth Souness did not leave a lot to work with, beyond those youngsters the club had developed and a couple of Dalglish's later signings who had matured.

TRANSFERS

Transfers In

All managers forage in the market they know best, but Graeme Souness had a strange habit of not only plundering leagues in which he'd managed, but also recruiting players who had previously played under him — and not always the best ones at that. For instance, when he later managed in Turkey and Portugal, and back in the Premiership with Blackburn, he bought ex-Reds Mike Marsh, Barry Venison, Stig Inge Bjornebye, Brad Friedel, Michael Thomas and Dean Saunders. Players he sold at Liverpool, like Marsh, Saunders and Venison, he ended up repurchasing when they were past their peak, although he did get the best from Friedel at Blackburn, who was originally brought to Liverpool by Roy Evans.

Whatever the reason for the failure of many of Souness' signings — and many did fail — it's fair to say that at the time they were purchased, quite a few made reasonable sense. He would regularly spend big money on established players who had done well in the old First Division/newly-formed Premiership. Perhaps these players just couldn't handle the step up to the biggest club in the land, or maybe Souness' management skills were woefully lacking. It's possible that some were simply not suited to the Reds' style of play; and then there's the likelihood that they were simply good top division players, but rarely *great* ones. Where was the real outstanding talent?

It seems there is evidence of a deficiency in Souness' scouting system throughout his career after leaving Rangers. Of course, there's the infamous story of Ali Dia, widely believed to be the worst Premiership player in its history when he briefly appeared for Souness' Southampton in 1996 — which seems to sum up the Scot's attitude to recruitment. Phoned by someone claiming to be former World Footballer of the Year George Weah, Souness was offered the African's cousin: Ali Dia, a Senegalese international who had previously played for Paris St Germain's first team. Of course, it was not Weah, and Dia was not Weah's cousin. Nor was he an international or a former *Ligue Une* player; he was little more than a parks player. With no chance to see him in a reserve fixture, Souness brought on Dia early in a Premiership match against Leeds United. So bad was he, Dia was himself removed on 53 minutes. Dia's one-month contract was promptly cancelled. Can you imagine many other top-level managers making such a bizarre mistake? (Souness has since criticised some of Rafa Benítez's signings, including Yossi Benayoun, saying he was 'not Liverpool standard'. *How dare he?* some might ask. Mischievous souls might suggest that some of Souness' signings at Liverpool made Dia look like World Footballer of the Year.)

At the start at Liverpool, Souness went in big and hard into the transfer market, just as he always had with tackles. In July 1991 the Scot paid £2.2m for Mark Wright, in what seemed an inspired move. Wright had excelled a year earlier at Italia '90 as England came within a penalty shootout of the World Cup Final. However, and perhaps crucially, it was as a sweeper, playing behind two stoppers that he excelled. Maybe this would be why Wright never found his best form under Souness in a 4-4-2, and only rediscovered his class in the mid-'90s, when Roy Evans adopted a formation with three centre-backs. In 1998, aged 35, Wright retired after 210 games for the Reds, having scored nine goals.

At the same time as he moved for Wright, Souness raided relegated Derby once again, this time for Welsh striker Dean Saunders, son of former Red, Roy. The English transfer record was broken in the process, as Liverpool shelled out £2.9m to partner the striker with his fellow Welsh forward, Ian Rush — the club's previous record signing. Saunders was a capable, busy striker, who could score goals without ever being particularly prolific. He scored 23 goals in his first season, but nine came in the UEFA Cup, against very substandard opposition, and four more followed in the domestic cups; meaning that only ten came in the league. Too often his control seemed lacking, and he couldn't utilise his pace on the break in a side that played possession football. Two more goals would be scored at the start of the following campaign before, in September 1992, Saunders was sold. As with later record-breaking signing Stan Collymore, Aston Villa came in and took the player off the club's hands, for about 85% the original fee, but by which time the transfer ceiling had risen. A couple of months after Souness signed Saunders, Ian Wright moved to Arsenal for £400,000 less; the Londoner may or may not have done as well at Liverpool, but he proved to be a far more effective Premiership goalscorer over the coming years.

Mark Walters arrived for £1.25m in August 1991, having scored a goal every 2.7 games at Rangers, but during his Liverpool career that ratio was a far less impressive one every 6.5 games, although quite a few of those appearances were as substitute. Walters was a fine player, but was always going to suffer by comparison with the recent memories of John Barnes at his best. Walters scored 19 goals in 124 games, but aside from 1992/93, when he scored 13 in 44, his contribution was too often lacking. He was released in 1996.

Michael Thomas looked like another shrewd signing, when he arrived in December 1991 for £1.5m. A box-to-box midfielder, the former Arsenal man, whose fame was cemented at Anfield two years earlier, would offer the kind of running his new midfield partner, Jan Molby, could only dream about. But as with John Barnes, Thomas suffered a debilitating Achilles tendon injury during the Souness reign, and emerged at the other side a diminished force. He would later establish himself in the Reds' midfield under Roy Evans, but as a holding midfielder whose job was to break up attacks and give simple passes. While not an outright failure, he did not live up to the expectations that came with a transfer fee that, by 2008 standards, would be the equivalent of around £15m. After 12 goals in 163 games, Thomas moved to Benfica.

Another midfielder arrived a few months after Thomas: Istvan Kozma, signed from Scottish football in February 1992. In the March of that year, 18-year-old Lee Jones was plucked from Wrexham for £300,000. Jones would later go on to prove a handy lower league player, but during his five years at Anfield he only made four appearances, all as a substitute.

The summer of 1992 showed no let-up in the rebuilding programme. David James arrived for £1m from Watford, for whom the 21-year-old had played almost 100 games. James was hugely talented, with the perfect physical attributes to be the very best. But the psychological side of the game would always hamper him — decision making, confidence and concentration. Capable of pulling off breathtaking instinctive saves, he fared worse when he had more time to think. It seemed that boredom crept in during games — he had to be involved, and would come for crosses when there was no need; although at least the defenders knew they had a proactive goalkeeper behind them, and not some timid soul rooted to his line. He also admitted spending too much time playing his Playstation, and not preparing properly for matches. Part of the problem was that he was still very young for a goalkeeper, and once he had made costly mistakes at such a high-profile club, he was mentally scarred. The cutting headlines — "Calamity James" — must have hit him hard. After 277 games, he was sold in 1999 to Aston Villa, for £1.8m.

When he was signed from Spurs in July, Paul Stewart, approaching his 28th birthday, had just made the PFA shortlist for Player of the Year. He had also recently won three caps for England; as such, it seemed that he was a player on the up. Souness paid £2.3m for the former striker who was now making his name as a holding midfielder. But Stewart never settled at Liverpool, where expectations were higher, and where he was expected to seamlessly transfer his midfield form from Spurs which, in itself, had come about after three years of failure as a forward. Injuries didn't help his stay on Merseyside; as a result, he seemed slower and more cumbersome without full fitness. In a midfield that could contain a now-overweight John Barnes and the considerable frame of Jan Molby, Liverpool were about as far from athletic as you could get. Julian Dicks and Neil Ruddock would soon add more weight to the back line, albeit in the wrong sense, while Ronnie Whelan was nowhere near as trim as in his youth. Within four years Stewart would leave on a free transfer, to cap another bad foray into the transfer market by Souness.

Rather than get better, Souness' signings only seemed to fare worse. Torben Piechnik was signed for £500,000 in September 1992. Piechnik was far from poor in terms of pedigree; he had only just helped Denmark, who hadn't originally even qualified for Euro '92 (but were allowed entry due to Yugoslavia's civil war), win the competition in one of the biggest upsets of all time. Part of their success was attributed to a lack of pressure; they weren't meant to be there, so they had nothing to lose. The same could never be said of a player joining Liverpool — there is almost always an expectation to win. The Dane started well enough, but deteriorated rapidly with a loss of confidence, and only played 23 times during two years at Anfield.

December 1992 saw Souness once again look to Scandinavia, with the signing of Norwegian international, Stig Inge Bjornebye, for £600,000 from Rosenborg. Bjornebye was never viewed as an outright success at Liverpool, but he was perhaps underrated and undervalued by many. It's true that his time at the club was very much an up-and-down process, with good seasons followed by bad. But the left-back/left-wing-back served the club well, particularly under Roy Evans, before being sold in 2000 for £300,000, a decent return on a fine, dedicated professional who was 31. In his eight years at the club, he scored four goals in 184 games.

Having failed to get Liverpool into the top five, Souness went all-out in 1993 to find the missing ingredients. It was a summer of big spending and, alas, massive failure. The Reds started the '93/94 season in excellent form, winning the first three games, but from that point it all fell away. None of his new signings made the kind of impact he was looking for.

Neil Ruddock was purchased from Spurs for £2.5m in July. Any player who gets 'self-styled hardman' put before their name should raise concerns. Perhaps contrary to this image, Ruddock was actually a very fine passer from the back, pinging balls out to the wing with his left foot. An imposing figure, his height made him useful at set-pieces at either end, registering 12 goals in a red shirt in 152 games. But too many times he let himself and the team down. Any time he was injured he returned heavily overweight — he claims to have piled on the pounds by just looking at food, but in that case, he must have spent every waking moment staring avidly at hamburgers, fries and pies.

More than 40 years after Bill Shankly tried to sign the striker's father, Nigel Clough was purchased in June for £2.275m. A talented player in the Peter Beardsley mould, the 27-year-old England international however didn't possess his predecessor's mobility and sharpness; in essence, he was *Beardsley-Lite*. Clough started brilliantly, scoring twice on his debut against Sheffield Wednesday and soon added a cheeky flicked goal at QPR. But his form then waned. His best game was against Manchester United at the start of 1994, when the Reds were trailing their bitter rivals 3-0 at Anfield. Clough popped up with two goals, before Ruddock equalised late on. After that, Clough drifted out of the picture, and was eventually sold to Manchester City for £1.5m in 1996, after just 44 games and nine goals.

In September '93 Julian Dicks arrived from West Ham, in a deal that saw him valued at £2.5m, but with two players — David Burrows and Mike Marsh — exchanged in *lieu* of cash. The introduction of the feisty 25-year-old Bristolian, as with Ruddock, was designed to add some aggression to the side. But it didn't really succeed in making Liverpool a tougher proposition. Dicks was a good Premiership player, but he never settled at Anfield, and left for less than half the amount paid for him after just one season.

Player	Quality	0.01pg	IN	OUT	FGV	VALUE	Ap	Details	
Rob Jones	8.30	2.43	-1	4	2	**13.73**	243	£300k 1991	Injured 27
All Managers' Average						**7.92**			
David James	6.44	2.7	-3	1.2		**7.34**	277	£1m 1992	£1.8m 1999
Stig Bjornebye	5.89	1.84	-1.8	0.4		**6.33**	184	£600k 1992	£300k'99 @31
Mark Wright	6.71	2.1	-7.6	5		**6.21**	210	£2.2m 1991	Retired @35
Dean Saunders**	6.35	0.61	-10	7		**3.96**	61	£2.9m 1991	1992 £2.3m
Michael Thomas	6.24	1.63	-5.2	1		**3.67**	163	£1.5m 1991	Rel. @31
Average	**5.1**		**-4.54**			**3.45**			
Nigel Clough	5.22	0.44	-6.1	3.6		**3.16**	44	£2.275m 1993	£1.5m@29 '96
Mark Walters	5.59	1.24	-4.3	0		**2.53**	124	£1.25m 1991	Rel. 1996
Istvan Kozma	2.59	0.1	-0.9	0		**1.79**	10	£300k 1992	Rel. 1993
Torben Piechnik	3.00	0.24	-1.5	0		**1.74**	24	£500k '92 @29	Rel. @31

Lee Jones	2.29	0.04	-0.9	0	**1.43**	4	£300k 1992	Free 1997
Neil Ruddock	5.72	1.52	-7.6	0.1	**-0.26**	152	£2.5m 1993	£100k'98 @30
Julian Dicks	4.06	0.28	-6.7	2	**-0.36**	28	£2.5m '93 Sw.	£1m 1994
Paul Stewart	3.59	0.42	-7	0	**-2.99**	42	£2.3m 1992	Rel. 1997

Key: *See page 51.*

Transfer Masterstroke

Souness did at least get one signing absolutely spot-on: Rob Jones. Just 19, the grandson of former Red Bill Jones arrived in October 1991 for £300,000, having already played close to 100 games for Crewe. Within days he was making his debut at Old Trafford. Jones was hugely impressive, showing no nerves — only pace, skill and determination. It was the first time that he had faced a player of the quality of Ryan Giggs, with the Welshman just starting out at the time, but Jones kept him quiet in a 0-0 draw. Giggs would later describe Jones as his most dogged opponent. When Jason McAteer arrived in 1995, Jones was switched to the left, as a wing-back. He'd played on that flank earlier in his career to great effect, albeit as a conventional full-back. Souness was inclined move Jones to left-back to deal with a particularly pacy winger, such as Aston Villa's speedster Tony Daley.

Jones' Old Trafford bow should have been the start of a brilliant career, but injuries limited the full-back to 'just' 243 appearances, 24 fewer than his granddad, and to only eight England caps. At first it was an issue with shin splints, perhaps a result of having played professional football at the age of 16; the condition caused him to miss Euro '92, having recently become an England international. In 1996 he would again be ruled out of the European Championships, this time with a cracked vertebra. It was so serious that doctors advised him to give up the sport altogether, at the age of just 24, or risk permanent disability. He rested for six months, and returned seemingly okay, but then persistent knee injuries started to plague him. In February 1998, a large swelling in his left knee needed surgery to repair, but it was not successful. Four operations later, and still it wasn't right. The end was nigh for one of the country's brightest talents.

Jones retired in September 1999, at the age of 27, having failed to regain his fitness during the briefest of spells at West Ham after Gérard Houllier released him that summer. Liverpool have had some fine right-backs since — Markus Babbel, Steve Finnan and Alvaro Arbeloa — but a fit and injury-free Rob Jones could have meant that none of those who arrived before 2005, when Jones should have been hanging up his boots, actually needed to be signed.

Expensive Folly

Where to start? Dean Saunders, £2.9m? Paul Stewart, £2.3m? Nigel Clough, £2.275m? Julian Dicks, £2.5m? In 2008 money, that's about £90m of talent, and it amounted to precious little. None of them lasted at the club for more than four years, and none was a regular in the first team for more than a single season. Saunders was the most successful, in terms of performances and recouped fee, while at least Clough had some very good games, even if he was on the whole a failure. Dicks, meanwhile, was steady if unspectacular. Which just leaves Paul Stewart — an expensive mistake if ever there was one. He cost 70% of the English transfer record — over £20m in current terms — and played just 42 times over his five year contract, only to be released for free at the end of it.

One Who Got Away

On November 6th 1991, after Liverpool's 3-0 victory over Auxerre in the UEFA Cup, Souness met France manager Michel Platini. The French legend told him he had a player who would like to play for Liverpool: Eric Cantona. Souness declined, citing the player's poor disciplinary record, which included throwing a boot in the face of a team-mate and, on another occasion, throwing the ball at a referee. Within a year Cantona, having helped Leeds win the title, would score a hat-trick in Leeds' 4-3 Charity Shield win over Souness' Liverpool, before moving onto even bigger success at Manchester United.

Was it Souness' biggest mistake? At Manchester United, Cantona proved to be a difficult character on the pitch (although a very successful one at that), but a consummate professional off it, teaching the younger players how to train and look after their bodies (as well as some fine kung-fu moves). It's easy to see why Souness declined, however. And whereas United were at the stage where they needed one extra spark within a talented and disciplined set-up, Liverpool were nowhere near.

Also with a strong Leeds connection, David Batty was a player Souness had been tracking in 1992, when he ended up going for the more physically imposing Paul Stewart. Leeds parted with Batty a year later, selling him to Dalglish's Blackburn, where, in 1995, he collected a league winners' medal.

Budget – Historical Context

Blackburn were building up a strong side under Kenny Dalglish, but they would peak once Souness had been replaced by Roy Evans. Arsenal signed Ian Wright in September 1991 for £2.5m, but they were still relying largely on home-grown stars; and anyway, the Gunners were becoming a fading force in the league. Leeds won the 1992 title with some young home-grown talents (David Batty, Gary Speed) and rejects from other clubs (Lee Chapman, John Lukic, Gordon Strachan), before promptly disappearing from the upper echelons of the league.

The big story, of course, was the emergence of the Reds' bitter rivals Manchester United. While Ryan Giggs had gravitated to the first team from the academy set-up, the side that lost the title at Anfield in May 1992 — Peter Schmeichel, Denis Irwin, Steve Bruce, Mike Phelan, Gary Pallister, Paul Ince, Bryan Robson, Ryan Giggs, Brian McClair, Mark Hughes and Andrei Kanchelskis — still had a very substantial average cost of 45% of the English transfer record. Nine of those players were Ferguson purchases, and clearly he was seriously bankrolled on his way to breaking the club's 26-year hex.

The side that Souness fielded against United on January 4th 1994, just weeks before resigning — Grobbelaar, Wright, Jones, Ruddock, Dicks, Barnes, Clough, McManaman, Redknapp, Fowler and Rush — cost on average 43.5% of the English transfer record; however, the five purchased by Souness — Wright, Jones, Ruddock, Dicks, and Clough — cost an even higher average of 58%. The Reds came back from 3-0 down to draw the game, but even that great Anfield night couldn't paper over a myriad cracks.

RECORD
FA Cup: 1992.

	P	W	D	L	F	A	%
Overall	**157**	**65**	**47**	**45**	**248**	**186**	**41.40%**
League	115	47	34	34	164	133	40.87%
FA Cup	13	5	6	2	17	11	38.46%
League Cup	16	7	7	2	38	22	43.75%
Europe	12	6	0	6	26	16	50.00%
Other	1	0	0	1	3	4	0.00%

CONCLUSION
Graeme Souness cared passionately about bringing success back to Liverpool. But perhaps his all-consuming desire hampered his efforts, making him impatient and causing him to lose both his temper and his perspective.

It took Alex Ferguson four years to simply get United out of the slump that they'd experienced after he arrived, and another three to land a first league title. A case could be made for saying that Liverpool's new man was simply following the same course. Souness himself used the example of Ferguson, and to this day feels he would have got it right in time: "Liverpool will always be a cloud over me. I know I would have got Liverpool right, but, you know, it took Fergie seven years at Manchester United." The changes Souness looked to make — related to diet and training — were becoming rife in England by the late '90s, but at the start of the decade it was another story. Was he ahead of his time? In that sense it seemed he had the right ideas, but perhaps didn't implement them properly, while facing resistance from the old guard. Had Walter Smith moved with him, he might have had more luck; as it was, Phil Boersma was not a top-quality coach.

Whatever the validity of his ideas on modernisation, the problem was that Souness' signings were so unsuccessful and the football often so uninspiring, that there was no leeway. Then there was the selling of his story to the *The Sun*. Michael Parkinson, the legendary journalist and broadcaster, understood the significance, despite no connection to Liverpool: "What he did was so crass, so insensitive and so plain bloody silly that he must still have been under the influence of the anaesthetic when the pictures were taken."

Souness might have been correct about eventually getting things right — in time, he *might* have rectified his mistakes and built a new side. But after three years there were no shoots of optimism — aside from the youngsters he'd inherited, and the purchased Rob Jones — that could be clung to. His subsequent career has shown him to be a fairly decent, capable manager, but a far from exceptional one. And in 1991, exceptional was what Liverpool FC needed.

"Anybody who plays for me should be a bad loser."

GRAEME SOUNESS

1994 - 1998
ROY EVANS

*"If you want to stand out, the way
to do it is to play for the team."*

ROY EVANS

INTRODUCTION

Roy Evans was a great Liverpool FC man. But there are four letters missing from the end of that sentence. He was not, alas, a great Liverpool FC man*ager*.

Some 20 years after John Smith had proclaimed that the 20-something would one day manage Liverpool, Roy Evans, by then a silver-haired middle-aged man, fulfilled the prophecy. In some ways he did very well: improving the team; introducing some flair and swagger; taking the team to two cup finals and winning one of them. Then there were two 3rd-place finishes, as well as two in 4th, and on two occasions the team at least contended the league title going into the final games (before falling badly at the last). But instead, his time is remembered as one of failure, and for the Spice Boy image his players acquired via their non-footballing activities. The squad he left was one of deteriorating talents and ill-discipline, with just a few bright sparks worthy of taking the club into the 21st Century.

Sometimes the divide between success and failure is so thin as to be the width of a wasp's wing. Roy Evans, and his Liverpool team, missed out on a place in the Champions League by the breadth of a post, and his fate was effectively sealed in the process. With virtually the last kick of the 1996/97 season Michael Owen struck a shot past the Sheffield Wednesday goalkeeper (admittedly an outfield player deputising for the red-carded no.1) that cannoned off the woodwork. A slight gust of wind from a favourable direction and the ball would have shifted a couple of millimetres in its flight, and started spinning, so that it then clipped the inside of the post and span into the back of the net. But ultimately it remained a shot off-target, and the goal, which would have guaranteed 2nd spot, did not arrive. Liverpool finished 4th. Better players could not be attracted without the kudos of the Champions League, and there was less money in the kitty. So close, yet so far.

Evans led the Reds to top-four finishes in each of his four full seasons. However, at the point when Gérard Houllier was introduced as his co-manager the team was showing signs of deterioration; in terms of points won, there had been an annual decrease: 74 (42 games), 71, 68, and finally, 65. While finishing position is the main thing, it was indicative of a weakening from two very strong campaigns.

The club was struggling to reassert its authority after decades of success. David James remarked that "We were always looking over our shoulder, trying to be something we couldn't be. There was a constant pressure to live up to Liverpool's history." Living up to the names of the past was always an incentive for Liverpool players; Ronnie Moran used to tell the likes of Souness, Hansen and Dalglish that their side wasn't as good as the great teams of a decade or two earlier — but Souness, Hansen and Dalglish *were* good enough; they responded as hoped, to prove Moran wrong. By the mid-'90s, it was painfully obvious that too many players simply weren't up to the standards of the past, and the pressure quickly increased. In some cases, it wasn't that the players lacked ability; James himself was a fantastic natural talent, but it wouldn't be until he'd matured as a person, and also sought the help of a sports psychologist, that he would finally be at the level that the Reds needed a decade earlier. By then he was elsewhere.

Ultimately, too many of that 1997/98 squad were players with no great future in the game at the very top. The Arsenal team of the same year contained a litany of names, including some older players, who would grace the highest stage for years to come: Bergkamp, Adams, Seaman, Anelka, Dixon, Winterburn, Keown, Parlour, Overmars and Vieira all had at least four or five — if not many more — years left at the top. Liverpool's squad was full of players heading rapidly for the lower divisions, propped up by just a handful of top-class players.

Situation Inherited

It's fair to say that Liverpool were in disarray in 1994, when Graeme Souness' reign came to an end. Roy Evans, his successor, inherited a handful of talented, young British players, including Robbie Fowler, Rob Jones, David James, Steve McManaman, Dominic Matteo and

Jamie Redknapp, but the squad left by Graeme Souness was, at best, a very mixed bag. Dampening the glow of these bright sparks were Nigel Clough (talented enough, but had lost his way), Julian Dicks, Mark Walters, Torben Piechnik, Lee Jones and Paul Stewart.

One bonus was that Mark Wright emerged from a difficult first three years at the club to show the kind of form he had displayed for England in the 1990 World Cup, but only after falling out with the new manager in preseason training. Wright went on to live up to his billing, albeit temporarily, in the twilight of his career, putting in a couple of excellent seasons at the age of 32/33. Neil Ruddock, another of Souness' expensive signings, was the epitome of inconsistency alongside Wright: some months lean and hungry, other months the hunger had clearly been sated at McDonalds.

Steve Harkness proved a decent option either at left-back or as one of the three centre-backs, but was far from remarkable, as his subsequent career attested. Stig Bjornebye was another player who found his feet under Evans, albeit in a very inconsistent manner. In 1994/95 he finally showed his full ability in a team that seemed to have some direction at last, but then a broken leg sustained just before the 1995 League Cup Final halted his progress. He missed most of the following season, but returned for his best year yet in 1996/97, when he provided countless assists from curling crosses with his cultured left-foot; unfortunately, it was a skill that seemed to desert him when his confidence was low, when he was more likely to pick out a red shirt in the Kop. That season, when the Reds made a decent push for the league title, he was deservedly included in the PFA Team of the Year along with McManaman and Wright.

Two Liverpool legends — Ian Rush and John Barnes — remained, albeit in a diminished form (although in Barnes' case, clearly this does not refer to his girth). Rush wasn't exactly still 'going strong', at least not when compared with his glorious pomp, but he was able to maintain a steady supply of goals and use his wily know-how to remain a very effective striker, and to help along the prodigy, Fowler. Evans helped Barnes rediscover his usefulness as a central midfielder, where his positioning and distribution could keep the team ticking over. It was a rare sight to see Barnes give the ball away, but for some fans there was a frustration that he was neither energetic nor a ferocious tackler. That said, he still weighed in with a few goals, most memorably the sublime overhead kick against Blackburn Rovers and the 45-yard 'pass' against Southampton that saw Dave Beasant scamper back across his goal-line in a vain attempt to catch the ball as it rolled inside the far post.

Michael Thomas was another player who lost his pace due to an Achilles injury, and like Barnes altered his game to a more one-paced, passing and breaking-up style; like a lesser version of Didi Hamann. Thomas filled in for Jamie Redknapp, but was distraught when a successful run of 20-odd games with him in the side came to an end and he was instantly dropped for the returning Redknapp for the 1996 FA Cup semi-final.

Jan Molby was still on the books, but never really featured under Evans. Ronnie Whelan, Steve Nicol, Bruce Grobbelaar, Torben Piechnik, Ronny Rosenthal and Julian Dicks were all sold or released in 1994, while Mark Walters lasted a couple of seasons, much of which was spent on loan. In 1994 Don Hutchison found himself on the wrong side of Evans and was sent packing.

Players Inherited Squad

Player	Quality	Age	Adj	Inheritance	Year	Age
Robbie Fowler (1)	9.43	0	0	9.43	1994	19
Steve McManaman	8.47	0	0	8.47	1994	22
Rob Jones	8.30	0	0	8.30	1994	22.5
Jamie Redknapp	7.41	0	0	7.41	1994	21
David James	6.44	0	0	6.44	1994	22
Dominic Matteo	6.29	0	0	6.29	1994	20
Michael Thomas	6.24	0	0	6.24	1994	27
Stig Inge Bjornebye	5.89	0	0	5.89	1994	24.5
Neil Ruddock	5.72	0	0	5.72	1994	26
Steve Harkness	5.35	0	0	5.35	1994	23
Don Hutchison	5.12	0	0	5.12	1994	23
Average	**6.49**			**4.79**		**26.4**
John Barnes	9.67	-4	-1	4.67	1994	31
Ian Rush (2)	8.76	-5.5	1	4.26	1994	32.5
Nigel Clough	5.22	-1	0	4.22	1994	28
Julian Dicks	4.06	0	0	4.06	1994	26
Jan Molby	8.59	-4	-1	3.59	1994	31
Mark Wright	6.71	-3.5	0	3.21	1994	30.5
Ronnie Whelan	8.61	-6	0	2.61	1994	33
Mark Walters	5.59	-3	0	2.59	1994	30
Lee Jones	2.29	0	0	2.29	1994	21
Paul Stewart	3.59	-1.5	0	2.09	1994	29.5
Steve Nicol	8.53	-6.5	0	2.03	1994	33.5
Torben Piechnik	3.00	-3	0	0.00	1994	31

Best XI

Player	Quality	Age	Adj	Inheritance	Year	Age
David James	6.44	0	0	6.44	1994	22
Rob Jones	8.30	0	0	8.30	1994	22.5
Neil Ruddock	5.72	0	0	5.72	1994	26
Mark Wright	6.71	-3.5	0	3.21	1994	30.5
Stig Inge Bjornebye	5.89	0	0	5.89	1994	24.5
Mark Walters	5.59	-3	0	2.59	1994	30
John Barnes	9.67	-4	-1	4.67	1994	31
Jamie Redknapp	7.41	0	0	7.41	1994	21

Steve McManaman	8.47	0	0	**8.47**	1994	22
Ian Rush (2)	8.76	-5.5	1	**4.26**	1994	32.5
Robbie Fowler (1)	9.43	0	0	**9.43**	1994	19
Average	**7.49**			**6.03**		**25.5**

Key: Quality 0-10; Age = -1 point for every year from 28 onwards, eg -4 for 31 year-old, and -1 point from 30 onwards for keepers, eg -4 for 33 year-old; Adj = adjustments for players either exceptionally fit/unfit for their age, or soon to leave; Inheritance = total out of 10. Excludes players not part of first team picture.

"The pride I feel is almost indescribable. I am a Liverpool lad. I stood on the Kop as a youngster and understand the football expectations of all our supporters."

ROY EVANS, 1994

State of Club

In the mid-'90s, Liverpool were still reeling from their fall from the summit, and trying to find a way of getting back to the top as quickly as possible. Following an external appointment, a return to the Boot Room philosophy was sought. Later, in 1997, there was a strong possibility of Kenny Dalglish returning as Director of Football. In the end Evans vetoed the idea, out of the (understandable) fear that the first bad result would lead to calls for Dalglish to resume his old management role, which would put both men in an awkward position.

As Gérard Houllier would later find, ex-players writing in the press could also pose a threat. "Former players have always had a pop," Evans said. "When that happens I am always disappointed. Most of them have tried the job of managing and failed. Now they know all the answers to the questions. Maybe they are in need of a few bob to say these things."

Assistance/Backroom Staff

Like Roy Evans, Doug Livermore had been a Liverpool player in the late '60s but failed to make the grade, playing just a handful of times more than Evans. During that time the two struck up a friendship. Livermore, who had started his coaching career by running the reserve teams of Norwich and then Swansea (working under another former Red, John Toshack), found himself working with Terry Venables at Spurs. When Venables became chief executive in an unusual move, Livermore and yet another ex-Red, Ray Clemence, co-managed the team for the 1992/93 season, at the end of which Venables, Livermore and Clemence were all sacked by Alan Sugar. Evans felt that his friend's outside experience would serve the club well, given that both Ronnie Moran and himself were Boot Room boys who knew only the Liverpool way. Sammy Lee was another whose coaching experience was limited to just Liverpool. Evans was also supported by Tom Saunders, who continued his role from the boardroom of assisting the manager with general administration, as well as being another wise old head to call upon for advice.

Management Style

Friendly, approachable and hugely likeable, Roy Evans will unfortunately be remembered for what went wrong at the club at the time. The football was easy on the eye, but there was a key problem. Despite his later protestations, discipline was a massive issue during Evans' reign.

Inevitably, plenty of those involved deny it was as bad as portrayed. And yet between them they will admit to a litany of unfortunate and down right idiotic incidents. These included: Steve Nicol drinking beer and eating a bacon sandwich one morning on a pre-season tour after being told there was an alcohol curfew after the previous night — his response was that it *still was* the previous night; Don Hutchison's drinking excesses that ended with a photo of a Budweiser bottle covering his beer-addled genitals; Steve Harkness going around putting faeces into other players' bags (in the name of 'team bonding'); Stan Collymore not turning up for training and refusing to play in the reserves; players not trying 'because it's only pre-season', and failing to maintain a healthy weight; and the now infamous pass-the-pound game, devised by Neil Ruddock. Apparently the captain would start the match holding a £1 coin, and this would be passed around whenever there was a corner/throw-in/free-kick. Whoever had the coin at the final whistle would have to buy the drinks that night. While not the crime of the century, it hardly shows players concentrating on the game and concerned with their own performances within it. No fan wants to watch robots perform, but 'characters' have to be performing at the highest level to justify their inclusion. Somehow it's hard to see Sami Hyypia, Dietmar Hamann, Pepe Reina, Xabi Alonso and Fernando Torres acting like that. If you're that keen on seeing personalities, then a few quid down the comedy club will serve up professional comedians at far better value than a match ticket. For ever-increasing entry prices, fans want *professional footballers*.

Fights, disputes and unrest will always occur at football clubs, but if they are isolated incidents they are not necessarily divisive. Some 'high jinks' will occur, and did so as recently as 2007, when Craig Bellamy took a nine-iron to John Arne Riise. Nine years earlier Jamie Carragher had shamed himself at the Christmas party. But these were one-off incidents during the leadership of Houllier and Benítez. Carragher knew in no uncertain terms that he would not be forgiven a repeat, while Bellamy signed his own exit papers with his actions. There were even problems during Bill Shankly's reign, with training ground bust-ups and disgruntled players, but the problems never lasted. Poisonous influences were banished.

There were a lot of youngsters on the scene in the mid-'90s, but also too much immaturity — and yet, ironically, this wasn't an accusation that could be levelled at the youngest of them all, Michael Owen. There just was not enough individual and collective responsibility being taken. When Houllier instilled a more disciplinarian regime in 1998, many existing players complained that it was too serious; and yet they were all happy to be picking up 'serious' wages that ran into tens of thousands of pounds per week. Fun and laugher at training grounds shouldn't be outlawed, and maybe Houllier was too strict, but if any professional wants a laugh, there are plenty of park pitches available.

It's not that Evans was especially weak — he wasn't; it was just that he wasn't *strong enough consistently enough*. He had a tough job from day one with the situation he inherited, but he made his task more difficult by buying players who only brought more trouble. Initially it was probably easier to lay down the law. A new man has licence to sweep his own broom. Given that Souness had been particularly combustible, Evans' brand of discipline would have seemed a little easier to bear. And while there are plenty of examples provided by Evans and some of his players of how ruthless the new manager could be — Wright and Dicks bombed from the first pre-season tour, players dressed down or eventually sold — it wasn't enough. No matter what Evans did, there remained too many indiscretions. It's not about ranting and raving and hurling tea cups, but commanding respect. Evans wasn't helped by some naturally disrespectful and disruptive characters — although some of them he himself purchased — but it is not the amount of discipline you get right that counts, but the amount that goes awry. That is what ultimately undoes all the good work.

Evans defended his stance in his autobiography: "The drinking culture was slowly changed with the introduction of foreign players into our football but you can't change entrenched habits overnight. Any problems I had were no different to those at other clubs. The culture has changed everywhere now but it's not down to managers like Houllier or Wenger; it's down to the players."

Evans' claim, however, does not tally with the way Wenger sorted out that Arsenal team, and in particular Tony Adams, who had a serious alcohol problem. There was a big drinking culture at Highbury, with Paul Merson another major culprit. There was no messing about by Wenger. Adams was turned around, Merson was shipped out. Wenger brought in foreign players with better habits to surround those stars worth keeping. It also ignores that Alex Ferguson had done the same thing a decade earlier, culling top players like Paul McGrath and Norman Whiteside.

"Graeme Souness had already tried to do it at Liverpool long before Gérard came along," Evans said, "and he'd had only a limited success because the British players weren't ready for it. They've realised the benefits of proper diet and conditioning over time but the biggest influence for change came from the foreign players."

Both Evans and Robbie Fowler have since said things like "if we were winning trophies, it wouldn't have been a problem" — which is true to a degree, but entirely misses the point that some incidents were *contributing to a failure to win trophies*. Surely it's like an athlete who eats 25 Mars bars a day and quickly puts on seven stone, turning around and saying "yeah, but if I'd won the race no-one would be mentioning that I'm morbidly obese and currently puking up blood in the long-jump sandpit". When you have a squad of players who already have fitness and weight issues, drinking can only make things worse. You sense a youngster with an ectomorphic body-type like Steve McManaman could run off any recreational excesses, whereas a more endomoprhic shape would pile on the pounds. The last thing Neil Ruddock should have been saying was "win or lose, first on the booze". Not only does it treat winning and losing as the same — what does it matter, we'll get pissed up and have a laugh afterwards anyway? — it's even more unforgivable if you are as naturally athletic as the average beached sea mammal. Modelling contracts, the persistent use of mobile phones at training, cream suits at Wembley, poor timekeeping — they seem small issues, but they did not add up to total professionalism.

For a while in the mid-'90s, Liverpool had a team every bit as good as Manchester United's — at least when it came to attacking. In 1995/96, United were outplayed at Old Trafford, and only scraped a late 2-2 draw with a dubious Eric Cantona penalty; at Anfield later that season the Reds dominated United in a 2-0 win, with the imperious Fowler placing two more picture-book goals past Peter Schmeichel. But in Alex Ferguson, United had the kind of taskmaster and disciplinarian who would curb the excesses of British footballers. Meanwhile, can you imagine a United player putting a piece of shit into Roy Keane's bag? (If one dared to, he'd end up in his own bag, the kind that comes with a toe tag.) In the '70s, there was a drinking culture at Anfield, as there was at most clubs, but it didn't stop the Reds being successful. At times the drinking sessions encouraged team bonding and alleviated the pressure, such as before the 1984 European Cup Final. But these were top-quality footballers, the best of their generation, and able to prove that their drinking did not inhibit their performances. As soon as you have footballers who fall short of those very high standards, then in order to compete with the best they need to do everything in their power to succeed. The sad thing from Liverpool's perspective is that Alex Ferguson curtailed the United drinking culture in the late '80s. It was almost a decade before such actions were taken at Liverpool. Souness had tried, and Evans tried too, but both failed. By that time, United — whose players still socialised — were more moderate in their libations. They won trophies first, and enjoyed a drink after.

Unique Methods

Roy Evans deserves some credit for trying to break away from the tried and tested Anfield methods with his 3-5-2 formation. He was looking to try something different, within the framework of the traditional pass-and-move philosophy. It didn't quite work, but it was an improvement on the preceding three seasons under Graeme Souness.

"You have to be flexible and fit the players you have available to you into the most effective system," Evans explained. "I played with wing-backs because I thought we had the players suited to playing in that style. It's not a case of saying one formation is better than another, it just depends on the skills of the players you have." This may be true, but plenty of top managers find the players to suit the system they like to play. It's a bit like the chicken and the egg: what comes first, the players or the system?

One drawback of Evans' formation was that playing with three centre-backs often meant three defenders marking one forward, particularly at Anfield; for some reason a switch of one to more of a midfield position rarely seemed to happen. Both Dominic Matteo and Mark Wright were very adept at bringing the ball out of defence, and were naturals as the 'sweeper' between or behind two stoppers, but neither seemed prepared to constantly forage further forward when there was just one opposition player in the vicinity.

At times there also wasn't an awful lot of variation to the play; the Reds seemed content to pass and pass, without ever working an opening. Perhaps this can be said of all patient passing teams who refuse to just lump the ball into the 'mixer', and has certainly been said of the recent great Arsenal sides (not that Evans' Liverpool reached such heights). But on the good days there was plenty of cut and thrust from McManaman, Fowler and Collymore who were, for a time, as potent as any strikeforce around. The wing-backs got forward well, and often delivered telling crosses for Fowler, whose heading was as good as anyone's.

With Barnes, Redknapp and Thomas the Reds could pass the ball quickly, and comfortably keep possession, but there was no central midfielder to get ahead of the play, in the way a young Thomas did at Arsenal. McAteer and Leonhardsen both made their names doing that very thing, but neither's all-round play was strong enough for the times when possession, rather than third-man running, was required. In the times he played there, McAteer looked lost. Having said that, it often wasn't necessary with the free role handed to McManaman in the 3-5-2 formation, in which the wiry Scouser became the focus of moves, playing between the midfield and strikers. Subsequently, the opposition felt they could nullify Liverpool if they stifled McManaman. Some teams deployed man-markers to follow him all over the pitch, and it tended to work.

The wing-back formation hasn't led to any significant success in English football, either back in its heyday of the '90s or since. Leicester and Middlesbrough won the League Cup playing this way — but then again, that was also all Liverpool won with the system. Germany had success at Euro '96, but otherwise examples are thin on the ground. Rafa Benítez has employed it on just a handful of occasions, and done so successfully, but it's not a formation he has ever been tempted to persist with.

Strengths
As a local lad and former Boot Room boy, Evans certainly knew the workings of the club, its history, and what it meant to the fans — all of which were a big strength. He is a good, honest man, and the players liked him; whether or not they fully respected him is another matter. Most seemed happy to play for him — a big plus — but it wasn't enough in itself when a few let him down.

Being a good guy should not be seen as a weakness, and you don't have to be a bad guy to be a winner; Brian Clough remarked that Bob Paisley was proof of this. But Evans was perceived as being too nice to succeed. "If Roy Evans wasn't happy," David James later remarked, "he would try and be happy for the sake of not being sad. There is no doubt that some of the lads at Liverpool took advantage of Roy." Jamie Redknapp said: "Some players took liberties with Roy Evans, which was wrong. Roy was a good man and didn't deserve that." It begs the question, why weren't more players standing up for the manager, and bringing the wayward stars into line? It's hard to imagine the likes of Smith, Yeats, Thompson, Souness and Dalglish allowing their peers to exploit the manager.

Another of the so-called Spice Boys, Jason McAteer, said of Evans: "I think he found it hard to drop or discipline players. We were all his boys. It was like a big, happy family. We were all very close, and Roy didn't like to hurt any of us by dropping us. We had some big characters there, and he found it difficult to deal with the Collymores and Ruddocks. It became very hard for him. I love him to bits as a bloke, but manager of that Liverpool team? He must have got up every day thinking, 'Oh God, I've got to give him a bollocking'. He must have hated it. The day came when he lost the will to fight. He really lost the mental strength to carry on, and left."

It was also to Evans' credit that he walked away when he did, stepping aside to let the new man put his own stamp on the club. It must have been heart-wrenching; feeling like walking out on a wife he still adored after almost four decades of marriage because she'd fallen in love with someone new. "I suppose it was natural after so long with the club to feel bitter and twisted about the way I left," he explained. "Part of me still wanted the team to do well because of my relationship with the players, but for a month or so I somehow needed them to lose so I could tell myself things were no better without me. That feeling didn't last. Eventually I told myself that they had had 34 great years out of me and I had had 34 great years out of them."

Weaknesses

With indiscipline already covered, the defensive frailties that haunted Liverpool during the '90s was the other major problem during Evans' time. And it wasn't for lack of spending, by both him and his predecessor. Wright and Ruddock were expensive in 1991 and 1993 respectively, while Evans' signings Babb and Scales cost big money in 1994. But with David James at that stage an immature, mistake-ridden keeper behind them, every centre-back was falling short in one way or another, and the unit never looked totally comfortable. The 3-5-2 system meant that when the wing-backs were caught upfield there were just three at the back, and two of those — Wright and Ruddock — were far from mobile. Babb *was* mobile, but prone to errors; he had great pace, but wasn't a natural reader of the game.

It could also be argued that Evans was not the greatest tactician. As with Kevin Keegan, another Shankly protégé who was in title hunts during the mid-'90s, there was a lot of excellent attacking play, but not a great sense of tactical flexibility. There had been a lot of great football thinkers at Liverpool over the preceding decades, but they preached a deceptive simplicity. Evans himself said: "Football is a simple game based on the giving and taking of passes, of controlling the ball and of making yourself available to receive a pass. It is terribly simple."

But you cannot keep using the same methods inexorably. The game changes, and the opposition wise up to your methods, and to new ideas they can adopt. There has to come a point where what worked in the past no longer has the same effect. By the mid-'90s, perhaps too much had changed within English football, and an incredibly long run of success could not be achieved with the ways of old; the same reason why, in 1959, Liverpool looked to Shankly for external inspiration and fresh ideas, rather then reverting to pre-war in-house ideas. That is not to say that Evans' ideas were completely out of date, and that he was some sort of dinosaur, just that Liverpool were not keeping up with swift developments within the game.

Perhaps Liverpool's approach of the '70s, which often revolved around having the best players (who played for one another) and not worrying too much about the opposition, could be exposed when the personnel wasn't quite up to scratch. Suddenly, with inferior players and a lack of total commitment, Liverpool needed some special ideas (or just divine intervention) to prevail. Or maybe Keegan and Evans simply weren't as good at identifying top-quality defenders and goalkeepers, and finding the balance. Both Shankly and Paisley signed and developed incredibly good defenders and keepers: Ron Yeats, Tommy Smith, Emlyn Hughes, Larry Lloyd, Phil Thompson, Phil Neal, Chris Lawler, Alan Hansen, Mark Lawrenson, Ray Clemence, Bruce Grobbelaar, *et al*. With players like that providing a solid platform, football becomes more simple.

A major criticism of Evans came from players like Patrik Berger and Stan Collymore — as well as from John Barnes, speaking out on their behalf — when complaining of a lack of instructions as to their tactical roles. "Go out and play your natural game" or "do what it was we bought you for" may have worked for Shankly and Paisley, but that often involved slipping new players into exceptional, well-drilled teams, and it also relied on the genius of those two managers to know exactly which players to buy. Berger was used to the continental approach of Slavia Prague and Borussia Dortmund, so adapting to English football required more assistance. Collymore, meanwhile, had made his name at Southend and Nottingham Forest from using his pace on the break; at Liverpool there was a lot more possession football. He wasn't clever enough to adapt. He also seemed unprepared to be a little fish in a big pond, playing his part; it had to be about "Stan the Man".

Deemed too soft in the centre of the park, the final throw of the dice was to introduce steel into the midfield, in the form of Paul Ince. John Barnes was sacrificed as a result. "I felt I was a sort of scapegoat for all Liverpool's ills when they phased me out," Barnes said. "The perceived wisdom was, 'Oh, Liverpool need a ball-winner in the middle of the park. Barnes and Redknapp can't deliver that so they should go for Ince.' But what was the point of having a ball-winner if bigger things weren't right? If timekeeping and players missing training was still an issue, then signing a new player didn't make any difference at all. They were going for the quick-fix solution and that's increasingly the way it is in football."

Ince added grit, and a few goals, but wasn't quite the leader that had been hoped for. Possession was conceded more often, so at times Ince was trying to win back balls he'd lost in the first place. He wasn't a Souness or McMahon, who could win the ball, but pass it beautifully too.

Historical Context — Strength of Rivals and League

The early-to-mid '90s were in many ways the dark ages of English football. The Premiership had been formed, but as yet clubs weren't making the most of the new money at their disposal, and the reintroduction of European club football showed that a gulf had emerged during the five-to-six year exile. The league was still predominately populated by English players, but the national team failed to make the 1994 World Cup, perhaps partly down to a limited manager in Graham Taylor, but also down to a squad that often included the likes of Andy Sinton, Paul Stewart, Carlton Palmer, Tony Dorigo, Tony Daley, David White, Lee Sharpe, Nigel Clough and Geoff Thomas. Scotland, meanwhile, had stopped producing the kind of players who had excelled at Liverpool over the decades. Bar the odd exception, the non-British players in the English top division were jobbing Scandinavians, such as Jan Arge Fjortoft and John Jensen. Wimbledon, with their crude tactics, were still a successful top flight club, having made it to the highest level of English football in 1986, a year after English clubs were exiled following the Heysel disaster. While the 'Crazy Gang' represented some of the more admirable traits seen in sport (spirited performances and the success of the underdog), their long-ball game and thuggish antics had the purists despairing. So it clearly wasn't a golden age for the English game. But by the mid-'90s the shoots of a revival were in place that would see the English national team reach the semi-finals of Euro '96, and, three years later, the first English team to win the European Cup after the exile. At the same time, Arsène Wenger's Arsenal were bringing a continental sophistication to the English game, and players like Gianfranco Zola, Gianluca Vialli, Ruud Gullit, Dennis Bergkamp, David Ginola, Eric Cantona and Juninho were wresting the sport back from the uninspiring cloggers.

When Evans took control at Anfield, Alex Ferguson had just ended United's 26-year wait for a title. Kenny Dalglish was at Blackburn, and Dalglish's leadership skills when combined with Sir Jack Walker's millions made for a very strong team, albeit one that was something of a flash in the pan. Blackburn's football wasn't as easy on the eye as Dalglish's great Liverpool sides of the late '80s, instead proving more of a throwback to the old British style of two wingers supplying a succession of crosses for two target-men, in the form of Alan Shearer and Chris Sutton; possibly the last time such a tactic has succeeded at the top end of English football. Former steel magnate Walker had shelled out £30m in transfer fees, breaking the English record for Shearer in '92 and then again with Sutton two years later. It worked: Rovers won their first senior title in 81 years. Blackburn finished 2nd in '94 before finally becoming champions in '95, at which point Dalglish surprisingly became Director of Football and the team instantly imploded, finishing 7th and 13th in the next two seasons, eventually suffering relegation in 1999.

Elsewhere, Leeds hadn't built on their surprise league success of 1992, and hastened their demise by instantly selling Eric Cantona to their bitter Pennines rivals, where the Frenchman won a second successive league title — the one that ended United's incredible drought. Arsenal had lost their way a little under George Graham after the league successes of '89 and '91, finishing 4th, 10th and 4th after that second title, and were soon recovering from the bung scandal that saw him lose his job in February 1995, a season in which Arsenal eventually finished 12th. In 1995 Bruce Rioch took charge, taking the Gunners back up to 5th, but his sole season is best remembered for the purchase of Dennis Bergkamp. And on Tyneside, Newcastle were riding the Keegan Rollercoaster, which was always spectacular until the unstable wheels came off. The Geordies had a very exciting team, but also a deeply flawed one, with an inability to defend.

So there were a number of teams all at a similar level, but precious few outstanding ones, and with both Leeds and Blackburn winning the title shortly after promotion, and Nottingham Forest finishing 3rd a year on from returning to the Premiership, it was (perhaps for the last time) a fairly equitable league. The time between 1995 and 1997 was perhaps Liverpool's best chance to win a 19th league title, particularly as Manchester United would only really go into serious overdrive on their spending from 1998 onwards, winning their famous treble a year later in 1999, while Arsenal moved ahead in terms of taking a continental approach with the appointment of Arsène Wenger. Evans' last season coincided with Wenger's first league title, and the sands had clearly shifted within the English game.

Then there was the expansion of the Champions League. When there were two English teams qualifying, Liverpool finished 3rd. When it was expanded to three, Liverpool finished 4th. Evans can point to the fact that these days, those finishes would have been good enough. While that is true, it ignores the fact that the *need* to finish in those spots brings extra pressure; it's easier to finish 4th if nothing is at stake, but far harder if you *have* to do so. For a team notorious for choking when the pressure was really on, it could have proved one more thing to fall short on; indeed, was it mere coincidence that every time the Champions League places were expanded, Liverpool always narrowly missed out? It's impossible to tell for sure. But exclusion meant missing out on the money and the prestige to attract a better class of footballer. With London proving a more popular destination for overseas stars, it was one more barrier stopping Liverpool from getting back to the very top.

Bête Noire

By now Manchester United were in their element, and Alex Ferguson was the man to beat. But in one-off games at least, Evans did do that on occasion. Joe Royle, the Everton manager, proved to be more of a problem, along with Duncan Ferguson, his big centre-forward. In '94/95 Everton won 2-0 at Goodison Park and drew 0-0 at Anfield; a year later the Toffees won 2-1 at Anfield, with the Goodison game a draw. The following season both games were drawn. Royle resigned in 1997, but Liverpool lost again at Goodison, this time 2-0, and yet another Anfield derby was drawn. Ironically, once the foreign managers arrived and with them a host of overseas players, Liverpool's record against the local enemy improved dramatically, with first Houllier and then Benítez winning games home and away.

Pedigree/Previous Experience

Roy Evans had enjoyed a number of years successfully running the Reds' reserve team. But as a first team manager, he had absolutely no Football League experience — just like three of his four predecessors, Paisley, Fagan and Dalglish.

Subsequent Career

Roy Evans went on to briefly assist Karl-Heinz Riedle at Fulham. He then spent six months as Director of Football at Swindon Town, working above Neil Ruddock, before a short spell as part-time assistant manager to Brian Carey at League Two strugglers Wrexham in 2007. He also began working alongside John Toshack with the Welsh national team in 2004, at a time when there were few top-class players left to choose from.

Of all those positions, only helping Wrexham to avoid relegation to the Conference in 2007 counts as a success, although the North Wales team could not hold out again in 2008, by which time Brian Little was in charge, with Carey as his assistant.

Defining Moment

The worst moment on the pitch, and the most remembered (usually in 3am sweat-soaked nightmares) was unquestionably the 1996 FA Cup Final against Manchester United, when Armani was the star of the Liverpool show. Kitted out like catwalk models in cream suits with red and white striped ties, the Reds would have been no worse served had Cindy Crawford, Naomi Campbell and Linda Evangelista been in the starting line-up. Not that United played much better. But they did just enough. Eric Cantona's scrappy late strike from David James' fumbled attempt at dealing with a corner put the game out of its misery, transferring that despair onto the travelling Kop. The Reds had twice outplayed United earlier in the season, with flowing football unfurling at pace. Robbie Fowler had scored twice in a 2-2 draw at Old Trafford and twice again in a 2-0 win at Anfield. Such delights were not on display at Wembley, where the suits would provide the abiding memory.

But the lowest ebb for Evans, and the moment when the writing was clearly on the wall, had to be the ignominy of joint-managership, whereby rather than be replaced in the summer of 1998 he was forced to share the job with Gérard Houllier, in what amounted to a *semi-*sacking. Evans claimed to have been in support of the idea of bringing in Houllier, but not in the role of joint-manager. The union started well, but lasted only four months once results deteriorated, and confusion amongst the players doomed the experiment to failure. Evans eventually quit in November 1998.

Crowning Glory

Beating First Division Bolton to win the League Cup in 1995 was hardly a highpoint in the history of Liverpool Football Club, but it was Roy Evans' only trophy as manager. As a game it wasn't a great spectacle, and Liverpool's second — and final — trophy of the decade came as had the first: against a team from a division below.

However, as a fitting epitaph to the times, the first 4-3 victory against Newcastle on April 3rd 1996 has to be the defining game of the Evans era. Just as Newcastle were famed for great attacking and comical defending under Kevin Keegan, then so too were the Reds under a fellow Shankly/Paisley disciple. There was some woeful defending as well as great attacking play in what was voted the best Premiership game of the '90s, and is yet to be bettered. For all the defensive shortcomings, the attacking play was still a joy to behold, and well worthy of an esteemed place in our memory banks. It is claimed that in football only the winners are remembered, but this is not strictly true; the football of Holland in 1974 and 1978 sees them live longer in the memory than the teams that won those World Cup finals, and the Liverpool and Newcastle sides of the mid-'90s, while not up there with Cruyff and co., will be remembered for the wonderful entertaining football they played that spring evening.

Legacy

The main legacy of Evans' time in charge was the successful progress of Michael Owen and Jamie Carragher. Injuries to Robbie Fowler cut short the striker's effectiveness, and incredibly, he was only 23 by the time his best days were behind him. Evans was later criticised for overplaying the 17-year-old Owen, when serious hamstring problems appeared two years down the line. It was a difficult situation for Evans, as Owen was desperately needed in the side. And in his first season, the striker played 44 games — hardly a definite case of overplaying when considering that some players can play 70 times in a season. But when it came to the players he bought, few would go on to flourish in the years to come.

TRANSFERS

Transfers In

It's fair to say that Roy Evans did not sign one single great, or consistently excellent player as a manager. Plenty of his signings shone in patches, and Stan Collymore looked like a world-beater on his day (alas, a wife-beater on others), but none was an enduring, unquestionable triumph. The best performers were either youth team graduates or those he inherited, such as Robbie Fowler, Steve McManaman, Jamie Redknapp, Rob Jones and Michael Owen.

Of those signed during his first year in charge, John Scales did well initially, at times looking very assured on the ball and a clever defender, but was prone to injuries and duly sold two years later, after 94 games. Phil Babb had his moments, but was mostly an accident waiting to happen (and that included colliding with goalposts). For £3.5m and £3.6m respectively, these were very expensive signings in 1994 — both breaking the English record for a defender. Scales left for £2.6m in 1996, but Babb exited on a free transfer in 2000, after 170 games, having been frozen out during the final two years of Houllier's reign.

Evans' second season in the transfer market was no more successful. Mark Kennedy never lived up to his supposed potential, nor made use of a surname synonymous with success at the club. Perhaps too much was expected of the youngster after a £2.3m transfer at the age of 19 — still a fairly big fee for a youngster now, let alone in 1995. Kennedy was sold to Wimbledon for £1.75m in 1998, after just 16 league games. He went on to have a fairly decent career, without ever being exceptional.

Boyhood Red Jason McAteer, signed from Bolton for £4.5m, was initially an exciting wing-back under Evans, but all energy and heart and no great intelligence. He didn't have the required skill to play in central midfield — his preferred position — at a club like Liverpool, where possession was the law. He only featured there a few times for the Reds, having made his name as a box-to-box player at the Lancashire club. However, he did well on the flank in the 3-5-2 formation, where he could use his great stamina to get up and down the pitch in what is possibly the most gruelling position in football — part full-back, part winger, but somehow expected to be in both places at the same time. He scored six times in 139 games for the Reds before moving to Blackburn for £4m in 1999.

In September 1996, Patrik Berger burst onto the scene with possibly the most exciting and explosive *immediate* impact seen by any Liverpool player, with the exception of Ronny Rosenthal. Following a few minutes as a sub in his debut against Southampton, Berger came on at half-time at Leicester a week later to rattle in two spectacular long-range goals, followed by two more in a 5-1 thrashing of Chelsea a week later (having bagged another two for the Czech national team in midweek). His performances put an extra 20,000 on the gate for the Cup-Winners' Cup game against Mypa 47, and he scored another wonderful goal, after nutmegging a defender. Expectations around the Czech were raised exceptionally high, and as a result, even though he had some fine years at Liverpool, particularly in the early part of Houllier's reign, he always seemed a slight disappointment. He scored 35 times in 196 games, including three seasons where he bagged nine each time, before spells at Portsmouth and Aston Villa upon his release in 2003.

Evans' luck in the transfer market was no better in 1997. Karl-Heinz Riedle, approaching his 32nd birthday when signed in 1997, was past his best and proved unsuited to the pace of the English game; quite reminiscent of Fernando Morientes in a number of respects, particularly physique and playing style. Like Morientes, Riedle had Champions League success under his belt: the German was fresh from scoring two goals for Borussia Dortmund when they beat holders Juventus in the 1997 final. That victory ensured Riedle would become one of a select group of players to win both the World Cup, which he had in 1990, and the European Cup. But such a pedigree didn't prepare him for the robust, physical nature of the Premiership. Riedle did okay at Liverpool, but was not a clear success; adding the professionalism that Collymore lacked, but without sufficient pace or energy. He played 76 times, scoring 15 goals, while his league ratio was one every six games.

Oyvind Leonhardsen, purchased from Wimbledon in June 1997 for £3.5m, was a leather-lunged athlete who couldn't seem to adapt to the 'Liverpool way', treating the ball like a hot potato. He was too accustomed to running onto flick-ons at Wimbledon and with the Norwegian national team; given that those sides bypassed midfield, he seemed unable to adjust to passing the ball *through* it. A very fine finisher, he just couldn't get involved in the game enough to justify inclusion in the team. He scored seven times in 49 games, before moving to Aston Villa (who spent the '90s signing Liverpool flops) for £3m.

American Brad Friedel went on to prove an excellent Premiership keeper at Blackburn, but never looked totally convincing during his 25 league games between 1997 and 2000. Costing £1m from Columbus

Crew, he perhaps suffered from the perennial curse of two no.1s fighting it out for a regular spot. Another player who did better after leaving Liverpool was Bjorn Tore Kvarme. The Norwegian started brightly, and looked like a talented, tenacious defender who was fearless in the tackle, but he lost his confidence and became something of a joke figure by the time he'd clocked up the last of his 54 appearances. He ended up doing well with high-flying Real Sociedad in *La Liga* after a spell in France, and therefore clearly wasn't a bad player, just one not suited to Liverpool.

Danny Murphy, however, would prove a very good signing, although another promising youngster who never quite lived up to the potential he was believed to possess. Having said that, the Liverpool fan had some fine seasons in the Reds' midfield under Houllier, scoring three winning goals at Old Trafford in four years and a corking strike in a victory at Goodison Park — which, in themselves, should ensure the beers are bought for him by Liverpudlians for the rest of his life. He scored 44 goals in 249 games, at a very respectable rate for a midfielder; Murphy also won a few medals and made nine appearances for England: so was hardly a failure in any way, shape or form. But in those initial years at the club, when he was meant to be a striker, he cut a frustrated figure, and was sent back to Crewe on loan by Houllier. Murphy had lost his way on and off the pitch, but he came back to enjoy four fine seasons. Rafa Benítez, surprisingly at the time, sold him for £2.5m in 2004, but the sale became understandable when Luis Garcia and Xabi Alonso arrived to join the midfield.

Stan Collymore aside, the big 'marquee' signing made by Evans was Paul Ince — one of those 'final piece of the jigsaw' transfers that turned out to be no such thing. The Reds had more bite and crunch in midfield with the inclusion of the former Manchester United man, brought back to England from Inter Milan in 1997 for £4.2m as he approached his 30th birthday, but conceded possession more frequently than with the more cultured Barnes in the side. Ince scored a fairly impressive amount of goals — the best rate of his career, with 14 in 65 league games — and was a success of sorts, but he was neither the final piece of the jigsaw or the all-conquering midfield hero that was anticipated. Ince only lasted a season under Houllier before he was shipped out in acrimonious circumstances, with the player admitting he wanted to punch the manager. It was rumoured that Houllier saw Ince as a disruptive force in the dressing room, and an ailing force on the pitch. Ince's son Thomas, aged 16, is currently a striker at the Liverpool Academy.

And then there was Evans' final summer, when he made two signings before the appointment of Houllier, at which point a third player was added. Evans two solo deals were not what the club needed; the re-signing of Steve Staunton, a free transfer, did not work out as hoped, and the frankly hopeless Sean Dundee, who cost £1.8m, had lost whatever confidence he had possessed in order to once top-score in the Bundesliga. He played five times for the Reds, and for Kopites, that was five times too many.

Vegard Heggem, earmarked by Evans and with the signing agreed by Houllier, had two fine seasons at right-back after a fee of £3.5m was paid to Rosenborg. He could have gone on to be Evans' biggest success in the years after the manager resigned, but injury robbed the Norwegian of a bright future. Aged just 24, he suffered a serious hamstring injury that would stop him appearing again for the Reds, and after three years of rehabilitation and several thwarted comeback attempts he called time on his career. He scored three times in 65 games, including a stunning solo effort at the Riverside Stadium.

Player	Quality	0.01pg	IN	OUT	FGV	VALUE	Ap	Details
Danny Murphy	7.55	2.49	-1	0.9		9.94	249	£1.5m 1997 £2.5m 2004
All Managers' Average						7.92		
Patrik Berger	7.69	1.96	-2.1	0	1	7.55	196	£3.2m 1996 Rel. 2003
Vegard Heggem	6.24	0.65	-2.3	2		6.59	65	£3.5m 1998 Ret. injured
Steve Staunton (2)	5.33	0.5	0	0		5.83	50	Free 1998 Rel. 2000
Paul Ince	6.17	0.81	-2.8	1.3		5.48	81	£4.2m 1997 £1m '99 @32
O. Leonhardsen	4.94	0.49	-2.3	2		5.13	49	£3.5m 1997 £3m 1999
Brad Friedel	5.50	0.31	-0.7	0		5.11	31	£1m 1997 Rel. 1999
Average	**5.45**		**-3.12**			**4.54**		
KarlHeinz Riedle	5.72	0.76	-2.4	0.3		4.38	76	£1.8m'97@31 £250k @34
Bjorn Tore Kvarme	3.78	0.54	0	0		4.32	54	Free 1997 Rel. 1999
Jason McAteer	6.11	1.39	-6	2.7		4.20	139	£4.5m 1995 £4m 1999
Mark Kennedy	4.06	0.21	-1.8	1.2		3.67	21	£1.5m 1995 £1.75 1998
John Scales*	5.91	0.94	-7	3.4		3.25	94	£3.5m 1994 £2.6m@30 '96
Stan Collymore**	6.44	0.81	-10	5		2.25	81	£8.5m 1995 £7.5m 1997
Sean Dundee	2.06	0.05	-1.2	0		0.91	5	£1.8m 1998 Rel. 1999
Phil Babb*	5.00	1.7	-7.2	0		-0.50	170	£3.6m 1994 Rel. 1999

Key: See page 51.

Transfer Masterstroke

Evans is the only manager in the last 50 years not to make one totally inspired signing. Of all 170 transfers covered in this book, his highest-ranked in terms of *Quality* is 42nd-placed Patrik Berger, with Danny Murphy just behind in 46th. With the exception of Souness, whose best signing, Rob Jones, is ranked 31st, and Joe Fagan's Jan Molby, ranked 25th, all other managers had at least one signing in the top ten, and at least two in the top 20. And in terms of *Value For Money*, it's even worse; Murphy, at 50th, is the highest-ranked Evans' purchase — more than 20 places behind every other manager.

So the success story for Evans is a toss-up between Patrik Berger and Danny Murphy, two players who gave the club good service, and who both scored a number of important goals. Each had an involvement in winning the treble in 2001: Murphy playing in every final, and Berger, returning from long-term injury, releasing the long-range "Paddy pass" that sent Owen away for the winning goal in the FA Cup Final against Arsenal. The pair shared 53 league goals in 318 Premiership matches, and were important members of Gérard Houllier's squad. Berger could certainly have been Evans' masterstroke, but a lack of instruction and, later, a number of injuries, stopped him being one of the Premiership's best players.

Expensive Folly

While not a total disaster on the pitch, and also offloaded for a reasonable fee, the signing of Stanley Victor Collymore was, in hindsight, an expensive mistake. If only he had come with a good psychologist, things might have been so different.

Collymore, Evans' most expensive signing — an English record at £8.5m — was the good, the bad and the ugly wrapped up in one idiosyncratic package. He had some sublime moments — bursts of skill and speed, and long-range curled goals — but his attitude was questionable at best, and his temperament was erratic. For a while Collymore and Fowler had an almost telepathic understanding, with the former supplying the latter with numerous crosses that were turned, with regularity, into goals. But the two did not get along, and it was a partnership fraught with tension — although Fowler denies that he had as big a problem with Collymore as the former Forest striker thought.

One person who did have a problem with Collymore was the manager. "It got to the point where we wouldn't know if he was coming in for training or not. He had refused to find a house in the area and was travelling up from Cannock every day for training. Then he started to miss sessions. Some days he would phone and tell us someone was sick, usually his mother, and it got to be a bit of a joke amongst the lads. Once the press got hold of it, it was hard to keep the lid on things. Then I wanted him to play a reserve game to help his match fitness and he simply refused. I fined him, as I had to, but it had no effect on his behaviour. When something like that happens, you start getting associated problems. The other players became unsettled by it, wanting to know what on earth was going on. It made things difficult for everyone."

Had Collymore lived up to his potential, he could have become a legend. The same can be said of so many Liverpool players during the

'90s, but Collymore was one of those rare players who seemed to have it all — but for that crucial something lacking between the ears. Evans, however, felt Collymore was simply the best he could be; the point being that all players have weaknesses of one kind or another, and for Collymore it was with his mentality. But unfortunately, it was too much of a weakness for him to justify breaking the English transfer record.

One Who Got Away

"We tried all sorts of options to solve the defensive problems," Evans later admitted. "You read all the suggestions in the papers from fans and journalists about who you should go for and so on but no one really knows the efforts that are put in. We tried to get the French guys Lilian Thuram and Marcel Desailly but we couldn't attract them."

Desailly, an outspoken character with impeccable standards, would almost certainly not have liked what he found at Liverpool in 1997 in terms of discipline, had he chosen the club as his destination. Having said that, he *was* what the team needed — a strong personality, an exceptional defender and a great professional. The idea was 100% right, but bringing in one or two would not be enough if it only left them disillusioned at what surrounded them. These top foreign players were choosing the more cosmopolitan appeal of London, with its additional closeness to the continent, and, for the most part, foreign coaches and managers. Liverpool needed a sea-change, not just a couple of continental stars. But you can't fault Evans for trying, with Riedle one such über-professional addition.

Another key signing that Evans missed out on was a key England international. "I wanted Teddy Sheringham to come and play in the area behind Robbie Fowler and Stan Collymore," he said, "but the board blocked the deal saying he was too old. I think Sheringham, who was at Spurs, was 28 or 29 at the time." Sheringham signed for Manchester United soon after, and was a big success at Old Trafford in their treble season; as for his age, he played a further decade in the top flight.

But one overseas star who might have been patient and helped the players adapt to a continental approach was Jari Litmanen, whom Evans spoke to in 1997. The Finn, an obsessional Liverpool fan, would eventually arrive at Anfield three years later, but by then injuries had made him a waning force. However, in '97 Liverpool were not in the Champions League — of which Litmanen was one of the true stars, and at the time its all-time leading scorer (albeit only since the rebranding five years earlier) — and the timing wasn't right. As much as he wanted to play for the club, he declined Evans' offer and moved to Barcelona.

Budget – Historical Context

By the standards of the day, Liverpool spent fairly big under Roy Evans. The Reds' outlay was £33m under his 'sole' managership between 1994 and 1997. £16m was recouped, leaving a net spend of £17m — a figure that seems fairly small now, when looking back from the current financial landscape, but at the time was no small beer. Also, this was still the time of relatively small squads. Spending tended to be concentrated solely on first-team players, with reserves very much just that — cheap alternatives to make up the numbers.

Evans' spending power can be seen in how he was able to break the overall English transfer record in 1995, having already twice broken the record for a defender with Scales and then Babb. With the signing of Collymore for £8.5m, he became the last Liverpool manager (as of 2008) to be able to set a new high-water mark in British transfer fees.

During the Evans' years, the net spend of Manchester United was just £2.1m. Part of this was down to the emergence of Ryan Giggs, Gary Neville, Paul Scholes, Nicky Butt and David Beckham; by contrast, Liverpool had already brought through Fowler and McManaman, two players who Evans made great use of, but it wouldn't be until 1997 that another youth graduate of such calibre emerged, in the form of Michael Owen. As well as the blossoming of his young starlets, Ferguson had already made a number of costly signings in the late '80s and early '90s: Gary Pallister, Peter Schmeichel, Roy Keane, Andrei Kanchelskis, Mark Hughes and Paul Ince were all signed while either Kenny Dalglish or Graeme Souness was managing Liverpool. While Ferguson spent £26.7m between 1994 and 1997, he also recouped £24.6m, much of it when selling off his first raft of expensive signings.

Andy Cole cost United £7m in January 1995, a new British tansfer record. Another -10 signing in the side was Roy Keane, who broke the record in 1993. Gary Pallister cost £2.3m in 1989, a -8.5 fee. By the time Ferguson really started splashing the cash, in 1998, Evans had been joined by Houllier in the dugout. The joint-managers spent a further £3m net, before Evans tendered his resignation. That summer, with Evans uneasy and Houllier unlikely to sanction any major transfers before assessing the squad, marked another point where United pulled away from the Reds.

By the mid-'90s, Liverpool's side was more expensive than that of the team that had usurped them at the top of the English game. United's 1996 FA Cup Final side — Peter Schmeichel, Denis Irwin, David May, Gary Pallister, Phil Neville, David Beckham, Roy Keane, Nicky Butt, Ryan Giggs, Eric Cantona and Andy Cole — cost an average of 35.2% of the English transfer record, as they secured that year's double. Liverpool's side — James, McAteer, Scales, Wright, Babb, Jones, Barnes, Redknapp, McManaman, Collymore and Fowler — averaged out at

44.5%. Including each team's three subs — Gary Neville, Paul Scholes and Lee Sharpe, to Liverpool's Rush, Thomas and Warner — only widened the gap; United's 14 averaged at 28.3%, to Liverpool's 45.7%. Only four of the starting XI were purchased by Evans, but McAteer, Babb, Scales and Collymore cost an average of 75.5% of the English transfer record. Yet their average *Quality* rating was just 5.86.

While Evans spent big, there were clubs that spent more money in net terms. Surprisingly, Arsenal were the biggest spenders, shelling out £39m and recouping just £12.9m between '94 and '97, making for a net spend of £26.1m. Since they had three managers over this period of time (George Graham, Bruch Rioch and Arsène Wenger), a higher spend is understandable to a degree, given that new managers are always looking to buy their own players to suit different ideas. Wenger inherited Dennis Bergkamp and David Platt, who cost £7.5m and £4.7m respectively in 1995, while David Seaman and Ian Wright were expensive signings at the start of the decade. The Arsenal manager added Marc Overmars for a fairly hefty £7m in 1997. Although some of Wenger's inexpensive youngsters, like Nicolas Anelka, would break through towards the end of 1997/98, the side that started that campaign averaged at 43.5% of the English transfer record. Wenger's spending would generally be regarded as frugal from then on, but he won the league that first time in 1998 with a very expensive side.

Newcastle were the biggest spenders in gross terms, laying out £51.9m; but the Geordies recouped £29.1m, resulting in a net spend of £22.8m. However, their side in 1996/97, when including Faustino Asprilla in addition to Les Ferdinand and Alan Shearer, cost an average of 49.7% of the English transfer record. Chelsea spent £33.6m, and recouped £12.5m, making a net total of £21.5m. Spurs, meanwhile, had an outlay of £28.5m, so fairly close to Evans' spending, but recouped £19.7m, making for a net spend of just £8.8m.

Blackburn, who were runners-up and then Champions in Evans first two seasons, had an expensive squad, but most of Dalglish's heavy spending had taken place in '92 and '93, although they did break the transfer record for Chris Sutton in 1994. Those expensive players were still in the side Evans had to try and overcome. Rovers' strongest XI in their title-winning team of 1995 had an average cost of 41.5% of the English record.

While Liverpool were able to get between 75-90% of their money back on some of Evans' more expensive signings, such as Collymore, Scales, Kennedy, Leonhardsen and McAteer, in "real" terms, their values had dropped more rapidly given the rise in the market. None of the players Evans bought saw their value soar, and several ended up leaving on free transfers. While signing players is about trying to blend a team to win trophies, and not simply about making investments, buying players who do extremely well but who can be sold once their usefulness wanes is both a great business *and* sporting model. In his first year at Arsenal, Arsène Wenger bought Patrick Vieira, Marc Overmars and Nicolas Anelka for a combined fee of £11m. All three players featured in league title-winning campaigns, and were later sold for a total of almost £65m; Anelka after having his head turned by Real Madrid, Overmars after overtures from Barcelona, and Vieira following nine sterling years of service. While Wenger has also signed a litany of disappointments of one kind or another over the years, he made such impressive profits on those 1996/97 signings that he could afford to reshape his entire squad in the coming seasons.

RECORD
League Cup 1995

	P	W	D	L	F	A	%
Overall	226	116	57	53	375	216	51.33%
League	172	83	46	43	280	173	48.26%
FA Cup	17	8	5	4	29	13	47.06%
League Cup	21	17	1	3	42	14	80.95%
Europe	16	8	5	3	24	16	50.00%

+ **Houllier & Evans**

	P	W	D	L	F	A	%
Overall	18	7	6	5	33	20	38.89%
League	12	4	4	4	19	14	33.33%
League Cup	2	1	0	1	4	4	50.00%
Europe	4	2	2	0	10	2	50.00%

CONCLUSION
So much promised, so little delivered in terms of actual achievement. The entertainment was often there, but the trophy cabinet was virtually bare.

Perhaps the Evans era could be summed up by the cutting banner "4th in a two-horse race" held up by United fans, referring to the 1997 title chase, when the Reds had led the table several times before the start of February. But that would be a cruel assessment, as is the 'Spice Boy' tag, which was only partly deserved by some of the players. Perhaps the same set of players working under a strict disciplinarian would have struggled to play with the same freedom — and such things can be important in producing good football. Ultimately, the lack of professionalism shown by some of the squad, allied to the temperamental weaknesses in very talented players like Collymore and James meant the Reds were perhaps always destined to fall a little short.

In hindsight, 1994 should have been when Liverpool appointed an Arsène Wenger-type figure. It's easy to say now, seeing how the game developed later in that decade, but that was the golden chance. It might not have been popular at the time, but it's not the job of the board to be populist. None of this is to say that Evans didn't 'deserve' to be manager; by the old criteria he clearly did. But had Wenger been lured to Liverpool in 1994 instead of moving from Monaco to Japan, Evans could possibly have still been working at the club now, in the way Pat Rice still assists the Frenchman at Arsenal. Instead, Liverpool waited until 1998, missing the boat on Wenger and one or two others.

There's no doubting that Roy Evans is one of football's good guys, and deserved better from several of his players. He also deserves respect for the part he played in the success of the 1970s and 1980s, as well as the fluent football his charges played once he finally became manager. But that's about as kind as history will get about the Bootle-born Boot Room boy — a fine football man who wasn't quite up to the biggest challenge in English football. It was a case of close, but no cigar.

"I think as soon as you get into this kind of job, somebody wants you out. That's the daft thing about it."

ROY EVANS

1998 - 2004
GÉRARD HOULLIER

"I used to stand on the Kop when I was here in 1969.
The atmosphere and passion on the pitch as well as the
terraces was intoxicating and Liverpool became part of
me from that day on."

GÉRARD HOULLIER

INTRODUCTION

More so than any other Liverpool manager, Gérard Houllier's
stewardship is characterised by two distinct periods, divided by a single
dramatic event: the building up of a very good side, and then failure as
he dismantled it following a near-death experience as his aortic valve
ruptured. Decisions made after that potentially fatal heart problem in
October 2001 were no longer laced with a Midas touch, and while it
may be merely coincidental, the *After* did not match up to the *Before*
in any way.

Situation Inherited

In the summer of 1998 Gérard Houllier walked into a club beset with
problems. Indeed, simply by taking the job *he instantly became one of them*.
With Roy Evans having lost control of some of his players and with
performances starting to stagnate, the club's hierarchy, breaking away
from all received wisdom, decided against sacking the affable manager
and instead appointed *yet another*. If too many cooks spoil the broth,
too many managers muddy the pitch. Things started well enough, as
the Reds won three and drew another in the opening four games —

including an emphatic, hugely stylish 4-1 win at St James' Park where the travelling Kop informed the new Newcastle manager Ruud Gullit that he could 'stick his sexy football up his arse'. Michael Owen, fresh from his France '98 World Cup success, scored a superb hat-trick, and a revitalised Patrick Berger added another. But soon problems began to arise. The next five league games saw three draws and two defeats. Players began to question who they should turn to, with the English players more loyal to Evans and the overseas stars seeing Houllier as their man; meanwhile, everyone was questioning why a winning side had been changed ahead of defeat at West Ham. A 5-1 thumping of Nottingham Forest, with Owen bagging four, suggested the Reds were back on track, but they then lost the next three games, including home fixtures against Derby and Leicester — really dire stuff. Defeat at Anfield to Spurs in the League Cup was the final straw, and Evans walked out on November 11th.

So it wasn't until mid-November that Houllier's proper stint as manager began; clearly he cannot be judged on those early months, as the decisions weren't solely his. However, unlike most managers he'd had several months working from within to assess the club and its players before taking full control. So he wasn't coming at the task cold. He had time to see what was wrong, before moving to implement great change in the summer of 1999.

Looking back, it's remarkable how many of the players Evans bequeathed to Houllier ended up in a lower division fairly quickly. Bjornebye, Harkness, Babb, Ruddock and McAteer were all in the First Division within a couple of years; either they'd lost their way, or, as was more likely, they were no longer good enough for the cutting edge of the top division as the English game began importing top foreign players at a greater pace. David James also ended up in the First Division with West Ham, but had enough ability to rise back to the top level and eventually proved himself one of the best in the land.

If the deadwood and journeymen were quickly offloaded, to make matters more difficult, three of the best players in Evans' legacy never amounted to much under Houllier, for one reason or another. The first to fall was Rob Jones, whose career was curtailed by an injury to his left knee in February 1998. Houllier offloaded the player to West Ham in 1999 after almost 250 games for the club but none under him. Houllier was pretty damning about Jones, saying he was sick of seeing him in the gym all the time (alluding to a lack of desire to get back playing), but the true extent of Jones' injury was apparent when, having only played one game for West Ham, he called time on his career, at the age of just 27. The finest British full-back of the '90s should have been at the peak of his powers under Houllier, but instead he was never able to feature.

Secondly, injuries in 1997 had robbed Robbie Fowler of his sharpness, and he barely played in Houllier's early years. Perhaps if Fowler had looked after himself better in those early days, and been better guided, he'd have either been less susceptible to some of the injuries (although many were impact damage from collisions, which are a fact of football life) but — more likely — he'd have been able to recover from them more quickly. Houllier could get to Jamie Carragher at a young enough age to have the defender adopt more professional methods, but Fowler was perhaps too far down a certain route for the manager's intervention. The two did not get along, even after Houllier made Fowler vice-captain, and eventually the striker was sold to then-rivals Leeds United in October 2001, in a shock deal, worth £11m.

Finally, Steve McManaman already had one eye on an exit before Houllier arrived, almost certainly because in 1997 Liverpool had agreed to sell him to Barcelona for a fee of £12m; when he turned up in Spain to talk over the move, he found that the Catalan giants had instead decided to sign Rivaldo, and that he was only a safeguard should the deal for the Brazilian fall through. Whatever the rights and wrongs of the player then running down his Liverpool contract to leave on a 'Bosman', you can see it from his perspective of having been made to feel like a piece of meat that was being traded; Liverpool could argue that in not having signed a new deal prior to the Barcelona approach, McManaman was already thinking of moving on. He would have his revenge on Barcelona by joining Real Madrid and twice winning the Champions League, even if he was a bit-part player by the time of the second success in 2002. That £12m — 80% of the English record — would have gone a long way towards helping Liverpool rebuild in 1997, but by 1999, following an injury-hit final season, the Scouser was on his way out of the club for nothing. "When the choice is between a hell of a lot of money and a hell of a lot of money," McManaman said, "the difference between the two sums, in reality, is not enough to sway you one way or another. I wanted to play abroad, full stop." With Paul Ince and David James two others in an England quintet destined for the exit, Houllier was almost starting from scratch when it came to building a Liverpool side that could challenge for honours.

Inheritance — Brains Trust
Squad

Player	Quality	Age	Adj	Inheritance	Year	Age
Steven Gerrard	9.93	0	0	9.93	1998	18
Jamie Carragher	9.36	0	0	9.36	1998	20.5
Michael Owen	9.29	0	0	9.29	1998	18.5
Robbie Fowler (1)	9.43	0	-1	8.43	1998	23
Patrik Berger	7.69	0	0	7.69	1998	24.5

Player	Quality	Age	Adj	Inheritance	Year	Age
Jamie Redknapp	7.41	0	0	**7.41**	1998	25
Danny Murphy	7.16	0	0	**7.16**	1998	21
David James	6.44	0	0	**6.44**	1998	26
Dominic Matteo	6.29	0	0	**6.29**	1998	24
David Thompson	6.14	0	0	**6.14**	1998	21
Jason McAteer	6.11	0	0	**6.11**	1998	27
Brad Friedel	5.50	0	0	**5.50**	1998	27
Average	**6.73**			**5.48**		**25.8**
Steve Harkness	5.35	0	0	**5.35**	1998	27
Phil Babb	5.00	0	0	**5.00**	1998	27.5
Steve McManaman	8.47	0	-4	**4.47**	1998	26.5
Stig Inge Bjornebye	5.89	-1.5	0	**4.39**	1998	28.5
Rob Jones	8.30	0	-4	**4.30**	1998	26.5
O. Leonhardsen	4.94	-1	0	**3.94**	1998	28
Bjorn Tore Kvarme	3.78	0	0	**3.78**	1998	26
Steve Staunton (2)	5.33	-2.5	0	**2.83**	1998	29.5
Neil Ruddock	5.72	-3	0	**2.72**	1998	30
Michael Thomas	6.24	-4	0	**2.24**	1998	31
Paul Ince	6.17	-4	0	**2.17**	1998	31
KarlHeinz Riedle	5.72	-5	0	**0.72**	1998	33

First XI

Player	Quality	Age	Adj	*Inheritance*	Year	Age
David James	6.44	0	0	**6.44**	1998	26
Jason McAteer	6.11	0	0	**6.11**	1998	27
Jamie Carragher	9.36	0	0	**9.36**	1998	20.5
Dominic Matteo	6.29	0	0	**6.29**	1998	24
Steve Staunton (2)	5.33	-2.5	0	**2.83**	1998	29.5
Paul Ince	6.17	-4	0	**2.17**	1998	31
Patrik Berger	7.69	0	0	**7.69**	1998	24.5
Jamie Redknapp	7.41	0	0	**7.41**	1998	25
Michael Owen	9.29	0	0	**9.29**	1998	18.5
Steve McManaman	8.47	0	-4	**4.47**	1998	26.5
Robbie Fowler (1)	9.43	0	-1	**8.43**	1998	23
Average	**7.45**			**6.40**		**25**

Key: *Quality 0-10; Age = -1 point for every year from 28 onwards, eg -4 for 31 year-old, and -1 point from 30 onwards for keepers, eg -4 for 33 year-old; Adj = adjustments for players either exceptionally fit/unfit for their age, or soon to leave; Inheritance = total out of 10. Excludes players not part of first team picture.*

In terms of *Quality*, Houllier inherited four players who scored 9 or higher, plus two more who scored more than 8: surely the nucleus of a great side? However, of the four 'outstanding' players, Fowler was never going to hit his very best form again, and Carragher was not an exceptional defender until *after* Houllier had been sacked — at the time he was more of a very steady full-back. But Steven Gerrard and Michael Owen were worthy of such high marks during Houllier's time. Gerrard, excelling for years in the club's youth ranks, was immediately given his debut and became the team's go-to player, while Owen, despite some limitations, was voted European Footballer of the Year in 2001.

Of the two players to score between 8 and 9 — McManaman and Jones — one was already intent on leaving, while the other would never play for the club again, so neither was a true part of Houllier's inheritance. As a squad, it was a fairly average collection of players. The poor quality of some of the other players made for a very unbalanced team, and the First XI scored the lowest mark out of 10 for *Quality* out of any of the teams inherited by a new manager (although only a fraction below the one Souness left to Evans, and the one Houllier himself passed on to Benítez). As an overall squad it was slightly stronger in terms of *Quality*, and considerably better than the one Houllier would leave for Benítez. Once adjusted for age, serious injuries and the desire to leave, the 1998 first XI dipped to an *Inheritance* average of 6.4. Houllier also inherited the 2nd-youngstest first XI, with an average age of 25.

State of Club

Despite hailing from a different country, Gérard Houllier had a very influential ally in the Liverpool boardroom in the key figure of Peter Robinson, the vice-chairman. Robinson forged a firm friendship with Houllier during the Frenchman's spell as a teacher in Liverpool in the late '60s. "I had known Gérard for a long time," Robinson said, "and we had established a friendship. We had kept in touch and I had followed his career and admired what he had done." Robinson went to lengths to stress that Evans had been very much involved in bringing Houllier to Anfield.

The problem was that Evans — and his players — expected the new man to come in to replace the retiring Ronnie Moran. Houllier had been working behind the scenes with France, and had just helped his country land the World Cup. It was not immediately apparent to Evans that Houllier was returning to the front line. In further changes at the club that summer, Rick Parry was appointed as chief executive. Robinson eventually left to become an agent in 2000, and the club lost one of its greatest guiding forces.

One of Houllier's main problems was not the club itself, but those ex-players who were by now filling up every vacant media position. "There are some players who get upset about what is said," he explained. "They just can't understand how a former player can be so critical of his own club. It always seems to be Liverpool under fire because, of course, so many former Liverpool players are employed by TV and radio. There are 22 currently working in the media as pundits — that's a whole squad. Sometimes I envy Everton because they seem to get support from their ex-players even through the hard times."

Assistance/Backroom Staff

When Gérard Houllier wanted an assistant with Liverpool connections, Phil Thompson's name was suggested to him by director Tom Saunders. At the time, not having an Englishman — and preferably a Scouser — in a key coaching position was almost unthinkable. It had been 39 years since the club appointed a manager with no previous Liverpool playing *or* coaching experience. The original aim to keep Roy Evans in tandem with Houllier highlighted the desire for continuity.

By the time he was ousted along with Houllier, and returned to his job as a Sky Sports pundit, Thompson's reputation was mixed. Clearly he was not as limited as many onlookers suggested — he wasn't merely a ranter and raver. He had amassed a wealth of experience as a player, and played under two of the greatest ever managers. However, there is also little evidence to suggest Thompson was a really great thinker on the game. It was clear that he was not particularly popular with many players — particularly the youngsters, who weren't used to such treatment — but then again, his role was the bad cop to Houllier's *bon flic*. Thompson fell out publicly with Robbie Fowler, the Kop's idol, and as such, the fans naturally sided with Fowler, even if where the blame lay wasn't clear. Ronnie Moran had previously been the archetypal bad cop, but success makes it easier to forge harmony. Or maybe Moran was just a more skilled and respected coach.

Thompson did lead the team for a number of months following Houllier's illness. But his performance is hard to judge for a number of reasons. There was the 'let's do it for the boss' reaction, when the team responded positively to the drama. Even then, Houllier was soon picking the team from his hospital bed and, later on during his recuperation, signing Nicolas Anelka on loan. By then the team had started to wobble badly, and it was only really when the manager returned that impetus was regained and the Reds ended the season strongly.

Sammy Lee seemed to be a more gifted coach. He was also there to motivate, but in a very positive sense; ebullient and infectious, he lifted the players. Lee chose to leave when Benítez arrived with his own assistant, and mixed a role on the England coaching staff with being second in command at Bolton. Lee eventually became manager at the Reebok at the start of 2007/08, but in trying to switch from direct to pass-and-move football, the Trotters struggled and he quickly lost his job. In retrospect, he might have wished to have stuck to being a top-class assistant, which more suits his talents; in 2008 he was appointed Benítez's no.2, and the pairing appears to offer a nice blend.

Patrice Bergues was perhaps the most important person behind the scenes during Houllier's time at Anfield. Bergues was a hugely popular and highly respected figure — Robbie Fowler, who doesn't have too many positive things to say about the staff from that era, described him as a "fantastic man". His departure in 2001, to become Director of Football at his old club Lens, came just a year before a big decline in the Reds' fortunes, and only one trophy — the League Cup — was won after he left. Ian Rush, who also had a minor coaching role at the club, felt that Bergues leaving was as much a turning point as Houllier's ruptured aorta a few months later. "When Patrice Bergues left in 2001, Gérard Houllier replaced him with Jacques Crevoisier and then Christiano Damiano, neither of whom commanded the same respect from players and other members of staff. That created extra problems for Gérard he didn't need. An assistant is supposed to handle some of the difficulties, not create new ones. It's impossible for a manager to be a friend of the players. He needs to keep a distance, and that's where assistants play a crucial role. Quite often, if they're not providing this link or are simply causing more irritation, they're having a counter-productive role and making life even tougher for the manager than it already is. I'm sure this happened in the last few years of Gérard's reign after Bergues left."

In 1999, fomer Hibernian boss Alex Miller was appointed as director of scouting, working with chief scout Ron Yeats. Yeats explained the process in early 2004: "I haven't got the last say who Gérard signs or doesn't. I go see them [the targets] and recommend them. Alec Miller, who was a manager at Aberdeen and Hibernian, does all the European tactics and looks at all the European players, thank goodness. I can't do two jobs. I've got 20 scouts in England and have to make sure they do their jobs. Alec also looks at all the European teams we're playing. A very, very technical man who does all the team reports on the opposition. Gérard trusts him." Miller would be promoted under Rafa Benítez to first team coach, although he left the club in the summer of 2008.

Management Style

Somewhat pertinently, Michael Owen described Houllier as a "manager in the wider sense" — a man, he felt, who could spot what was wrong in any organisation, but who was not a great tactical thinker. Houllier was less a training ground, hands-on boss, and more a general manager with philosophies that enabled success to be planned for; he tried to provide the players with what he hoped was the right environment for them to succeed. He was a disciplinarian, but without the hysterics of someone like Graeme Souness.

While Liverpool was not a totally unprofessional club under Roy Evans, teams elsewhere were raising the standards of fitness, athleticism and abstinence required to be successful. Houllier described the difficulties he encountered upon arriving in England. "The problem here is that players think they can drink. Maybe they could once, but the game demands so much more now, not just physically but mentally because of greater tactical awareness. If you drink, you lose half an inch, then an inch, then half a yard, then a yard [— *of pace*; he didn't mean the players all ended up resembling Sammy Lee]. Your brain also becomes gradually slower to react. And in the process you lose the chance to progress from being a Premiership player to a top-class player. I compare top-class players to racing cars. Drinking alcohol is as silly as putting diesel in a racing car."

Houllier also felt that the younger players in England were susceptible to bad influences. "What stuns me here: a young player comes into the game, looks the part. He's not a drinker, looks after himself. Then, as soon as he gets into the first team, he thinks that to show he's a man he has to drink. In probably every other country, the young player actually becomes more serious about the game. He'll do anything he can to improve and stay in the team."

Jamie Carragher was seen as something of a tearaway in the late '90s, although this was almost certainly something of an exaggeration. But he still needed guidance with regards to acting with the utmost professionalism — which came after the 1998 Christmas party, at which his drunken antics made the front pages of the Sunday tabloids. Some 500+ games later, Houllier's direction looks justified. Carragher has every chance of moving ahead of every other Liverpool player in the appearance table, with the possible exception of Ian Callaghan.

Jason McAteer, who didn't last long under the new regime, later detailed his experiences with Houllier: "Obviously the board thought discipline was lacking and Gérard came in. We never saw eye to eye. I wanted to play football, week in, week out, and he wasn't prepared to give me that. He didn't like the Spice Boys thing, and I think he was under pressure to change all that. If you look at Liverpool now, there's none of my old team left. Sometimes I lie in bed at night thinking, 'I bet he wishes he had half that team now'." This last point is debatable — it's hard to see Houllier craving some of those players at *any* point in time, even as things fell apart towards the end.

Houllier was obsessed with the small details of running a club. Gary McAllister explained his take on the manager's methods: "At Liverpool I sometimes wondered why, oh why, Gérard was so pernickety, but over time I realised that taking care of so many small things in training and preparation carries through into games. If you've been focused and disciplined all week you're more likely to stay disciplined when you're hanging on in the final few minutes of a vital match."

Despite his image as a taskmaster, Houllier hated confrontation. During their ill-fated partnership, Houllier left the delivery of bad news to Evans. The pair had agreed to jointly inform McAteer that he was being dropped. "I went to tell Jason the news and had to do it by myself because Gérard was nowhere to be seen," Evans said. "It's a shitty job at the best of times." Evans subsequently found Houllier having a cosy chat with some of the club's hierarchy, and when asked why he wasn't where he was supposed to be, the Frenchman claimed to have forgotten. For a man who focused on every small detail, it was a strange excuse.

Also, players were not allowed to show their disappointment in front of the new manager. "He didn't like having to deal with players expressing anger or frustration," Evans explained. "He thought it showed a lack of respect for management and he had to be the dominant character. My own view is that you want to see players hurt when they're dropped or when they're substituted. Any self-respecting professional should be."

Clearly it's about getting a balance. A manager needs to be the boss, in total control. And players need to know their place. But there has to be some kind of dialogue, a willingness to hear ideas. And a manager needs to understand that disappointment at being omitted from the team, or at being substituted, is normal. There is of course an unacceptable level of dissent that any player can show towards his manager, but that's not the same as merely expressing frustration. Good players should be keyed up, wanting to play. Robbie Fowler accused Houllier of buying meek characters who would gladly accept his decisions, but again this is about getting a balance. If players disrespect the manager and undermine his decisions, then that is working against the team. However, you need players with some kind of character and backbone.

Unique Methods

Gérard Houllier was the first Liverpool manager to employ rotation with fitness in mind, although in his case it was limited mainly to the strikers. Before Houllier arrived, team selection was based on form, and fitness, on the day. Now it was about trying to plan for a long season. In particular, Robbie Fowler suffered with the notion of rotation, given that he was dropped — or 'rested' — after scoring goals, and tended to sit out more matches than he started. But maybe that was more about him coming to terms with no longer being the first choice striker at the club; any manager will always have in his mind the identities of his preferred players, and Fowler was now third-choice.

Houllier's main ethos was about the team, and equality. His philosophy on this was sound: "To me, the team is more important than any individual member of the squad, and the players have to realise that and accept that my priority is to pick a side with the best possible chance of winning each match."

He wanted the players to bond: "I want camaraderie. Players have to get on well, be friends." But that was clearly not the case — at least in his later years at the club. "I won't let anybody raise a finger against the togetherness of the team otherwise I chop it immediately," he said. El Hadji Diouf had another take on it. "The squad was not close-knit. The French were on one side, the English on the other and the Czechs on the other. [It must have been a triangular room he was referring to...] The players had enemies among themselves and Houllier never got the respect of any of them." French defender Djimi Traoré had a slightly different view on Houllier: "He was much appreciated by the Englishmen and I can see why. But a lot of the French players didn't have a chance to play and express themselves. We had to work twice as hard to play." Of course, a number of English players resented Houllier too. Even allowing for the grudges that can build up at a club when disgruntled players are out of the first team, it doesn't paint the picture of a unified club.

Strengths
Having never been a top-class player himself — merely a non-league forward in France — Houllier's methods were not about passing on his genius or experience of high-pressure situations on the pitch, but rather creating the right environment for the players to thrive in. He used his acumen and common sense to work on players' weaknesses, to give them the best chance of succeeding.

Take the example of Michael Owen's left foot— or lack of it. Quite why it took so long for someone to notice this glaring weakness in an otherwise superb finisher's armoury is a little baffling, but Houllier seriously addressed it. Owen was always effective, but a predictability about which foot he would use gave defenders a chance to snuff out his threat. Even if a player is never going to be anywhere near as good with his weaker foot, no matter how hard he practices, a willingness to use it when it's the only foot that can naturally strike the ball from a certain position is such an advantage, particularly as it gives defenders doubts. By the end of 2001, Liverpool were winning the FA Cup because Owen was confident enough to take on Tony Adams on a side that the defender wasn't expecting and finish with inch-perfect precision with his weaker foot.

There was also Houllier's physical work with the players. Another problem with Michael Owen was his weak hamstrings, emanating from a problem in his lower back; in 1999 he missed five months of football after a serious tear appeared at Elland Road. The injury had been treated, but not the cause. Houllier sent Owen to Germany to see Hans Müller-Wolfhart, Bayern Munich's club doctor, and a man who'd treated Jürgen Klinsmann and Brazil's Ronaldo, as well as sporting stars José María

Olazábal, Paula Radcliffe, Kelly Holmes and Maurice Greene. Owen was still dogged by various injuries after leaving Liverpool in 2004, but Müller-Wolfhart's work meant that his hamstrings were rarely a problem.

Meanwhile, it's easy to forget how injury prone Steven Gerrard was as a youngster, before Houllier sent him to France to see osteopath Philippe Boixel. Maybe Houllier wasn't the best tactician and was an imperfect judge of players, but he ensured Gerrard would be free of problems for years to come with methods that would not have been sought by many other managers at the time. So many players get into a destructive cycle of injuries, and some never recover; whatever happens after 2008, Gerrard was able to enjoy at least six years of almost constant football thanks to the osteopath.

"Boixel changed my back into a better shape," Gerrard explained. "I was struggling to repeat games because it was making other parts of my body get niggling injuries. When I know I'm not going to get injured, that's when I play my best stuff. Before, I was going on to the pitch and just thinking about what minute I was going to come off, and not that I was going to finish the game." In January 2002, Boixel, who also treated Zinedine Zidane, gave Gerrard a clean bill of health — one that was presciently accurate. "You can say he is cured of that trouble. He can now play as often as Liverpool wish him to. These players are like Formula One cars. They need constant attention to ensure they deliver peak performance. The repetition and high intensity of matches means their bodies must always be under review."

Weaknesses

At first, Houllier seemed a canny operator. He made Liverpool harder to beat, and masterminded numerous victories against Everton and Manchester United, with the latter often achieved through defending deep and hitting on the break. The ball was moved swiftly from back to front, at times bypassing the midfield. When the ball was kept on the ground, the counter-attacking was fast and effective, although a tendency to hit too many long balls placed a big onus on the front two.

But as time wore on, it became apparent that there was no Plan B. There was no real development of other strategies, no variations to the play. Liverpool's new style had initially surprised teams used to setting up against a possession-based outfit, but in time it became predictable. The aim was to get Michael Owen in on goal, and what had been an excellent weapon became, to all intents and purposes, the only weapon. The tactics were limited; there wasn't enough flair in the final third, not enough movement between defence and midfield, or midfield and attack. It all got very one-dimensional. If Owen didn't score, often only Heskey was well-placed on the pitch to chip in with goals, but aside from the treble season, that was something he failed to do often enough.

Despite not often moving from his rigid tactics, Houllier did employ a good system against teams who played with three centre-backs, often putting Danny Murphy, Vladimir Smicer or Jari Litmanen in a free role behind two strikers; but in like-for-like 4-4-2 match-ups — which was most games — there was a lack of playing 'between the lines'.

A big problem with Houllier's 4-4-2 was the defence sat deep and the midfield were positioned almost on top of it. The reliance on direct forward balls made it was harder for midfielders to get goals from open play. Gary McAllister scored six times in the treble season, but three were penalties and the other three were direct free-kicks. Steven Gerrard scored ten, but it was far and away his best season for goals under Houllier; he tended to average around six, compared with the 18 he has averaged since 2004. Danny Murphy also scraped into double figures on a couple of occasions, but again, his best season came when McAllister had moved on and he took direct free-kicks and penalties; almost 20% of his Liverpool goals came from spot-kicks.

At times Houllier tried to change the personnel and add flair players, introducing first El Hadji Diouf and Bruno Cheyrou, and then Harry Kewell. But the team failed to flourish, with Kewell fading after a bright start, and the other two offering nothing of any note. Smicer was another flair player who impressed only in fits and starts.

Perhaps another failing of Houllier's was placing too much blame on players making mistakes; famously, David Ginola still feels Houllier called him a 'criminal' after his sloppy pass ended up costing Houllier's France a place at the 1994 World Cup; Houllier had said making such a *pass* was criminal, which is clearly different, but perhaps as a result of that night, he became famed for a safety-first style. Getting the balance between cutting out mistakes by playing 'percentages' and trying to keep possession — and taking risks in the final third, in order to unlock defences — is key to success. Any defender can find Row Z, but while that's appropriate at times, at others it's not — ultimately, it's conceding possession. Liverpool simply stopped playing the ball out from defence in any way, shape or form; Hyypia and Biscan made attempts early in their days at centre-back, but both soon cut out the dribbling. Everything started going long, even though neither Hyypia nor Henchoz were passers of the calibre of Ruddock and Agger. Players stopped leaving their set positions, making play more rigid and predictable. For instance, when Emile Heskey played on the wing — something he'd done at Leicester and with England — he tended to still be out wide when the ball was with Liverpool on the opposite flank. It was as if, rather than get into the box and gamble as any wide player should, he was staying in position for when the move broke down. Maybe this was a failing of the player, in that he was never the most proactive, but compare it with how Dirk Kuyt, a less naturally gifted player, would bust a gut to get into the box to become an additional striker.

Historical Context — Strength of Rivals and League

Gérard Houllier arrived in England when Arsenal were starting to emerge as a force under Arsène Wenger, and Manchester United were still in a position to challenge for the league title. Wenger had arrived in 1996, and by the time Houllier was appointed, Arsenal had just won the league and FA Cup double.

But Wenger's path to a first league title was in part down to the weakness of the opposition. The managers of the day were Gianluca Vialli, an unproven player-manager, who had replaced another unproven manager, Ruud Gullit, at Chelsea halfway through the 1997/98 season; and at Liverpool, Roy Evans, a great servant for the club, but a rookie manager who was perhaps better suited to a support role. None of these managers went on to have successful careers. Meanwhile, two powerful teams of the mid-'90s, Newcastle and Blackburn, had lost important managers and swiftly imploded.

Leeds United started to emerge as a force in 1998/99, managed by another rookie, David O'Leary, whose managerial career now looks more of an illusion based around Leeds' chronic overspending. The Yorkshire club began to spend massively at the turn of the millennium, but within a handful of years would find themselves in the lower divisions. Newcastle were revived under the canny leadership of Bobby Robson, as some experience returned to the pack challenging Manchester United and Arsenal. United, meanwhile, grew incredibly strong in Houllier's first season in charge, as Ferguson won the treble with his expensively-assembled new team.

Chelsea, who gained strength from the mid-'90s onwards, only emerged as an über-force in 2003 with the arrival of Roman Abramovich as the new owner; before that, Claudio Ranieri had been doing a fairly decent job as manager since his appointment in 2000. But Ranieri had always been a bit of a 'nearly man'; someone who won the occasional cup and got teams to 4th in the table, but never beyond. In 2003/04 he finally took a team higher, but was promptly replaced after Chelsea finished 2nd; in the years since, he has managed one 3rd-placed finish, with Juventus, but failed spectacularly after succeeding Rafa Benítez at Valencia.

Bête Noire

Unlike other Liverpool managers, Houllier's *bête noire* was not a rival manager. He had a good record against most other clubs, winning his fair share of games against Everton, Arsenal, Manchester United and, at home at least, Chelsea. Houllier's *bête noire* was one of his own players.

His relationship with Robbie Fowler started on a rocky footing, and deteriorated rapidly from there. Fowler helped Houllier land the treble of 2001, scoring in two finals, two semi-finals and bagging a brace in the final 'final' at The Valley to belatedly end the Reds' Champions League exile, and the manager had earlier made him the club's vice-captain. But the two became staunch enemies. Fowler was absolutely stinging in his attacks on Houllier in his autobiography, detailing the story of a man he saw as forcing him out of his beloved Anfield. It had been known well before its publication that Houllier used young local journalist Chris Bascombe, new to a role covering the club for the *Liverpool Echo*, as a way to publicly criticise the player. Bascombe was forbidden from praising Fowler, even when he played brilliantly; more bizarrely, Houllier adopted the same tactic with Michael Owen years later, by which time Bascombe had wised up to the manager's motives.

The most controversial of all Houllier's moves was the sale of Fowler in October 2001. At the time it was a shock to all Kopites; Fowler was unquestionably the player they most adored, despite the fact that Owen had been more effective and prolific for four years and Gerrard was emerging as a world-class midfield force. It was even harder to take as 'God' was sold to Leeds United, at the time one of Liverpool's closest rivals in the league. The £11m fee was pretty sizeable for a player plagued by injuries in the previous half-decade, but Kopites wanted the player, not the cash. Hindsight proves Houllier right in certain aspects of the sale; Fowler, while still possessing massive natural talent, was past his best due to the curse of injuries, and it was a good price for a player who had become third-choice at Anfield. The problem was that the manager spent virtually every penny on El Hadji Diouf — which was like getting a large cheque for your ageing BMW, which could still get you from A to B in at least *some* style, and buying an overpriced, faulty Fiat Uno, complete with wobbly wheels and more than a few loose screws.

The problem Houllier faced was that Fowler was 'untouchable' in the eyes of the fans, and that's always dangerous for the man who has to decide who plays. It seems pretty certain that Fowler was not an easy character to deal with, and one who made mistakes, but at the same time his account of Houllier's behaviour paints the picture of a man who couldn't cope with confrontation or deal with players on the straightest of levels.

Pedigree/Previous Experience

At the point when he joined Liverpool, Houllier had been away from the club scene for ten years. He had suffered a torrid time as the manager of the French for their 1994 World Cup qualifying campaign, having joined the national set-up in 1988 as technical director and assistant-manager. He took over from Michel Platini as team manager in 1992, but with qualification for USA '94 looking assured — France needed just one point from matches against Bulgaria and Israel — the wheels fell off. Drawing in the final minute against Israel, David Ginola lost the ball, and *Les Bleus* lost a goal. Houllier resigned, and returned to a technical role with the French FA; he was later commended for his contribution to the country's success at the 1998 World Cup.

Never a professional player, Houllier had served a thorough apprenticeship in the dugout, starting at the age of 26, in 1973, as player-manager of Le Touquet. It was with Noeux-les-Mines, whom he joined three years later, that he started making waves, taking the small northern club into the French Second Division with two consecutive promotions. He moved to Lens in 1982, again winning promotion, and sealing qualification for the UEFA Cup. Paris Saint-Germain was his next destination in 1985, and PSG won the French title the following year — his only league championship prior to 2006.

Subsequent Career

After a year out of the game, Houllier took charge of Lyon in 2005, succeeding Paul Le Guen. The club had been French champions for the previous four seasons, so Houllier's two further titles in his 24-month spell at the club are hard to judge; he added nothing new to the equation, but at the same time he maintained success. His brief was to make the club a European force, so strong were they domestically when he arrived. The club had been threatening to take the Champions League by storm, but never quite made that final step. Houllier failed to change that, although Lyon made it to the quarter-finals in 2007, losing to AC Milan; a year later they were defeated in the last 16 by Roma. Lyon won the league yet again after Houllier resigned, which either proves that Houllier did a good job in helping things along, or that the club were far too dominant in a league where no real challengers existed.

Defining Moment

The ruptured aorta suffered by Houllier during a home match against Leeds United can be used to define a 'before' and 'after'. He was able to cleverly manage the situation at first, so that his return several months later was a boost to the team and the fans as he unexpectedly made his way to the dugout for the crucial Champions League game against Roma. But a handful of months later, when the season was over, things began to go very wrong. It may all be coincidental, but the team hit a swift decline, dropping from 2nd place in 2001/02 to 5th a year later.

Then there was the substitution of Didi Hamann in the Champions

League quarter-final against Bayer Leverkusen in April 2002, replacing the defensive midfielder with Vladimir Smicer. Liverpool were being overrun in midfield, and replacing the man protecting the back four was an odd move; however, there can sometimes be merit in bringing on a more attacking player who can keep hold of the ball and take the game to the opposition. Liverpool needed to hang on to an away goal advantage, but the German team continued to flood forward, and the Reds lost 4-3 on aggregate. This is often seen as a key moment in Houllier's reign, and while that's undeniable, it also gets overplayed, as does the performance of Hamann — it wasn't one of his better nights, yet his display has been retrospectively described as "masterful" by one newspaper, as the myth of Houllier's grand folly expands. It should not be forgotten that it was just one moment in one game when the Reds, despite leading the tie, were under the cosh.

The summer of 2002 was almost certainly a more defining moment in the history of modern Liverpool — a crossroads where the right path had to be taken. Houllier spent fairly big, as he had in 1999, but this time the quality of his signings was woefully lacking. This is illustrated by the decision not to permanently sign the on-loan Nicolas Anelka, and instead buy El-Hadji Diouf. To compound matters, Houllier had shown interest in Cristiano Ronaldo, but a deal could not be struck. It's easy to think that Ronaldo and Anelka would have given Liverpool the necessary pace, skill and cutting edge, while handling the pressure, but it wasn't to be.

Subsequent history suggests that this was the summer in which there was no margin for error. Spending reasonably big in 2002 also left insufficient funds in 2003, at which point the Frenchman's budget for 2004 was also partly allocated, with the prearranged deal to bring in Djibril Cissé from France. Houllier might have called time on the trio of Diouf, Diao and Cheyrou in 2003, but he was intent on sticking with his failing crop of *Ligue Une* imports. Between the summers of 2002 and 2004, Manchester United, Arsenal and Chelsea added the following players: Cristiano Ronaldo, Wayne Rooney, Cesc Fabregas, Robin van Persie, Gael Clichy, Kolo Toure, Joe Cole, Luis Saha, Damien Duff, Claude Makelele, Didier Drogba, Arjen Robben and Petr Cech.

Liverpool added only one successful player: Steve Finnan, a very reliable full-back, but not a match-winner.

Crowning Glory

The treble achieved by Houllier's men in 2001 means it will always remain one of the better seasons in Liverpool's history, although its true value as an achievement is hard to ascertain. Do people remember Arsenal's 1993 vintage, when the FA and League cups were won, or 1989, when 'just' the league trophy was secured? Clearly it's the latter.

Can you combine a number of cups to equal the feat of one league campaign? After all, Liverpool played two-thirds of the amount of games that the Premiership entails — so almost a season in itself — and didn't lose a single tie across those 25 games (although some individual matches were lost). On the other hand, plenty of teams — Stoke, Slovan Liberec, Rapid Bucharest, Rotherham, Crystal Palace, Tranmere, Wycombe and Birmingham — were not on a par with top-division teams from England or from Europe's other major leagues. Those inferior teams counted for eleven of the cup games that season. For all the weak teams faced, the remainder of the games involved some high-level opposition: Roma, Barcelona, Chelsea, Leeds United and Arsenal, spread across all three competitions.

Ultimately, it will always fall short of the greatest achievements in the club's history. But it was still a very unique success: the Reds becoming the first English club to play every single cup game possible in a season. After the lean years of the '90s, it felt extra-special, as three trophies were won in the space of three months, when the previous three were attained over a period of eleven years. For that, Houllier deserves credit and respect.

Legacy

In Houllier's eyes, he was heavily responsible for the Reds' success in Istanbul in 2005. From his perspective, it's easy to see why: seven of those starting against AC Milan were players he had purchased, and a further two he'd helped nurture; not to mention squad players like Biscan and Sinama-Pongolle, who had made telling contributions *en route* to the final, and, of course, Didi Hamann, who came on to help change the game. However, some of them were playing far better by then than they had under the Frenchman's guidance. Clearly the experience gained through the treble of 2001 benefited some of those who played in Istanbul four years later; but from that success, only Gerrard, Carragher, Hyypia and Traoré were in the starting line up in 2005, while Smicer and Hamann came on as subs. So while there was an element of Benítez benefiting from the three trophies won in that landmark season, it was a team that included several players with no great experience of cup finals. Furthermore, two of the most important players had been Benítez signings: Xabi Alonso and Luis Garcia.

Above all else, it was the tactical acumen of Benítez that saw the team through to the final, as he set up the limited players at his disposal in a way that would allow them to stop the opposition, and provide a platform for the better Liverpool players to flourish. Once Benítez had cleared out many of those players, they found themselves struggling to hold down first-team places at far inferior clubs.

TRANSFERS

Transfers In

As with his overall record — and therefore perhaps it is no coincidence — Houllier's transfers can be broadly split into two sections. It's fair to say that his dealings as sole manager had an inauspicious start, with the £1.5m capture of 30-year-old former French international, Jean Michel Ferri, from Turkish football. Rumoured to be Houllier's 'mole' because he was almost never seen on the pitch (perhaps because he was tunnelling under it?), the midfielder was sold to Sochaux for the same fee soon after, following just two substitute appearances.

Frode Kippe, a £700,000 signing in January 1999 from Lillestrøm, was a 21-year-old defender with promise, but more of a gamble for the future than a sure thing. He returned to Lillestrøm in 2002 after two substitute appearances, and won the Norwegian league's Defender of the Year award in 2007. More successful was the signing of Djimi Traoré, for £550,000 in February 1999. Traoré never developed into the Thuram-like centre-back hoped for, but the investment was still shrewd. Prone to errors, he was still a very handy squad player over a number of seasons — quick, good in the air, and with the best recovery tackle in the league (due to his extra-long legs), but he caused a lot of problems for himself with his poor control and lack of concentration. Benítez sold him to Charlton for £2m in 2006, meaning a nice profit was chalked up on a player who never quite made the grade.

Houllier's raft of investment in 1999 was significant, as he set about putting his stamp on the club by signing a number of players. Two of those to arrive in 1999 — Sami Hyypia and Didi Hamann — went on to reach a kind of legend status at the club and win every trophy available with the exception of the Premiership, while two more — Vladimir Smicer and Traoré — would win as many medals as the more celebrated duo, and also feature in Istanbul in 2005.

Hyypia, who had been on trial at Newcastle in 1995, proved the imposing centre-back the Reds had lacked since 1990, as he spent the next decade shoring up the defence. Lacking any real pace, his game was about anticipation and positioning, while he instantly cured what had been a weak point in the Liverpool team for a number of years — a lack of aerial ability. Composed on the ball, his passing from the back was usually good, unless forced to look long. His days in Dutch football as a holding midfielder with Willem II had ensured he was calm in possession, something often seen when at the other end of the pitch.

Didi Hamann, already regarded as an impressive talent after stints with Bayern Munich and Newcastle, matured into one of the world's top midfield shielders, with only Claude Makelele, of Real Madrid and subsequently Chelsea, arguably more respected in the role during the German's peak years. It took Hamann, who cost £8m in July, a while to make his influence felt at Liverpool, where his lack of goals and all-action style failed to catch the eye in the manner that might be expected from such an expensive player. But in time his simple but hugely effective style would come to be greatly appreciated during his seven years at the club. Hamann scored eleven goals in 283 games, but it will be his defensive work that lives longest in the memory. He was released in 2006, whereby he joined Bolton but, sensing he'd made a mistake, was transferred to Manchester City just 24 hours later. Where Liverpool had handed him a free transfer, Bolton were able to make a £400,000 profit; but Liverpool had already got good value for money from the German.

In July, Vladimir Smicer was signed for £3.75m from Lens in France. A clever player who specialised in playing behind the main striker — a role in which he ultimately scored 27 international goals — he spent much of his Liverpool career on the wings or on the bench. The fact that the Czech midfielder-cum-striker holds the record for highest number of substitute appearances for Liverpool, totalling 74, tells the story of his time at the club: a *nearly* player, with lots of ability, but not a lot of consistency, no doubt hindered by a proneness to injury. However, the Czech saved his best for last: helping Liverpool win the 2005 Champions League as an early substitute, popping up with a stunning goal (his 19th in 184 games) to bring the score back to 3-2, followed later by a coolly taken penalty. It had been a largely frustrating time for Smicer at Liverpool, and he was already set to leave on a free transfer, but the popular player ended with the biggest smile possible as he smoked a fat cigar in Taksim Square following the game.

Of the six remaining signings from 1999, Stephane Henchoz was the most successful, performing very well as a mainstay of Houllier's back-line. There were few better players at defending their own box than the Swiss centre-back, who would throw himself in front of any shot and excel at desperate lunging tackles when the cause looked lost. But lacking pace, he was far less assured defending a higher line, and aware of this, he was prone to dropping too deep. This made it harder to play good football from the back, and invited the opposition to play in front of the Reds' box. After 205 appearances, Henchoz was released by Rafa Benítez in 2005, for whom he never played a competitive game.

At times Sander Westerveld and Titi Camara looked like good signings during their brief times at the club, but neither lasted as long at Liverpool as expected. Westerveld, the promising young Dutch keeper who joined from Vitesse Arnhem for £4m, had just played his part in the winning of five trophies (three 'proper', two ceremonial), and been Man of the

Match when defeating Manchester United in the recent Community Shield when, at the start of September 2001, his future was made clear as Houllier signed two goalkeepers on the same day. Westerveld, who played 103 times for the Reds, was an excellent shot-stopper, but also prone to a few too many mistakes, most memorably punching an own-goal at Stamford Bridge and fumbling a Dean Holdsworth shot at the Reebok Stadium — an error that, as far as Houllier was concerned, was the final straw. Westerveld also tended to stay rooted to his line at corners and free-kicks, perhaps in order to avoid making obvious errors (such as, say, punching a cross into his own net), but this meant he stopped commanding his area.

Meanwhile Camara, a maverick figure signed for £2.6m, had scored a few goals in his first season (nine in 33 league games) and looked a clever player capable of breaking down defences with his skill and movement. He famously played for Liverpool just hours after his father died, scoring the winning goal against West Ham (the team he'd soon join), before sinking to his knees in tears at the Anfield Road end. But he fell out with Houllier at the start of the following season, after slipping down the pecking order, and ended up at Upton Park with Liverpool recouping their money.

Another African, Rigobert Song, was, like Camara, bought in 1999 and sold a year later to West Ham for a fee in the region of £2.6m. Song had some fine moments, without ever being totally convincing in his 38 appearances. He came back from the 2000 African Nations Cup with a poor attitude, and played like his mind was still back on his native continent, and as such was promptly offloaded.

There's not a lot that can be said about Erik Meijer, a free signing from Bayer Leverkusen, other than, in true rhyming fashion, he was a trier. Better at rousing the crowd than scoring goals (none in the league in 24 outings, with his only two strikes coming at lowly Hull City in the League Cup), he gave his all in his hugely limited fashion, and was warmly appreciated for his efforts. The fact that he cost nothing, and didn't outstay his welcome, meant he could be loved in a cult-idol kind of way, rather than become an annoyance.

Much more was expected of Emile Heskey following his arrival in March 2000. The Leicester City striker was seen as a key signing, as attested to by his £10.5m fee, a new club record. Having linked well with Michael Owen for the England U21 team in a game against Greece, Houllier, a spectator that night, sought to reunite the pair. The immediate effect wasn't as expected: the Reds failed to score a single goal in the final five league games, and missed out on the Champions League to Leeds as a result. But the following season the pair combined to excellent effect, as the club landed a trio of cups and finally qualified for the Champions League. Heskey's goals dried up somewhat towards the end of the season, but he still bagged 22, to go with Owen's 24. Heskey's form was inconsistent from then on — at times unplayable, at others unbearable — and he was sold by Houllier for £6.5m in 2004, after scoring 60 goals in 223 games.

One very exciting and controversial signing was that of Christian Ziege, brought in from Middlesborough for £5.5m, but with the Reds accused of tapping up the German. Liverpool were fined £20,000 by The Football Association for making an illegal approach. It was reported that as a result of the ruling the eventual fee was closer to the £8m 'Boro had been holding out for. Ziege had ability in abundance, but he was most accustomed to being a wing-back. He was marginalised after a mistake at Elland Road cost the Reds victory, and only started 20 games in his one season at Anfield, before being sold to Spurs in 2001 for £4m.

Nick Barmby was another controversial signing, the first Evertonian since 1959 to make the Blue-to-Red switch across Stanley Park, as Liverpool agreed a £5.75m fee with their neighbours in July 2000. Barmby duly obliged with a goal against his former club in the first Mersey derby of the season, and hit eight in total in his first year. He lost his way in his second season — a problem which started at the end of the first, when he missed the final ten games due to injury, during which Danny Murphy came to the fore. In 2001/02, with Murphy continuing to do well and Barmby struggling with injuries, the former Evertonian, whose busy, clever style was never really seen to its best effect at Anfield, was sold to Leeds United for £2.75 million.

Still, at least something *was* seen of Barmby; something that can barely be said of Bernard Diomède, a World Cup winner with France just two years earlier. In his three seasons at the club, the £3m signing from Auxerre played just four times. Perhaps things might have been different had his spectacular overhead kick on his debut at home to Sunderland been allowed to stand; the ball crossed the line, but the officials did not award the goal. Had the French winger got off to a flying start, he might have been able to build on it; instead, he disappeared into virtual anonymity.

In September 2000 19-year-old French full-back Gregory Vignal was signed from Montpellier for £500,000. The youngster was soon in the first team, impressing on his league debut at home to West Ham. Perhaps he felt he had 'made it', and got cocky — but clearly he had not. He promised so much, but as with Houllier's other young French signings, he didn't amount to what was expected at Anfield; to a degree this is natural, with precious few promising teenagers developing into top-class first team pros at any club, but the law of averages suggests maybe one or two should go on to thrive. He was released by Liverpool upon Benítez's arrival, after 20 games.

Two of the very best bits of business undertaken by Houllier came that summer, and as Bosman deals, neither cost a penny. Both Gary McAllister and Markus Babbel helped take Liverpool up a level the following season, and had a large impact on the winning of three trophies in 2001. Alas, neither player would last long in the first team, for very different reasons. Babbel had a superb first season after arriving from Bayern Munich at the age of 28. Although he could play at centre-back, he spent the season in the right-back position. A fine overlapping full-back, he wasn't especially gifted on the ball in technical terms, but had enough intelligence to use it wisely. He popped up with six goals, and really thrived as the season reached the business end. But then things quickly changed, as the right-back slot started to look cursed. Like Rob Jones and Vegard Heggem before him, Babbel's career was under threat before he was 30. The German defender fell ill with Guillain-Barré Syndrome, a potentially deadly neurological condition, which left him completely debilitated. He spent the rest of the next season having to learn to walk again. While he made what could be termed a full recovery with regard to the illness itself, he was never able to find the levels of fitness needed to be a top-class Premiership player. He then fell out with Houllier, who was angry at the player's attitude in the reserves; in fairness to Babbel, he appeared to be frustrated at a lack of his old strength and stamina. He went on loan to Blackburn in 2003/04 and played 25 league games at centre-back, and ended up breaking Milan Baros' ankle in an accidental collision. After that moderately successful loan spell he was released by Liverpool in 2004, and ended his career with Stuttgart in the Bundesliga.

If the early demise of Babbel was unforeseen, no-one could argue the same of Gary McAllister, given that he was already 35 when he arrived. Houllier said Liverpool would have won a lot more trophies had the Scottish central midfielder arrived at Anfield a decade earlier. It was something of a shock when he signed, having been at lowly Coventry City, a side he would help condemn to relegation in his first season at Liverpool with a trademark precision free-kick. McAllister had scored 13 goals in his final season at Highfield Road, and was a consummate professional; as such, there was life in the old dog yet. While he didn't start his Liverpool career too impressively, he improved as the season went on, and just when things began to reach boiling point in a remarkable campaign, he came into his own. The following campaign saw McAllister's influence wane, but having turned 37 on 25th December 2001, his decline was inevitable. He returned to Coventry after 87 appearances for the Reds, playing a further 55 times in the First Division, before retiring. Few players have been as warmly appreciated in such a short spell at Anfield.

Having had great success with two free transfers, Houllier showed that he found it harder when the fees got bigger; very few of his expensive signings paid off, and certainly not to the degree expected. Many of his best signings — McAllister, Hyypia, Babbel, Finnan and Nicolas Anelka (on loan) — were either cheap or free. Only Didi Hamann bucked the trend.

Central midfielder Igor Biscan arrived at the tail end of 2000, costing a fairly hefty £5.5m from Dinamo Zagreb. The tall Croatian had been compared with Ruud Gullit by Osvaldo Ardiles; alas, at times he played more like Rudy Giuliani. After a disappointing first three years at the club, Biscan managed a rebirth of sorts, as a centre-back — offering the pace that neither Hyypia or Henchoz possessed, but not the consistency. Following the arrival of Rafa Benítez, Biscan cemented his cult-hero status. Getting to play in his favoured central midfield berth, where his ability to run with the ball was more evident than had been seen under Houllier, he was a very handy option for the Spaniard, particularly when Xabi Alonso was out with a broken ankle. Ultimately, Biscan's future, after a very mixed time on Merseyside, was always going to lie elsewhere. With his contract up he was released, having played 118 games and scored three goals.

Having already done exceptionally well with two free transfers, Houllier went for the hat-trick in the 2000/01 season when, in January 2001, he signed Jari Litmanen, a world-class talent in his pomp, from Barcelona. It was shortly before the Finnish forward's 30th birthday, but his game had always been about intelligence, not pace or hard running. The recent doubts about Litmanen had always been with regard to fitness, and he was soon injured at Liverpool too, resulting in him missing the crucial run-in to the season. There's no doubt he was a disappointment of sorts, in that he never produced his old Ajax form, but all the same he scored nine goals in 43 games for the Reds, finding some good form in his only full season at the club in 2001/02, particularly in Liverpool's inaugural Champions League campaign — a competition he'd won seven years earlier. His arrival was perhaps indicative of Houllier trying to go for more technical strikers, but in the end Owen and Heskey were still the preferred choices.

One of the most stunning days of transfer activity in Liverpool's history took place on Friday August 31st 2001, when, with the deadline hours away, Jerzy Dudek and Chris Kirkland were signed from Feyenoord and Coventry City respectively. Dudek, a 28-year-old Polish international described by legendary Dutch coach Leo Beenhakker as the best keeper he'd seen in 30 years, cost £4.85m, while the 20-year-old rookie Englishman cost £6m, with the potential to rise to £9m. There were rumours that one of the keepers was signed by mistake; that, in a game of brinkmanship, Houllier had wanted either one or the other, but inadvertently ended up with both. Clearly, this is a little hard to believe, given that the raw Kirkland had yet to prove he was ready for the pressure of being a first-team regular at a big club. As a result of the new arrivals, Sander Westerveld quickly went from first choice to sitting in the stands, and five months later was sold to Real Sociedad, who, with a certain young Xabi Alonso in their ranks, finished 2nd in *La Liga* in 2003. Kirkland promised much, but played only 45 times in four years, and left as a disappointment of sorts. He was 6' 6" as a teenager, but was far from athletic and slow off his line. A great shot stopper, and imposing when commanding his area, his main problem was an inability to stay fit for longer than a few matches at a time. At the age of 24, he was sold to Wigan Athletic for £3m.

Dudek had been pretty much impeccable in his inaugural season, making his first mistake in the final weeks of the season at home to Blackburn. Not the tallest or broadest, his agility was that of a gymnast — cat-like seems to be the usual goalkeeping epithet. But no goalkeeper can be judged until he comes through his first really tough period. The key is how they deal with costly mistakes, which are sooner or later made by even the very best. And in Dudek's case, it was not good. In his second season he started to drop a few clangers, which escalated into howlers. While Dudek's fate was sealed when Benítez moved to sign Pepe Reina in the summer of 2005, the Pole at least got to savour one great high. Winning a Champions League medal is one thing, but to do so as the hero is something special. Dudek made one absolutely incredible point-blank double save from AC Milan's Andrei Shevchenko, and then denied him, and his team-mates, in the penalty shootout that ensued. He moved to Real Madrid on a free transfer in 2007, after 186 games, to continue life as a bench-warmer.

Another signing from the summer of 2001 was John Arne Riise, the promising young left sided Norwegian. Riise, who cost £3.7m from Monaco, had been deployed as a central midfielder in France, but it was on the flank where he made his mark at Liverpool. His tenacity, indefatigable stamina and thunderous shooting initially made him a firm favourite with fans. Despite his limitations — anatomists have yet to confirm the existence of his right foot, while he has no trickery whatsoever when it comes to beating a man — he managed to remain in Benítez's plans for four years, despite his style being more suited to Houllier's counter-attacking approach. Possibly one of the most one-footed players ever to play the game, he did however score a stunning goal with his right foot in the Nou Camp to consign Barcelona to a home defeat; however, he will also be remembered for a last-minute own-goal in the semi-final against Chelsea in April 2008, that ultimately cost Liverpool a place in the final, when he refused to use his right foot to clear. Two months later he was sold to Roma for £4m, after 31 goals in 348 games.

The young Czech striker Milan Baros arrived in December 2001 from Banik Ostrava for £3.2m. At first considered overweight and out of shape, not a great deal was seen of the new talent for the remainder of that season. But eventually he forced his way into the first team picture, starting 22 times in '02/03, and making a further 20 substitute appearances, registering 12 goals in the process. The year between June 2004 and 2005 was an absolute dream for the striker. In Euro '2004 he won the Golden Boot as top scorer, although his side crashed out at the semi-final stage. He started the new season — Benítez's first — in fine fettle, and while his league form fell away in the new year, and he failed to score in all but one of the post-group Champions League games, he ended the season as a European Cup winner. Ultimately a lack of goals, and a tendency to play with his head down, running into blind alleys with little awareness of team-mates, meant that Benítez was inclined to look elsewhere. Baros started the following season at Anfield, but was soon sold to Aston Villa for £6.5m, as Liverpool doubled their money. He left having scored 27 goals in 109 games, but only 66 of which were starts.

Another shock signing was that of French *enfant terrible* Nicolas Anelka, in a loan deal from Paris Saint-Germain that included the option of the Reds making it permanent at the end of the season. It didn't help that he was in no way match fit when he arrived, having been frozen out in Paris, and it took him ten games to break his duck — albeit against Everton, which is always worth more in the eyes of the fans. He gradually improved as he found his sharpness, and produced a quite glorious display as the Reds routed Newcastle 3-0 at Anfield in a game delayed by floodlight failure. It seemed he'd done enough to make the move permanent. But just as Anelka's arrival was a shock, so too was Houllier's decision to instead opt for the less-proven El Hadji Diouf.

Defender Abel Xavier arrived in January 2002 from Everton, costing £800,000. He scored on his debut, in a 6-0 win at Ipswich, but only played a further 20 times for the Reds, with very mixed results. With a white beard, the Portuguese international possessed more than a passing resemblance to King Neptune, and at times played like a 2,000-year-old man who had just dragged himself from the bottom of the sea.

Which brings us to the point where Houllier really started to mess up; the summer where it all went horribly wrong. In what he would later admit to being his biggest mistake, Houllier signed El Hadji Diouf from Lens for £10m. If Anelka was tarred with a bad reputation, Diouf's was arguably worse, after a tearaway teenage existence; something which, on top of inferior ability, made the signing all the more baffling when hindsight is applied. While he'd end up having some good games on the wing at Liverpool, most notably in the 2003 League Cup Final victory over Manchester United, he was ultimately a big failure, particularly in his time as a striker; three league goals in almost 60 games tells its own story. Snarling, spitting and pouting, Diouf quickly became an embarrassment to the club. He never played for the first team under Benítez, and after a successful loan spell at Bolton, where he scored nine times in 27 league games, the Trotters made the deal permanent, for a fee of around £4m.

With Diouf arrived another Senegalese who'd done well at the 2002 World Cup, 25-year-old Salif Diao. The tall midfielder cost £5m when signing from Sedan; after a decent start, the word *sedan* summed up his later years: sat on the bench, getting splinters. If Diouf was skilful but possessed of a bad attitude, Diao was the opposite: a solid, likeable character and fine athlete, but not a great footballer. At the time it was remarked from a high-ranking French coach that Diao was the 'new Vieira', but in truth he was little more than the new Robbie Savage. The £5m investment dwindled away to nothing when he was released at the end of his contract, to play his football in the lower divisions with Stoke City.

Having got the new Savage instead of the new Vieira, Houllier swiftly captured not the 'new Zidane' he promised but, rather painfully, the new Bernard Diomède. In truth, the comparison with the greatest player in the world at the time did nothing to help Bruno Cheyrou, although fans at Anfield for the pre-season game against Lazio, in getting their first proper glimpse, thought the comparison might have been valid. Cheyrou, a goalscoring midfielder who cost £4.5m from Lille, had talent, but absolutely no conviction in the rough and tumble of Premiership life. A propensity towards injuries didn't help him either. He is a prime example of a young player doing well in an environment where he has had time and space to blossom and develop, but who cannot cope once thrust into a new arena with the burden of a relatively large price tag (and in his case, a needless comparison). He moved back to France after 48 games for the Reds, having scored five goals.

One interesting signing was that of Bayern Munich's French teenage midfielder, Alou Diarra, on a free transfer. While Diarra was totally unsuccessful at Liverpool in playing terms — he spent his entire three years out on loan, even becoming a French international in the process — he was sold for £2m in 2005 by Benítez when the superior Sissoko was lined up. As a bit of business, and that alone, it was successful.

Back in 2001, Liverpool had announced they would be signing young French duo, Anthony Le Tallec and Florent Sinama-Pongolle, from Le Havre. The pair had excelled at the World Under-17 Championships that year. Le Tallec was awarded the Silver Ball as the second-best player, while Sinama-Pongolle, his cousin, won the Gold Ball as France won the tournament. Both players, aged only 16 at the time, would stay at Le Harve until 2003, when they were deemed ready to bring over to England, for a combined fee of £6m. Le Tallec played some steady games in his inaugural season, but as a thinking striker in the Teddy Sheringham mould, he was always likely to blossom later in life; by contrast, Sinama-Pongolle, who was also skilful and clever, had the pace to make more of an immediate impact, something he did in the final months of 2003. Neither was totally convincing, but given their age and the fact that they'd just arrived in England, it was a very promising first season for both. But then Houllier was sacked, and everything changed. Having failed to settle at St Etienne when loaned at his own request, Le Tallec found himself back in the Liverpool squad, and would feature in seven games during '04/05. Most surprisingly, he was put into the starting line-up for the crucial game against Juventus at Anfield, which the Reds won 2-1, with the young Frenchman having a hand in Luis Garcia's stunning goal that made it 2-0. But that was about as good as it got for Le Tallec; more loan spells followed, before he was sold to Le Mans for £1.1m in 2008. Sinama-Pongolle was faring much better during Benítez's first year, until he suffered a serious knee injury, which curtailed his season at the mid-point. It was a bitter blow for a player starting to show some real form. Sold to *La Liga*'s Recreativo Huelva for £2.7m in 2007 after a very successful year on loan (before a move to Atletico Madrid in 2008), his time in England will be best remembered for two crucial contributions as a substitute in games that looked lost — against Olympiakos and Luton Town — but which, thanks to his goals, would start a run that led to silverware. For these contributions, and a few more special moments, Sinama-Pongolle will be fondly remembered, but not without a sense of regret about how much more he might have delivered.

Having had his fingers badly burned by his foray into the French market for major signings in 2002, Houllier turned his attention to proven home-grown talents who were ready to go straight into his first team. While Steve Finnan and Harry Kewell were born outside of the UK, in Ireland and Australia respectively, both had come through the youth systems of English clubs. Finnan had established himself as one of the Premiership's best full-backs: a very steady defender who, at the other end of the pitch, could also put in a telling cross with either foot. The Irish international cost £3.5m from Fulham, but he initially struggled to find his best form. It was only in his second season, with the arrival of Rafa Benítez, that Finnan began to hit his stride. He maintained those standards for the next two seasons, with remarkable consistency; it was only in 2007/08, whilst struggling with niggling injuries that contributed to a loss of form, that his performances grew patchy. Meanwhile, some really tough competition for his place meant he was no longer a shoo-in

— Alvaro Arbeloa impressed, and Jamie Carragher, the player Finnan had replaced at right-back, switched to the position in certain games. Kewell, meanwhile, experienced the opposite trajectory to his Liverpool career. The Australian, signed for a bargain £5m from cash-starved Leeds United, started in superb goalscoring form, hitting double figures halfway through his first campaign. But in terms of performances and fitness, that was as good as it got. Kewell was involved in all of Liverpool's landmark occasions over the next three years, but suffered injury problems that consigned him to the periphery of each. He had the faith of Benítez, but without a miracle worker to help the winger stay fit and sharp, he was always fighting an uphill battle to stay in the team. He limped out of the first three finals under Benítez — League Cup, Champions League and FA Cup — and, following yet more injury woes, was only fit to enter the fray as a sub in the fourth, another Champions League Final. He managed to stay fit for two-thirds of 2005/06, and played very well at times, particularly in the FA Cup semi-final as Chelsea were beaten 2-1, but another injury, this time picked up at the 2006 World Cup after an effervescent display against Croatia, meant that he would barely be seen again in the next 18 months. Benítez gave him plenty of chances in '07/08, but Kewell couldn't find his best form. What was in theory an excellent signing by Houllier turned out to be a massive disappointment. In 2008 Kewell signed for Galatasaray.

Player	Quality	0.01pg	IN	OUT	FGV	VALUE	Ap	Details
Sami Hyypia	9.33	4.45	-1.7	7		19.08	445	£2.6m 1999 Age 34
Markus Babbel	7.44	0.76	0	2	1	11.20	76	Free '00 Rel illness
John Arne Riise	7.22	3.48	-2.1	1.3	1	10.90	348	£4m 2001 £4m 2008
Jerzy Dudek	7.28	1.86	-2.6	2	2	10.54	186	£4.85m 2001 Rel. @34
Dietmar Hamann	8.89	2.83	-5.3	4		10.42	283	£8m 1999 Rel. '06 @33
Steve Finnan	7.39	2.17	-1.2	1	1	10.36	217	£3.5m 2003 Age 32
Gary McAllister	8.28	0.87	0	0		9.15	87	Free 2000 Rel. @37
Milan Baros	6.06	1.08	-1.1	2.2		8.24	108	£3.2m 2001 £6.5m '05
All Managers' Average						7.92		
Vladimir Smicer	6.39	1.84	-2.5	2		7.73	184	£3.75m 1999 Rel. @32
S Henchoz	7.28	2.05	-2.3	0		7.03	205	£3.5m 1999 Rel. @30
Nicolas Anelka	6.78	0.2	0	0		6.98	20	Loan exp.
Djimi Traoré	4.94	1.41	-0.4	0.7		6.65	141	£550k 1999 £2m 2006
Harry Kewell	5.72	1.39	-1.7	0	1	6.41	139	£5m 2003 Rel. 2008
Ft S Pongolle	5.72	0.66	-1	0.9		6.28	66	£3m 2003 £2.7m 2006
Jari Litmanen	5.78	0.43	0	0		6.21	43	Free 1999 Rel. 2002
Average	**5.59**		**-1.96**			**6.00**		
S Westerveld	6.50	1.3	-2.7	0.7		5.80	103	£4m 1999 £2m 2001
Chris Kirkland	6.00	0.45	-2.1	1		5.35	45	£6m 2001 £3m 2005
Titi Camara	5.67	0.37	-1.7	1		5.34	37	£2.6m 1999 £1.5m '00

Abel Xavier	4.78	0.21	-0.3	0	**4.69**	21	£750k 2002 Rel.2003
Rigobert Song	4.00	0.38	-1.7	1.7	**4.38**	38	£2.6m 1999 £2.5m '00
Christian Ziege	5.11	0.32	-5.3	4.2	**4.33**	32	£5m '99 £4m @29 '01
Gregory Vignal	4.29	0.2	-0.3	0	**4.19**	20	£500k 2000 Rel. 2005
Erik Meijer	3.53	0.27	0	0	**3.80**	27	Free 1999 Rel. 2000
Djibril Cissé*	5.94	0.79	-4.9	1.9	**3.73**	79	£14.2m 2004 £6m '06
Emile Heskey*	6.50	2.23	-7.3	2.2	**3.63**	223	£11m 2000 £6.5m '04
Anthony Le Tallec	4.11	0.32	-1	0	**3.43**	32	£3m 2003 Rel. 2008
Nick Barmby	5.83	0.58	-4	0.9	**3.31**	58	£6m 2000 £2.75m '02
Igor Biscan	5.50	1.18	-3.7	0	**2.98**	118	£5.5m 2000 Rel. 2005
Bruno Cheyrou	3.71	0.48	-1.3	0	**2.89**	48	£3.7m 2002 Rel. 2006
El Hadji Diouf	3.83	0.8	-3.4	1.2	**2.43**	80	£10m 2002 £3.5m '05
Salif Diao	3.33	0.61	-1.7	0	**2.24**	61	£5m 2002 Rel. '05
Jean Michel Ferri	2.00	0.02	-1	1	**2.02**	2	£1.5m 1998 £1.5m '99
Frode Kippe	2.11	0.02	-0.4	0	**1.73**	2	£650k 1999 Rel. 2002
Bernard Diomède	2.76	0.05	-2	0	**0.81**	5	£3m 2000 Rel. 2003

Key: *See page 51.*

Transfer Masterstroke

A case could be made for both Gary McAllister and Didi Hamann, two central midfielders with contrasting styles and with a chasm in transfer fees. But the clear winner has to be Sami Hyypia, a bargain £2.6m capture from Willem II in 1999. Without any pace to lose, he has endured due to sheer defensive nous, and at the age of 34 in 2007/08 enjoyed one of his best seasons, featuring in almost 50 games when he was expecting closer to 15. Covering for the injured Daniel Agger, it was a sign of how well he was doing at the start of 2008 that the arrival and impressive form of Martin Skrtel did not consign the Finn to the reserves, but instead saw Jamie Carragher shift to right-back on several occasions, so that all three could feature. In April 2008 Pepe Reina sang the praises of the big Finn: "People say that he is not quick, but did Emmanuel Adebayor get past him with speed very often in three games against him? I don't remember it if he did." While it looks unlikely that Hyypia will reach the 500-game brigade (he is on 445 going into 2008/09), he still stands in the top 20 appearance makers for the Reds, and a one-year contract extension will see him complete at least a decade at the club. Incredibly, the centre-back played every minute of 57 consecutive European games for the Reds from November 2001 to February 2006, and passed the 100 European appearances mark soon after. Given his many towering performances in Europe, he will be remembered as one of Liverpool's best-ever centre-backs — praise indeed considering those who have gone before him. Never was he better than on the way to the club winning its fifth European Cup in 2005.

Expensive Folly

It's hard to know how Djibril Cissé would have fared had he ever got to play for the manager who had coveted him for two years, and who agreed to pay a club record £14.2m for his services. More suited to Houllier's tactics, and as a fellow Frenchman, there would have been a lot less uncertainty surrounding Cissé, and a lot more faith from the manager. Then there was the horrific broken leg suffered at Blackburn early in Benítez's tenure, followed by an almost identical injury just before the 2006 World Cup — at a time when Liverpool were set to recoup £8m from his sale back to France; in the end, the player departed to Marseilles for £6m a year later, after a loan spell that was part of his recuperation. Tall and explosively quick, the Frenchman had an excellent goalscoring record in France (and has scored a lot of goals there since his return), but lacked game intelligence and was forever running offside. Without the confidence he'd built up over a number of years at Auxerre, and with the weight of being Liverpool's record transfer, he never found his stride. He also seemed to take Benítez's rotation of strikers personally, although in 2008 he remarked that he had no ill feeling towards the Spaniard over his sale.

But Cissé was not Houllier's biggest mistake. For all his faults, Cissé made some telling contributions, scoring a penalty in the Champions League Final, as well as a crucial and technically adroit goal in the FA Cup Final, not to mention 19 in total during 2005/06, when he played many games on the wing. Cissé also had some undeniably bad luck that made it harder for him to shine. El Hadji Diouf may have cost £4m less than Cissé, but he delivered nowhere near as much, in far less extenuating circumstances. Both players left Liverpool for £6m less than they cost, but at least Cissé left behind some warm memories, unlike the unpopular Diouf.

One Who Got Away

Like a man who thinks he has caught a moth rather than a Red Admiral, Nicolas Anelka was the player who was most firmly within Houllier's grasp, only to be carelessly released. But there was perhaps an even greater mistake made a year later, albeit one for which the club's hierarchy must share the blame. In his autobiography, Phil Thompson admitted that Liverpool were offered Cristiano Ronaldo for £4m at the end of the 2002/03 season, shortly before he eventually joined Manchester United for £12m. Thompson had been very impressed the first time he'd seen the youngster, but less so on a return visit. While interested, Liverpool were shocked by the player's demands of a yearly salary of £1m tax-free. Thompson explained: "We had just signed Florent Sinama-Pongolle and Anthony Le Tallec, both on far less than

Ronaldo's aspirations. And we would have had anarchy if the other players had found out how much we were considering paying for an 18-year-old kid." While trying to work out a compromise with the player's agent, Ronaldo excelled against United in a friendly, and Alex Ferguson's players said that they simply had to sign the youngster. Thompson explained that he was sitting in a lounge at Anfield having some lunch and looking at the big TV screen when he heard of the development. "Up came the news United had signed Ronaldo from Lisbon for £12.2m. Gérard and myself nearly choked on our food." It was a massive missed opportunity, and even if Ronaldo had failed to find his feet at Liverpool, it would at least have stopped United possessing someone who would develop into one of their best-ever players by the age of 23.

Of course, the less said about Houllier's apparent desire to recruit an ageing Dion Dublin in 2004 the better.

Budget — Historical Context

In 1998, Liverpool were still relatively cash rich, but times were changing. Houllier arrived just three years after the transfer record was last held by the club, and within a year had purchased Dietmar Hamann for £8m (53%), and nine months later, Emile Heskey for almost £11m. Heskey, who cost 73% of the English transfer record, was the closest the Frenchman would get to the spending of the rivals at Old Trafford; his other two expensive strikers, El Hadji Diouf and Djibril Cissé, cost 34% and 49% respectively.

Manchester United's spending went up a level in 1999 from where it had been the previous decade — ever since Ferguson had bought several expensive players between '86 and '89. In the new millennium the United manager broke the English transfer record three times: paying £19m for Ruud van Nistlerooy in 2001, £28.1m for Juan Sebastian Verón in 2002 and £29m for Rio Ferdinand later that same year. The starting XI defeated 2-0 by Liverpool in the 2003 League Cup Final had five home-grown players, but also four who had at one time broken the English transfer record (the other being Roy Keane). The average cost was 42%, compared with Liverpool's 24%. Unfortunately for the Reds, that victory was achieved with a 5th-place Premiership finish, while United won the league.

Leeds United also overtook Liverpool in terms of spending. Their squad from 2001/02 had three players — Rio Ferdinand, Robbie Fowler and Robbie Keane — who cost more than any Liverpool purchase until 2004. Youth team graduates Harry Kewell, Ian Harte, Gary Kelly, Paul Robinson, Stephen McPhail and Alan Smith helped keep down the average cost of the 16, but there was also a litany of mid-range signings — Olivier Dacourt, Lee Bowyer, David Batty, Nigel Martyn, Mark Viduka, Michael Duberry, Seth Johnson and former-Red Dominic Matteo — dating back to 1996 in the ranks. On average, the 2001/02

16-man squad cost 30.6% of the English record, which, in 2000, they themselves had set with the capture of Ferdinand. By contrast, Liverpool's strongest XI in 2001/02 cost only 23%, while substitutes like Anelka, McAllister and Litmanen took the cost of the 16 down to 19.7%. Leeds' overspending became legendary. Jobbing full-back Gary Kelly was given a contract worth £40,000 a week following their run to the Champions League semi-final at the start of the millennium, a figure he was still earning when the club was relegated to the third tier of English football. Then there is the apocryphal tale, which may actually be true, of Seth Johnson being advised by his agent to hold out for £13,000 a week from the Elland Road club — who promptly made their opening offer at £30,000 a week; in the end, Johnson's agent said "Okay, make it £37,000 a week and he'll sign". Leeds won nothing, and never finished above Houllier's Liverpool after 2000. Leeds were living the dream, but soon experiencing a nightmare.

But as soon as Leeds fell from grace, Roman Abramovich was on the scene, pitching up ominously in west London.

RECORD
League Cup, 2001, 2003
FA Cup, 2001
UEFA Cup, 2001
Community Shield, 2001
European Super Cup, 2001
Champions League Qualification 2001, 2004

	P	W	D	L	F	A	%
Overall	307	158	75	74	516	298	51.47%
League	216	108	54	54	354	212	50.00%
FA Cup	19	12	2	5	32	15	63.16%
League Cup	18	11	2	5	50	24	61.11%
Europe	52	26	17	9	78	45	50.00%
Other	2	1	0	1	2	2	50.00%

+ Houllier & Evans

	P	W	D	L	F	A	%
Overall	18	7	6	5	33	20	38.89%
League	12	4	4	4	19	14	33.33%
League Cup	2	1	0	1	4	4	50.00%
Europe	4	2	2	0	10	2	50.00%

CONCLUSION

It seems certain that fans will always remain split over the contribution of Gérard Houllier. Between 2000 and 2002, Liverpool were a very strong team, formed from a squad brimming with talent and experience. The Reds won three major and two minor trophies in 2001, and finished 2nd in the league a year later — the highest since 1990. It's just either side of this period where the problems existed. Beforehand, there was the joint-managership farce with Roy Evans — according to David James, "When the two systems clashed it was like Halley's Comet hitting the earth." And afterwards there was the final two years of his reign, when the football grew ever more predictable and league results faltered to the point where the Champions League was missed in 2003/04, and only narrowly guaranteed for the following season. The team was now struggling in the UEFA Cup, and aside from the League Cup victory over Manchester United in 2003, the domestic cups were not providing much respite either.

Unfortunately for Houllier, the good and the bad will be remembered in equal measure. You cannot analyse one without acknowledging the other, and as such, Houllier's time will be considered a mixed affair: success and failure sit snugly side-by-side.

"There are those who say maybe I should forget about football.
Maybe I should forget about breathing."

GÉRARD HOULLIER

2004 -
RAFAEL BENÍTEZ

*"Rafa Benítez reminds me of Shanks. He understands the game,
how to get the best from individuals, how to change a game with
substitutions and his tactics are sound. He has gradually built a
squad that looks far stronger than last season, combining class,
pace, excellent movement and strength in depth."*

TOMMY SMITH ON RAFA BENÍTEZ, 2006

INTRODUCTION

It's possibly fair to say that Rafa Benítez's methods have been
questioned more than those of any manager in the history of English
football: rotation, zonal marking, defensiveness, players out of position,
and so on. Of course, visionaries in life — be they in sport, art, music
or politics — tend to be more greatly appreciated retrospectively, when
their ideas have proven inspired and their influence can be traced.
Life is not usually kind on those 'geniuses' who think differently, such
as Vincent Van Gogh, Charles Darwin, Sir Isaac Newton, Plato and
Paul Merson. In Spain, Benítez suffered the same criticisms before his
Valencia side won two titles in three years. At Liverpool, such league
success remains elusive, but within four years of his arrival the Reds
were ranked the no.1 team in Europe according to UEFA's coefficient.

From the moment Benítez arrived in England the press seemed to
have it in for this foreigner with his unusual ideas. *The Daily Mirror*'s
Brian Reade, speaking on LFC TV in late 2007, suggested that there
was a press agenda dating back to 2004, when journalists had wanted
to see one of the main English managers given such a key position; men
like Alan Curbishley and Sam Allardyce (both of whom, incidentally,
have hardly covered themselves in glory having subsequently tried

their hands at bigger clubs), and the less said about another name mooted — Steve McLaren — and his chance at the big time, the better. Others saw Benítez as another version of Gérard Houllier, the man he was replacing; where Houllier filled the club with Frenchmen, Benítez was buying mostly from Spain.

Struggles in his first season only further cemented the antipathy towards the Spaniard, who was the opposite of Chelsea's Jose Mourinho's larger-than-life personality; the colourful Portuguese was largely loved by the media for his ability to make their jobs easier, but Benítez was seen as cautious and cagey. By the January of his first campaign, Benítez had suffered defeat at Burnley with a weakened side, and with the team languishing below Everton in the league, there was an almost unprecedented talk of crisis at the club.

Within five months Liverpool were crowned champions of Europe.

Situation Inherited

When Rafa Benítez pitched up at Anfield in June 2004, he found a playing staff tearing itself apart at the seams. Michael Owen, the team's top scorer for seven seasons, was looking to move on, while Steven Gerrard, the subject of a £30m+ bid from Chelsea, was for the first time considering life away from his beloved Reds. Jamie Carragher, the third member of the core local trio, was also unhappy, although not looking to leave. Factions had arisen between the French-speaking players and those from England. Qualification for the Champions League had been secured on the final day of the previous season, but hopes weren't high. This was a team that had just had a miserable season in the Uefa Cup, losing tamely to Marseilles — the side comfortably beaten in the final by Benítez's Valencia.

Benítez knew Liverpool fairly well, having faced Houllier's men four times in two years. The first was in the summer of 2001 in Amsterdam — coincidentally, his first game in charge of Valencia — in a pre-season friendly which the Reds narrowly won. Then came the two games that mattered most: it was the autumn of 2002, and Liverpool were not so much beaten in both as thoroughly humiliated. The games, in the group stage of the Champions League, were lost 2-0 away and 1-0 at home, but the ease of the victories was what marked them out. Another preseason friendly in August 2003, at Anfield, in which Valencia yet again triumphed 2-0, was further confirmation that Benítez had shaped a special side. In all but the first of those four games Liverpool barely got a touch of the ball. Valencia, known as the 'Crushing Machine', were like a boa constrictor that squeezed the life out of its prey. There was no breathing space for a red shirt, while the white shirts swarmed in packs, attacking and defending as a perfect unit.

In 2006, Dietmar Hamann pointed out the dissimilarities between Houllier and his Spanish successor. "There's a huge difference. We train harder, we train for longer and we work harder than we used to. Everything is about tactics as well. You know that they know what they are doing and that's the main thing. We work on tactics almost every day and if you look at our goals-against record, that is a massive improvement." Referring to the Anfield encounter in the Champions League, the German midfielder explained, "We played Valencia a few years ago when Rafa was in charge there and that was probably the hardest game ever for us. It was hard to get the ball and once we had it, we couldn't play. We got beat 1-0 at home and I think we only had half a chance through Emile Heskey. We were completely outplayed and couldn't get anywhere near them. When you see the way they train us now, you can see why Valencia played the way they did."

Players Inherited

Technically Benítez inherited Michael Owen, but the player was already as good as out the door. That left Steven Gerrard and Sami Hyypia as the two outstanding talents rated at 9+ by the Brains Trust, although a third, Jamie Carragher, would rise into that bracket in the coming seasons. Didi Hamann, at 8.89, wasn't far off, but the mixed quality of the squad can be seen in how the next-highest ranked player in terms of *Quality* was Steve Finnan, with 7.39. Most damning, the attacking players were rated average at best. With this in mind, it's perhaps no wonder that the Reds failed to score many goals, and Benítez, as he had been at Valencia, was labelled a negative coach.

The squad had a nice average age, but that was undermined by the lack of quality in depth. The First XI was rated as the second-worst of all those a new Liverpool manager inherited in terms of *Quality*, and the squad was believed to be the worst. But when age is taken into account, the *Inheritance* rating gives both the squad and the First XI a slightly more respectable appearance. While the players weren't the best, there was at least some potential to get a few years' service out of the players or offload them (as seen with Traoré, Diarra, Diouf, Kirkland, Cissé and Sinama-Pongolle) for bigger fees than the nominal amounts that could be gained for players on the wrong side of 30.

Squad

Player	Quality	Age	Adj	Inheritance	Year	Age
Steven Gerrard	9.93	0	0	9.93	2004	24
Jamie Carragher	9.36	0	0	9.36	2004	26.5
John Arne Riise	7.22	0	0	7.22	2004	24
Danny Murphy	7.16	0	0	7.16	2004	27
Dietmar Hamann	8.89	-4	2	6.89	2004	31

Player	Quality	Age	Adj	Inheritance	Year	Age
Sami Hyypia	9.33	-3.5	1	**6.83**	2004	30.5
Steve Finnan	7.39	-1	0	**6.39**	2004	28
Stephen Warnock	6.29	0	0	**6.29**	2004	22.5
Milan Baros	6.06	0	0	**6.06**	2004	22.5
Chris Kirkland	6.00	0	0	**6.00**	2004	23
Djibril Cissé	5.94	0	0	**5.94**	2004	23
Florent S Pongolle	5.72	0	0	**5.72**	2004	19.5
Harry Kewell	5.72	0	0	**5.72**	2004	26
Igor Biscan	5.50	0	0	**5.50**	2004	26
Average	**6.07**			**5.46**		**25.5**
Jerzy Dudek	7.28	-2	0	**5.28**	2004	31
Djimi Traoré	4.94	0	0	**4.94**	2004	24
Gregory Vignal	4.29	0	0	**4.29**	2004	23
Stephane Henchoz	7.28	-3	0	**4.28**	2004	30
Anthony Le Tallec	4.11	0	0	**4.11**	2004	19.5
El Hadji Diouf	3.83	0	0	**3.83**	2004	23.5
Bruno Cheyrou	3.71	0	0	**3.71**	2004	26
Salif Diao	3.33	0	0	**3.33**	2004	27
Vladimir Smicer	6.39	-4	0	**2.39**	2004	31

First XI

Player	Quality	Age	Adj	Inheritance	Year	Age
Jerzy Dudek	7.28	-2	0	**5.28**	2004	31
Steve Finnan	7.39	-1	0	**6.39**	2004	28
Sami Hyypia	9.33	-3.5	1	**6.83**	2004	30.5
Jamie Carragher	9.36	0	0	**9.36**	2004	26.5
Djimi Traoré	4.94	0	0	**4.94**	2004	24
Steven Gerrard	9.93	0	0	**9.93**	2004	24
Dietmar Hamann	8.89	-4	2	**6.89**	2004	31
Harry Kewell	5.72	0	0	**5.72**	2004	26
John Arne Riise	7.22	0	0	**7.22**	2004	24
Djibril Cissé	5.94	0	0	**5.94**	2004	23
Milan Baros	6.06	0	0	**6.06**	2004	22.5
Average	**7.46**			**6.78**		**26.4**

Key: *Quality 0-10; Age = -1 point for every year from 28 onwards, eg -4 for 31 year-old, and -1 point from 30 onwards for keepers, eg -4 for 33 year-old; Adj = adjustments for players either exceptionally fit/unfit for their age, or soon to leave; Inheritance = total out of 10. Excludes players not part of first team picture.*

State of Club

In many ways Benítez experienced the opposite of what Shankly encountered. Back in 1959, the club was stable enough behind the scenes, but the infrastructure was a mess. Come forward five decades, and Benítez would eventually have to deal with unprecedented unrest in the boardroom, but at least the facilities were state-of-the-art. There wasn't the money of previous decades, in relative terms, although David Moores did his best to support the manager before he sold the club. But Moores was growing increasingly out of his depth in a new era, in which mere millionaires were no longer rich enough; football clubs were now owned by *billionaires*.

In selling the club to Tom Hicks and George Gillett, Moores was conceding that his race was run. But within a year of the sale, the leadership of the club was an on-going saga in the back pages of every newspaper. The two American billionaires fell out with each other in no uncertain terms; in the process, rifts were growing between Benítez and Rick Parry, and between Parry and Hicks — with the latter, in an unprecedented act, calling for the former to resign.

Benítez had found out in November 2007 that his job was on the line with league results slipping and qualification for the last 16 of the Champions League in the balance (although it would later be redeemed brilliantly, with 16 goals scored in the final three games). In January 2008 he discovered that the club had gone so far as to have informal talks with former German manager and Spurs striker Jürgen Klinsmann — meaning the club was once again making headlines for the wrong reasons. Two months later it was revealed that Hicks and Gillett were no longer on speaking terms, and again the whole sorry situation was played out to a watching world, this time with Hicks roundly criticising Parry. Gone was the old Liverpool way of keeping problems behind closed doors, although by the summer of 2008 it *appeared* all parties concerned had worked hard to bring an end to the discord, and had reached some kind of truce. (Time will tell on that score; at the point of going to print, Benítez and Parry had publicly fallen out and then publicly reconciled.)

So it was to Benítez's great credit that, after an autumnal slump and a sticky January (both coinciding with the height of the in-house fighting), he managed to return focus to the team and have it comfortably secure a top-four finish and lead it to yet another Champions League semi-final; although it was almost certainly easier to run the team when the power brokers began arguing with each other and left him alone. Without the unwelcome distractions in the middle of the season, when the players were put under extra pressure with one bad result capable of seeing the manager sacked, much more might have been possible.

Assistance/Backroom Staff

For over a decade, Rafa Benítez had what he felt was the most trusty of lieutenants, in the form of Pako Ayestaran. Popular with the players, Ayestaran was the man with whom they worked most closely, while Benítez kept his distance in order to maintain his authority. With the two Spaniards virtually inseparable throughout the previous eleven years, it was a massive shock when Ayestaran left the club at the start of the 2007/08 season.

In March 2008, Benítez told Guillem Balague and *The Times* the reasons behind the departure. "Pako was much more than a physical trainer, he was my friend and someone I trusted for many years ... One day I found out that he had serious contacts with other teams and that seemed to me a betrayal towards me and the club that I couldn't accept. He told me he wanted to leave the same day that we played against Toulouse [in August 2007], so I lost someone I trusted greatly, a key member of my staff at a crucial moment in the pre-season."

Ayestaran's departure preceded a 6-0 drubbing of hapless Derby County, which suggested all would be okay, but was more a case of papering over the cracks, albeit in style, against woefully substandard opposition. Then came a two-week international break, and from then on Liverpool's title hopes started to disintegrate. It wasn't necessarily that Ayestaran himself — *that it could only be Ayestaran* — was key to squad harmony, but any time a liked and respected key member of the coaching staff leaves, particularly under a cloud, uncertainty is created. Back-room staff often change in football; Alex Ferguson has got through countless assistant managers, including Brian Kidd, Steve McLaren and Carlos Queiroz (twice). Each time Ferguson has come back to win a league title, but not without disruptions and a transitional phase.

When Benítez arrived with Ayestaran as his second in command, Sammy Lee, the first team coach with an eye on the assistant's role, walked out to join Bolton as Sam Allardyce's no.2. But four years later, it was Lee replacing Ayestaran. "When a club the size of Liverpool comes in for you and when a manager of the magnitude of Rafael Benítez wants you then you can't say no," Lee said upon his appointment. "When I found out they were interested in me I was really thrilled ... I've been around Melwood this morning and seen a lot of old faces but a lot of new faces as well. There are some great people here and I can't wait to get working with them. It's so nice to be back."

Lee is positive, infectious, but also knowledgeable. Perhaps because of his unimposing stature he is not an authority figure, not a leader, hence why he didn't succeed as a manager. (If there is such a thing as Napoleon Complex, Lee doesn't seem to fit the bill; he doesn't seem power-hungry and dictatorial.) Changing a predominantly long-ball team to a passing one overnight (as he tried to do at Bolton) was always a massive task, and in the space of two months would possibly have been beyond even someone like Arsène Wenger. Lee will certainly help fill the void left by Ayestaran's departure.

Within nine months of Ayestaran leaving, a second key member of the coaching staff was on his way out. Alex Miller, an important figure at the club since arriving in 1999, was offered a massive pay rise to manage JEF United Chiba in Japan. In June 2008 Mauricio Pellegrino, who had failed in a brief time as a Liverpool player but whose presence off the field had a great impact, was appointed as Miller's replacement.

Miller, who had previously undertaken scouting and technical duties with the club, had seen those roles evolve and develop into the forming of an entire unit. As well as coaching with the reserves, Angel Valdes heads up the Technical and Video Analysis Department at Melwood. Since 1991, Angel has been a Doctor of Sports Science, having taught football to degree level at the University of La Coruna and to Masters level in three other Spanish Universities. He explained the role of the new unit: "There are five of us. Two travel all around England watching games, another one elaborates scouting reports of the opposing teams, there is a video editor and then myself. I coordinate and analyse our play. I try to compile all the information possible about our football so that Rafa can analyse it later and use it as he sees fit in order to increase the team's performance, which is what it's all about."

The influence of Benítez's Spanish contingent doesn't end there. As well as helping Pepe Reina and his understudies, Xavi Valero, the goalkeeping coach, has also helped Fernando Torres with his analysis of opposition keepers: "We've a Spanish goalkeeping coach," Torres said, "and he has been a genius at telling me every week exactly what kind of task lies in front of me in the following match. Nobody has ever worked with me like this before. It's outstanding. Basically, I know days before the next game exactly the best way to finish a chance against the keeper I'm about to face. Xavi Valero tells me precisely what each keeper tends to do — stay big, go down early, if they have a preferred side they try to push you to. It's vital information. I've refined the way I take chances as a result."

Management Style

If there's a single quote that sums up Benítez's management style, it is one in which he detailed the different ways a defining characteristic of his can be analysed. "You can't win games only on passion and for me, it is important to be calm and analyse every situation. One of my problems, or maybe my qualities — I don't know — is that I want to analyse games before, during and after. If you have a lot of passion during the game, you don't think of problems and solutions. Players look to the manager for solutions."

Perhaps there will never be a better illustration of this attribute than in the Merseyside derby at Goodison Park on October 20th 2007. Steven Gerrard, along with Jamie Carragher the Scouse heartbeat of the side, but unlike Carragher the go-to man in rescuing lost causes, had got Liverpool back into the game by surging forward to win a penalty, which Dirk Kuyt duly converted to draw the teams level. The Reds, experiencing a sequence of results that had seen them lose at home to Marseilles in the Champions League and drop two points at home to Spurs in a third successive league draw, were feeling the pressure. The good start to the campaign was faltering, and until Gerrard's intervention, derby defeat was looming. Fifteen minutes after Gerrard's game-turning burst, Benítez did the one thing that was virtually unthinkable, and which no other manager in world football would probably have dared do: he substituted his captain, and brought on a raw 20-year-old Brazilian *for his debut*. It was an incredible decision, but also a move that had some logic, particularly when referring back to the manager's own words about using the head rather than the heart. There's nothing wrong with passion, up to a point — indeed, the game thrives on it — but once it causes you to lose your head, you become a liability. It had caused Gerrard to be sent off in a recent Anfield derby.

Gerrard wanted to win at Goodison. Desperately. The subject of sick taunts from the home faithful, in Benítez's eyes he was trying *too* hard. He was haring about all over the pitch, and the shape of the team wasn't as Benítez wanted it. Everton were down to ten men following the penalty, but the Reds weren't making the extra man count — they needed patient passing to drag the Blues out of position. Once Lucas replaced Gerrard, the team calmed down, playing as a cohesive unit, and not as one player trying to do it all whilst his team-mates looked to him at every turn. Possession was no longer being squandered cheaply. Liverpool suddenly created more chances and began to get the upper hand, until, in the last minute, Lucas' goal-bound shot was punched off the line by Phil Neville; denying Benítez the ultimate vindication. But Kuyt, showing real *testikels*, stepped up once again, and the spoils were Liverpool's. Had the result not come off — and what looked a valid penalty claim for Everton in the dying moments might have seen the score level once again, had the referee not waved away the appeals — Benítez would have come in for some serious criticism. As it was, even with the three points in the bag, he received a heap of condemnation for *what might have happened*. But the point was, he made an incredibly brave decision (and bravery is not a quality attributed to him by his critics), and it paid off. End of story. The substitution helped Liverpool play better, and the substitute helped created the winning goal. Only if Liverpool had lost would he have deserved the flak that came his way.

This is perhaps at the root of the distrust of Benítez within the English media, where a bloodied Terry Butcher is the epitome of the British bulldog spirit on which subsequent generations have been brought up. Foreign cunning is still not entirely trusted, with English football as a whole rooted in passion rather than thought.

Unique Methods

Rafa Benítez's strong sense of purpose and belief in his own ideas have led to much criticism over the years; particularly with regard to his rotation policy. Before him, at the turn of the millennium, Chelsea manager Claudio Ranieri was labelled the 'Tinkerman', but the criticism was taken to a whole new level with Benítez. Whether or not you agree with his methods, the Spaniard clearly deserves far more respect for his approach, given the success it has brought him since arriving at Valencia in 2001. No-one had a better record in *La Liga* during his time at the Mestalla — even though the press in Spain criticised his rotating — and since arriving at Liverpool, no-one in Europe has a better record in the Champions League. AC Milan's record is virtually equal — one European Cup, one runners-up, one further semi-final, one round of 16 exit — but Liverpool edge them out a fraction in UEFA's all-important coefficient over the period. Irrespective of emotion and opinion, these are facts.

The benefits of rotation remain — and always will remain — impossible to prove, especially when assessing one game at a time. The 'proof' Benítez will call upon is how his teams always end the season fresh and in top gear, and how, with far less financial resources than Chelsea and Manchester United, finishing the season strong in Europe (in which he also rotates) would always be his best route to success — despite an equal, if less realistic, desire to win the league. In 2007/08, the managers of the top four, bar Arsenal, had all made on average between 3 and 3.5 changes per league game, going into the final stretch of the season. Arsenal's Arsène Wenger had made less than two, and it was his team that tired the most dramatically in the spring, and who was the first to fall out of contention for both of the main two trophies on which they are judged. Of course, it doesn't mean that a lack of rotation *definitely* cost Arsenal; but perhaps it did. Either way, Wenger seemed to remain bulletproof while Benítez was derided.

Benítez's detractors highlight dropped league points in the first half of the season when certain key players were rested. This of course presumes that Liverpool would have won those games; as if no full strength team ever dropped points. Judging rotation needs something similar to clinical trials, where you have two test groups — one trying one medication, the other trying either an alternative or a placebo. But you can never play the same game of football twice; once the ball is rolled from the centre-spot, cause and effect makes for something as unique as a snowflake or the human fingerprint. Indeed, even if you picked the same two teams to face each other over and over again, you'd either get radically different results, or the same result achieved in myriad different ways. Short of a parallel universe, no-one can say for sure when rotation fails or succeeds. Relative to the cost of his squad and those of his rivals, Benítez's record in the league is in keeping with money spent. The teams to beat Liverpool to the league title during his time in England — Chelsea and Manchester United — did so with more expensive sides.

Benítez explained his reasons for rotating to Spanish journalist Guillem Balague in an excellent interview for *The Times* in March

2008. "First, if you rotate a squad it means you believe in your players and trust in their ability to perform. You want everyone to feel they are working together to achieve our goals. If we win it is thanks to the efforts of everyone, however small their contribution. Look at Vladimir Smicer, who did not play a lot for us [in '04-05] but scored one of the goals that allowed us to win the Champions League. Every manager with a team in European competitions and with international players, with so many games to play, rotates his squad — call them changes, rotations, they all do it."

This is undeniably true. Alex Ferguson 'rests' players, while Benítez is always 'tinkering'. Ferguson 'keeps a strong core', while Benítez 'makes scattergun changes'; except players like Reina, Gerrard, Carragher and Torres (who was rested just twice in the league before April), as with United's key men, were virtual ever-presents when fit in the league and Champions League, unless it was the end of the season and the final league position was not under threat. Again, it's an issue of perceptions.

Benítez continued: "Things have changed in terms of physical demands. The decision to rotate starts by watching my team train — that is a priority for me. I see which players have energy and what players need to rest. You look at a player, talk to your staff, to the doctors, try to analyse the situation and then you chat to the footballer, although he will almost always say that he is ready to play. So sometimes you have to read between the lines to gauge whether they are really fully fit and if they are more tired than they are letting on."

While fitness issues are important to the manager, a key strategy for Benítez is his desire to have as many different options and approaches as possible, in order to be unpredictable. He doesn't like being second-guessed, and while this may lead to a lack of cohesion at times, and accusations of over-thinking things, the ability to change a winning formation and opt for someone like Peter Crouch in the second leg of the quarter-final against Arsenal — and for the tall striker to play a key role in a 4-2 victory — shows how exploiting an opposition weakness, such as the Gunners' inability to deal with a target-man, can be more beneficial than simply sticking with the tried and tested each week.

"We want to use two or three systems during the season," Benítez said in the summer of 2008. "The key isn't the system itself, but how the players adapt on the pitch. It doesn't matter if it's 4-3-3 or 4-4-2, it's the role of the players that counts. At the beginning of last season we were doing well with 4-4-2, so if the players can read the game and understand things, then it's easier to change the system. Now we have more options at full-back, with Degen, Finnan and Arbeloa on one side and Dossena, Aurelio and Insua on the other. We have players with different qualities. You can't use too many systems — two or three maximum — and the key is to teach the players how to adapt to each system."

Another often noted fact about Benítez is that he only names the team an hour before the kick-off, a method first used at the club by Kenny Dalglish. This way there's no excuse for any player in the 18-man squad not being ready for the game. It makes sure everyone is desperate to play, and should there be any late injuries, he doesn't have to call on people who have switched off or, thinking they're not playing, failed to prepare for the match properly. It also makes it harder for the opposition to get an idea ahead of the game. It can be argued that it hampers understanding, but the team can still be prepared in training, which these days is longer and more detailed, if everyone knows their role.

He almost preaches the opposite of the old Liverpool maxims — "same team each week", and "let the opposition worry about us" — and as such it has led to criticism, particularly from those who cannot see the need for change and progress. But back in the halcyon days, Liverpool undeniably had the best team and were in a position of total domestic domination. While certain methods were right for Paisley in the '70s, with his supreme team and the slower intensity of games, when Benítez arrived in England the best players were generally at Manchester United, Arsenal and Chelsea, and those three clubs had deeper squads, too. Benítez took over a team that had just finished 30 points adrift of the champions, ending up 4th having just previously finished 5th; he inherited a team that had also been poor in Europe in the previous two seasons. Initially, for every top-class player Benítez added to the side, his rivals in the top four were adding one, if not two of their own, to what were already superior squads. For every £10m Benítez spent, Chelsea spent £30m, while Arsenal and Manchester United had begun quarrying some of Europe's best young kids when Gérard Houllier was still in the middle of his reign. So it was clear that Benítez was not going to win the league on the strength of his team alone; he needed to ally clever thinking to good players, and to try and make the most of his ability to both surprise the opposition and to keep the energy levels of his team high. If it means playing Steven Gerrard on the right, as he did to win 2-1 in Barcelona and 4-2 at home to Arsenal in European Cup quarter-finals, he will do so. But of course, for every bold decision that does not pay off, the manager is instantly open to more criticism. It's the same with zonal marking at set-pieces; teams concede frequently when man-marking, but in this system different culprits *on the pitch* get the blame each time, depending on which individual was at fault. However, if zonal marking fails to work because a player fails to react, or because of a goalkeeping error, then it's seen as the manager's fault for persevering with a supposedly flawed system. This despite the fact that for almost two years, until the 2007/08 season, Liverpool had the league's best record for defending set-pieces.

Strengths

Benítez is very much a hands-on coach. It was not an unusual sight in early games to see the new manager walking onto the pitch following victory, and rather than salute the jubilant Kop, approach a player, put his arm around him and point to specific areas of the pitch, taking him back through mistakes.

Most players who have worked under Benítez claim that they have improved. Some were just happy to get a new direction, after the Houllier years limped to an end. Steve Finnan's dramatic improvement may have simply been a case of having settled into the club — he was, after all, voted the league's best right-back when at Fulham — but he certainly found supreme consistency in the Spaniard's first three seasons.

Steven Gerrard also improved. Part of that process was simply maturing, having still only been 24 when Houllier was sacked. But the captain also changed the way he played. At first it was a painful process, as he sought to run free and do everything; something he still does on occasion, but on the whole he is now more disciplined. Benítez wanted that energy channelled, to have his main man play in a more continental style. Gerrard learned to stop recklessly diving into tackles, and having averaged around six goals a season up to 2004, he averaged 18 over the next four campaigns.

Perhaps the greatest improvement came from Jamie Carragher, a versatile defender who had spent several seasons in either full-back position, having originally struggled as a young centre-back. Benítez wasted little time in ousting Stephane Henchoz and placing Carragher beside the commanding Sami Hyypia. By now, Carragher was a mature player, and able to better handle the position. While not exactly lightning-quick, his extra pace made him an improvement on the Swiss, as did his ability on the ball; never the best going forward at full-back, Carragher used the ball with surprising accuracy when able to look left or right, rather than just infield. Thanks to the influence of Benítez, Carragher was soon regarded as one of Europe's finest centre-backs.

Ryan Babel is another who claims to benefit from the manager's approach. Midway through the baptism of fire that is a young Dutchman's first Premiership season, he said: "I'm learning so much here and again I can see that it's often the small details that make the difference." It was interesting, because this was no rookie from a backwater club where coaching was limited; this was a product of the famed Ajax Academy, a player who'd already played almost 20 times for Holland, and who, crucially, had been personally trained by the legendary Marco Van

Basten before the two were reunited when the latter became the Dutch manager.

Angel Valdes also gave an insight into Benítez's attention to detail. "[I've learned] A lot," he said. "For example, the importance of the small details in tactical work. On a tactical level, he is one of the best managers in the world. But the best thing is that despite having been so successful he never allows himself to relax or rest on his laurels. His level of self-demand is the same now as it was when I met him while he was working with Real Madrid's youth teams. He's always looking for ways to improve, to apply the latest technologies as a means to support performance. He is talented from a tactical analysis standpoint but besides that he has the labour and dedication. For me, being a part of his staff is a mixture of satisfaction for being alongside one of the best and of responsibility, because the level of demand we set ourselves is very high."

One of the most interesting insights into the methodical planning of the manager came from Fernando Torres. "Rafa calculates everything," he said, "including runs and flights of the ball, and studies it on his computer. If he tells you to stand five feet from the penalty spot, it's not in your best interests to be six feet from it! He'll show you that the extra distance makes the difference between a goal and a missed chance — and it has worked for me. The proof for me is I had never scored a club hat-trick in my life before joining Liverpool, but I've since got three, against Reading, Middlesbrough and West Ham. Rafa explained everything to me before I even signed — how we would play, and what our aims were. He even gave me a work schedule in advance."

Weaknesses

While some see it as one of Benítez's weaknesses, his man-management skills could also be viewed as a method of motivation. Like Shankly before him, Benítez keeps his distance from the players, with the other coaches there to deal with them on a more personal level. Benítez has received criticism for his treatment of Steven Gerrard, but he refuses to single out players for special praise. Gerrard claimed in his autobiography that Benítez had never gone out of his way to give him a pat on the back, but clearly it helps keep him hungry. Ian Rush said that Bob Paisley never gave him a 'well done', and that relationship didn't work out too badly in a sporting sense.

Another interesting insight came from Alvaro Arbeloa: "I didn't know where I was in my first week with Liverpool," he admitted. "It went badly, and the image I remember from those early days is of the manager criticising everything I did, from the way I did some basketball practice to how I played my football. My first fortnight at the club was inhumane, but I am grateful to him now for filling me in on how the team works. It is a well-run club and I found it easy to adapt to their way of working. People say the manager is grumpy but I have only seen that once. He is serious-minded, though, and I can assure you nobody enjoys themselves during the training sessions. There is a great seriousness about them because that is where we go to work."

It's clear that Benítez is not an easy man to work with. He has exacting standards, and doesn't mollycoddle players and their egos. But the key thing is that his playing staff *respect* him. At Valencia plenty of his charges openly loathed him, but would still play for him — because he enhanced their careers and won them trophies. He tests players, pushing them to the limit, and those who cannot cope are quickly shown the exit. Interestingly, few have spoken out against him after leaving the club, as you would normally expect from players nursing bruised egos. Fowler, Cissé and Crouch all suffered exclusions from the team under the Spaniard, but each seemed to accept that it was not personal.

Jamie Carragher is one of those strong characters who have flourished under Benítez. "Everything he does," the vice-captain said, "is geared to keep us improving. He is very critical, never one for praising people. No matter how good a game you've had, he picks you up over something you've done wrong, which is why there's no chance of complacency creeping in. He puts you in your place very quickly if you get carried away with yourself. He is just a perfectionist."

Fernando Torres is another who respects Benítez's approach. "He has great powers of seduction," he said, "and makes crazy demands on us. At the end of training, when we are all tired, he can still make us repeat routines 20 or 30 times. Nobody is sure of his first-team place at Liverpool. Rafa is merciless, and anyone who wants to play in matches has to earn the right in training. It is different to Spain, where only an earthquake can change the pecking order at a club. You soon learn the Liverpool way of doing things. If you train like an amateur you end up dropped to the bench for the next game."

Benítez is also seen as a negative, defensive coach. There is some truth in the observation, inasmuch as he tries to build from a platform of solidity and stability, and at times this can make him appear cautious. His reputation stems largely from his Valencia team winning the league with a top scorer managing just six goals; the title was won on the back of countless clean sheets. But two years later he regained the title with a much greater balance. In terms of keeping it tight at the back, Benítez has the joint-best defensive record out of any Liverpool manager's first 150 league games. His side has so far conceded 119 goals in the top flight — level with Bob Paisley. But allied to this Benítez has looked to find a balance between defence and attack. In 2007/08 the Reds managed 119 goals in all competitions, the most of any English team.

Historical Context — Strength of Rivals and League

The obvious difference from anything his predecessors faced has been the Abramovich Factor. Not even just a billionaire, the new Chelsea owner was on his way to being a *trillionaire*. Gérard Houllier had to face the West London riches for just one season, but for Benítez it is an ongoing issue. Furthermore, Chelsea also appointed a top-class manager in Jose Mourinho, something Claudio Ranieri never quite was. Managerially, Chelsea appeared weaker in 2007/08 under Avram Grant, but by this stage the team was an experienced, well-oiled machine. Manchester United were a mega-rich club with an entrenched manager and an expensive playing staff. Now owned by the Glazers, they possessed a squad full of £15-30m players. Arsenal were going through something of a transition, with the departure of Robert Pires, Freddie Ljungberg, Sol Campbell, David Seaman, Patrick Vieira and Thierry Henry within a few years, and seemed low on cash. But once the Emirates was built they had a licence to print money, and a young team of players sourced before Benítez arrived in England began to come of age.

And that was it with regards to the rivals; by the time Benítez arrived in England, a 'big four' was developing, with the Reds admittedly a very distant fourth at that point. The problem was that, unlike at any time in the past, all three of the other teams were amongst the best in Europe; once Mourinho arrived, all three had top-class managers, two of whom had been in charge of their club for one-to-two decades. Arsenal had won the league in 2004 without losing a game, and two years later were beaten Champions League finalists. United had been champions in 2003, and by 2007 and 2008 were winning the domestic title once again, while making the Champions League semi-final in 2007 and winning the trophy in 2008. Chelsea garnered two league titles, in 2005 and 2006, and were Champions League semi-finalists in 2004, 2005 and 2007, and finalists in 2008. Keeping Liverpool in the top four was not the biggest challenge, although an improved Everton made it nervy at times, but overtaking Chelsea and Manchester United was nigh-on impossible. In 2005/06, Liverpool finished with 82 points, and won 66% of their league games (the 2nd-best total in the club's history, better even than the legendary 1987/88 side), but still only came third. In 2007/08 Liverpool lost only four league games, one of the club's lowest-ever totals, and the fewest for 20 years, but it still left the Reds in 4th. The gap of 11 points behind the Champions was the lowest in six years, and a massive improvement on 2003/04's 30-point deficit, but made no difference to the league position.

Bête Noire

There's only one obvious candidate here. Perhaps it was a case of familiarity breeding contempt, as Liverpool faced Chelsea no less than 16 times in Benítez's first three-and-a-bit seasons. Chelsea's manager for those games, Jose Mourinho, had been appointed at the same time as Benítez, and had reportedly been the original target of the Liverpool board. Both were Iberians coming to England on the back of great success as underdogs, and both were failed footballers who were methodical in their preparations. But whereas Benítez was serious and studious, Mourinho was flamboyant and cocky. In many ways it was a modern day version of Bob Paisley versus Brian Clough: the introvert versus the extrovert.

At first, Mourinho, having inherited a stronger squad (Chelsea having just finished 19 points ahead of Liverpool), and then spent with largesse to bolster it, was the clear winner. His Chelsea side won the first two league encounters 1-0, and the Carling Cup Final 3-2. The fourth game — the Champions League semi-final first leg — finished 0-0 at Stamford Bridge. But by the end of game five — the second leg — Benítez had won the match that mattered most. Tensions simmered from then on. Mourinho criticised Liverpool for using the height of Crouch, yet his team continually searched out the towering Drogba; the Portuguese even used to send on Robert Huth, a giant, artless defender, at the end of matches to play as a forward, something Benítez mocked.

In April 2008, six months after the Portuguese was sacked, Benítez explained how he was glad that the two didn't have to face up anymore, not least because of the tiresome press brickbats. "The media might miss Mourinho, but not me. At the end of the day, the players are the key more than the managers. Managers can talk before the game but, during the game, the players make the difference. The best thing for a manager to do is not create any mess so the players can just play."

Mourinho also constantly moaned about the 'ghost goal' Luis Garcia scored to win through in the first semi-final encounter. While it was hard to tell for sure if the ball crossed the line, the referee admitted just days later that had he not given the goal, he would have awarded Liverpool a penalty for Petr Cech's foul on Milan Baros, and sent off the Czech keeper. With 87 minutes still to play, that was hardly a favourable decision for the 'Special One'. Meanwhile, Chelsea had numerous beneficial decisions in the 16 encounters: Tiago punching the ball off the line from under the ref's nose; the bizarre penalty given by Rob Styles that led to the referee being suspended; Frank Lampard breaking Xabi Alonso's ankle, and then Eidur Gudjohnsen diving to get the Spaniard suspended from the semi-final second leg; and Pepe Reina being sent off for merely touching Arjen Robben's face, with the Dutch winger falling as if suffering the prolapse of his major organs. (Afterwards, Benítez joked that he was unable to do his press conference as he was off to see Robben in hospital.)

As Benítez attested, Jose Mourinho was a friend of sorts until he started losing. By the end of the duels, Liverpool's boss was increasingly coming out on top, until Mourinho was sacked at the start of 2007/08 following a draw courtesy of Styles' terrible refereeing decision. While the Liverpool/Chelsea clashes continued with tiresome regularity — making five every season since Benítez arrived — they were clearly less colourful without the presence of the Portuguese. Chelsea even got their belated semi-final victory in May 2008.

Pedigree/Previous Experience

It's fair to say that with regard to prior managerial experience, Benítez was the most qualified of all Liverpool's managers. Indeed, four of the eight appointments had no previous league management experience, while Shankly had managed only at lower division clubs. Souness had an excellent record in Scottish football, but at that stage it was not a particularly strong league, unlike in the '60s and '70s. Houllier had won a French league title, in 1986, but between then and his appointment in 1998 he had been behind the scenes at the French national team. So Benítez's two *La Liga* titles and UEFA Cup marked him out as a man with excellent pedigree.

What he did not possess was experience of English football, beyond facing Liverpool and Arsenal in the Champions League. Far from insular, he had visited Premiership teams in the late '90s as part of his education. But it was still a fairly difficult transition once actually in charge of an English giant, not least because he had to master a new style of football, while turning the team he inherited into a more possession-based outfit, with what was essentially a mixed bag of players.

Defining Moment

The Olympiacos game on December 8th 2004 is rightly seen as one of those miracle nights at Anfield. Trailing 1-0 at home to the Greek side, Benítez needed to see his team score three second-half goals or face elimination. He made changes, and each time he brought on a sub, they seemed to score or create a goal. And with six minutes remaining, Steven Gerrard struck a wonder-goal that even had dyed-in-the-very-bluest-wool Andy Gray in raptures. But this game was still a month before the club was described as being in crisis following defeat at Burnley, and as such, it was only a turning point in Europe. In the interim, the Reds put together some good results, but also lost big games at Everton, Chelsea and Manchester United before the Turf Moor debacle.

But Olympiacos allowed a series of further 'turning points'; without beating the Greeks, there would have been no unexpected victory over Juventus, and no 1-0 semi-final win over Chelsea in the best atmosphere experienced at Anfield in decades. And that led to perhaps the greatest turning point of all — half-time at the Ataturk Stadium, when a shattered dream was somehow revived in front of incredulous fans.

Crowning Glory

There can only be one moment — a night that will probably never be topped. If Rome '77 was the greatest night in the club's history, given that it was the historic first European Cup win, then Istanbul can arguably top it on account of the sheer drama and unexpectedness of the outcome. Were Benítez to go on and land a league title, it would possibly eclipse the 2005 Champions League success in terms of achievement, but it's hard to imagine it causing such unbridled delirium. Coming back from 3-0 down against an imperious AC Milan side had people all over the world rubbing their eyes in disbelief. If Rome '77 was the story of a great side confirming its supremacy, Istanbul was that of a fairly average side performing brilliantly to win against all odds.

Legacy

Not yet applicable, of course, but were Benítez to be replaced, or resign, then he would leave a young, talented squad with bundles of potential.

If there's one thing that Benítez has paid particularly close attention to as part of his managerial duties, it is the thorough and systematic development of the club from top to bottom. The first team is vitally important, but the reserve and youth sides are given every bit as much attention. Scouting has become an almost obsessional crusade. Like Gérard Houllier, Benítez has a background in youth development. Unlike Houllier, Benítez did precisely what was needed at Liverpool. In retrospect Houllier's efforts look a little half-hearted — a few French teenagers recruited here and there, but no great scouring of the world; compare this with how his compatriot Arsène Wenger was not only picking up talented kids from his homeland, but going to Spain to steal Cesc Fabregas from Barcelona, not to mention having a firm eye on the entire African continent. For years, Manchester United had been bending the rules to get English kids from beyond the allowed radius. But Liverpool seemed to be set on producing kids only from the surrounding area, and with many of the best ones, given their allegiances, as likely to opt for Everton (as seen with Wayne Rooney), there just wasn't enough top-quality talent filtering through.

Which brings us to one man, and a battle Benítez won that his predecessor had lost. Steve Heighway was a great servant of Liverpool FC, a passionate Red, and a good, intelligent man. For years he had done a brilliant job as youth development officer. But football was changing, and in trying to cling to his admirable ethics and morals, he was keeping Liverpool both insular and rooted in the past. If Merseyside was throwing up a Gerrard, Carragher or Rooney every couple of years, his inclination to keep the youth team local would have been vindicated; but the best local lad to make it through to Liverpool's first team in almost a decade was Stephen Warnock, a decent, committed but distinctly unremarkable player when compared with the kind of quality needed to keep pace with the competition. Benítez was frustrated that, bar only one or two exceptions, the club weren't even producing 'rejects' capable of Premiership football; he noted how Spain's *Primera Liga* was full of around 40 players who had come through the Real Madrid system.

It wasn't about giving up on the local kids, but about only taking the very best ones forward. Without the riches of Manchester United or Chelsea — both of whom were growing increasingly wealthy — getting the world's best young players before a big fee became involved was the best way to challenge, particularly as those two clubs, along with Arsenal, were hardly hanging around on that front themselves. Importing talented, hungry youngsters from across the globe should also benefit the best Scouse lads — training and playing with better players should only elevate their abilities, and the increased competition should in theory lead to a removal of any complacency. Where Arsenal and Manchester United had been taking players away from Barcelona's youth team before the Catalans were allowed to secure them on permanent deals, Liverpool joined in the act, moving for the talented playmaker/striker Daniel Pacheco in 2007, and then 'robbing' Real Madrid of their Argentine prodigy, Gerardo Bruna, soon after. These were the type of player Liverpool's Academy was just not producing.

The fact that the youth team, replete with Benítez signings, won the FA Youth Cup in 2006 and 2007, and then, with a team of teenagers, romped to the 2008 reserve league (Northern Section) title in 2008 — before beating Aston Villa 3-0 in the all-England playoff — showed that the manager was on the right track. Heighway's local lads, including Stephen Darby and Jay Spearing, were a big part of that success, but it also relied heavily on players sourced by Benítez and his scouts from other parts of Britain, as well as those from Europe, Africa and South America. By the summer of 2008, it seemed that Benítez had talented youngsters for every position in every single age group from 16 to 20.

At this stage, it doesn't mean *too* much. After all, given the tender age of those recruited, it's yet to bear too much first-team fruit. But it's far better to have the potential on tap, ready to trickle or flow through, whoever the manager may be. Just as it took Liverpool and Manchester United at least five years to produce successes after their youth systems were both originally overhauled in 1986, it's still too soon to expect first-team regulars. But several teenagers have already held their own in the senior side on occasion, while players like Pacheco, Insua and Nemeth appear to have that something special to take them all the way. And at the very least, Spearing, Plessis, Hobbs, Anderson and Darby, like Danny Guthrie who was recently sold to Newcastle for £2.5m, look very much like Premiership players in the making.

TRANSFERS

Transfers In

Going back to the start of modern Liverpool, Bill Shankly had a very firm idea of the kind of player he wanted. Geoff Twentyman explained that any targets "have to have the temperament as well as the talent." In that sense, Benítez was keen on not making the same mistakes as some of his more recent predecessors. "The key," he said, "is to sign the right players with the right mentality — a winning mentality. Competitive players, players who are desperate to come here to win something."

Benítez's success and failure in the transfer market seems to correlate directly to how much he spends. Cheap signings have proved either hit or miss — which is no bad thing, on balance — but unlike a lot of managers, the more expensive ones have generally been worth every penny. Perceived as having spent very big, even before the outlay of 2007 and 2008, the truth is that Benítez has spent frugally by comparison with Chelsea and Manchester United (the only two teams to finish consistently higher). Having initially dealt in quantity, the Spaniard was able to recoup a lot of his expenditure. By February 2008, Benítez had bought the club's most expensive defender (Skrtel £6.5m), midfielder (Mascherano £18.6m) and striker (Torres £23m), but it was still a small outlay compared with that of his rivals down the M1 and East Lancs Road.

But it didn't start too well. Josemi, Malaga's right-back, was purchased for £2m in July 2004. He was offloaded 18 months later in a swap deal for Jan Kromkamp, after his bright start faded away. Tough and rugged, he seemed intent on diving into tackles rather than staying on his feet, and as a result picked up a number of yellow cards and an inevitable red at Fulham in October 2004. He left after 35 appearances.

Antonio Nunez, valued at £2m as part of the Michael Owen deal, was another cheap punt that ultimately didn't pay off. A serious knee injury sustained in his very first training session meant that it was November before he made his debut, and as such was always playing catch-up in terms of sharpness and adaptation. Like Josemi, Nunez returned to Spain as Liverpool got their money back. But the former Real Madrid winger, who was steady rather than spectacular, did have a handful of really effective games, not least as a sub against Olympiacos, when he had a hand in two of the three crucial goals. He scored once in 27 games.

But it was around the time that the Owen-Nunez deal took place that Benítez struck gold with two more Spaniards. Luis Garcia and Xabi Alonso arrived at the end of August, with the season already underway. Both instantly settled into the team and into English football. While Garcia would ultimately frustrate and marvel in equal measure, his contribution to the reaching of major cup finals cannot be overlooked; he was a 'pop up' player, one who arrived on the scene at the right moment with the right response, scoring 30 times in his 121 appearances, only 55 of which were complete games. At £6m, the former Barcelona squad man became a scorer of invaluable goals, a real big-game contributor, be it continental occasions, semi-finals or blood-and-thunder Merseyside derbies. A mixture of slack passing and super-sharp thinking, his benefits outweighed his drawbacks and loose drag-backs. Injury halfway through his final season denied Liverpool a key player in the latter stages of the Champions League, and he departed to previous club Atletico Madrid for £3.5m in 2007.

While Garcia impressed in fits and starts, Alonso, the cultured central midfielder who cost £10.5m from Real Sociedad, proved a more consistent key component, in his first two seasons at least. Perhaps it was the jaw-dropping impressiveness of his passing in his first season that left standards too high to live up to, or maybe fans simply took his presence for granted, but from then on there was talk of underachievement. What is almost certainly true is that opposition managers did their best to stop the Basque getting time on the ball; the easiest way to thwart Reds' attackers was to ensure that the playmaker didn't have a chance to pick them out. Serious injuries saw two seasons fragmented: a broken ankle sustained against Chelsea on New Years' Day in 2005, and a broken metatarsal in September 2007, which robbed him of almost 20 games. With 14 goals from 163 matches, including two consecutive amazing efforts from his own half, he has proved capable of weighing in with a few strikes from a holding midfield position.

The transfer window of January 2005 gave Benítez the chance to reinforce his squad, having had a few months to assess those he inherited. Mauricio Pellegrino, a free transfer, was one of those who arrived, but it's fair to say that his influence was felt more off the pitch than on it; hence his later re-appearance as first-team coach. The ageing Argentine, a mainstay of Benítez's Valencia defence, was too far gone in years to cope with Premiership football — he was 33 — although he did produce a couple of excellent displays in amongst the general shakiness.

A lot more was expected of Fernando Morientes — the £6.5m signing from Real Madrid. But the 28-year-old Spaniard was a disappointment. He wasn't in any way *terrible* — he just failed to hit the heights seen for Real, Monaco and the Spanish national team. It was no surprise when he returned to Spain in the summer of 2006, moving to Valencia for £3.5m, and, once back in his element, he scored more than twice as many league goals upon reaching the 41-game mark, the total he played for the Reds.

Scott Carson, aged 19, was signed from Leeds United for £750,000 — a veritable bargain for a player presciently labelled a future England international. While his Liverpool career would amount to just nine games, it would include the Champions League quarter-final against Juventus just months after his arrival; he made one glaring error, but also pulled off a smart save, and Liverpool progressed 2-1 on aggregate. The next year the tall, toothy Cumbrian was understudy to newly-arrived Pepe Reina — a superior keeper who was not much older (just three years), but who had already played almost 200 career games to Carson's handful. Carson spent his third year on a season-long loan at Charlton, where he excelled in the role of busy shot-stopper as the London side suffered relegation. His fourth season was spent loaned to Aston Villa, where there was greater expectation, but still not the pressure associated with keeping goal for Liverpool; all the same, it was an important step up in his education. Liverpool received £2m for the loan, meaning the Reds had made a handsome profit even before his sale to West Brom in 2008, which netted a further £4m.

The summer of 2005 was Benítez's first chance to dip into the full, open market having had a year to work with the players he inherited. As well as those destined for immediate inclusion in the first team, he began scouting youngsters, many of whom would go on to help the club land its first FA Youth Cup for a decade.

Antonio Barragan signed for Liverpool in July 2005, picked up from Sevilla for a nominal compensatory fee (believed to be £250,000) as the youngster had not signed a professional contract in Spain. The talented 17-year-old right-back became the Reds' youngest player in the European Cup when he came off the bench against CSKA Sofia, but that was his only taste of action. In the summer of 2006 he was sold to Deportivo La Coruna, for £680,000, where he soon made the senior side. The fee was initially reported to be as high as £1.7m, but the lower figure was believed to have been decided upon in order to give Liverpool the chance to buy back the player in 2008 or 2009. Jack Hobbs was just 16 when Liverpool made an approach to Lincoln City, offering £750,000 for a mere boy — admittedly one who stood 6' 3" — who had already played in the football league, albeit for just a few minutes. Hobbs soon featured in some pre-season games, and made his full debut in September 2007, having just turned 19. He made a handful of appearances, and performed very well given his age and inexperience, before being sent on loan to Scunthorpe and then Leicester to further his education. Other youngsters arrived in the summer of 2005, such as Godwin Antwi, who had just turned 17, was snapped up from Real Zaragoza; Antwi would partner Hobbs at centre-back on the way to winning the 2006 FA Youth Cup, and has since been loaned to Accrington Stanley, Hartlepool and Tranmere. And Miki Roque, another member of that successful youth side, was signed from Lleida at the age of 17; the young Spaniard featured in one first team game, coming on as a substitute against Galatasaray in the Champions League, in what was a dead rubber with progress already assured. In 2007/08 he spent a year on loan at Spanish second division side Xerez CD, having previously played four games for Oldham in a brief loan spell.

With the Reds freshly crowned Champions of Europe, major things were expected in the transfer market. For some fans it was a disappointment, in that there were no big name signings — Luis Figo was pursued but chose Inter Milan — and in a couple of cases, players who had suffered plenty of derision in recent years ended up at Anfield. Bolo Zenden had enjoyed two impressive seasons at Middlesbrough, as their playmaker, but the former PSV Eindhoven and Barcelona winger had been fairly mediocre in his spell at Chelsea. Once a pacy young wide-man, he would prove steady but unspectacular during his stint on Merseyside, after arriving on a free transfer. He started very well on the left-hand side, but a serious injury sustained in November 2005, soon after scoring in two Premiership games, curtailed his first campaign, and from then on he was never more than a squad player. The Dutchman, with 53 caps, saved his best Liverpool performance for the Champions League semi-final against Chelsea in May 2007, having faced each of his previous clubs (bar Middlesbrough, obviously) *en route* to Athens. However, he was disappointing in the final itself, and released immediately after, with 47 Liverpool games to his name.

There was plenty of dismay amongst some sections of the Liverpool support when Benítez stumped up £7m for Peter Crouch, a 6' 7" striker famous for not scoring many goals. But the 24-year-old was on the up, having just scored 16 in 24 Premiership games for Southampton, as well as recently making his England debut. Crouch, so ungainly, is a player who is easy to misjudge; his touch is not just good 'for a big man', but it's good for a forward of any size. His best game for Liverpool was the 4-1 victory over Arsenal in March 2007, when he scored a 'perfect' hat-trick, notching with a header, a close-range right-footed finish, and a stunning left-foot goal having turned the Arsenal defence inside out. His record of 42 goals in 134 games is particularly impressive seeing as one third of those games were as a substitute; so while his record is one-in-three, in terms of starts it's one-in-two. His England record is even more outstanding: 26 games, but only 14 starts, and 14 goals; this for a player roundly mocked and jeered when he first played for his country. At Liverpool he suffered following the arrival of Fernando Torres in 2007; both players like to be the furthest forward, with Crouch there to use his height and Torres looking to get in behind teams, but the modern game means someone has to play in the 'hole'. With this in mind, Crouch, despite nearing the end of his contract, was sold to Portsmouth for £11m in July 2008 — meaning a nice profit on a player who had given a lot to the Liverpool cause.

While Benítez made bids on players in excess of £10m, including Simao Sabrosa, it was signings for around half this amount that were most common that summer, as he sought to rebuild every aspect of the squad. Along with Crouch came two young players from Spain: José Manuel 'Pepe' Reina, a £6m signing from Villarreal, and Momo Sissoko from the manager's old club, Valencia, for £5.8m. Both enjoyed excellent debut seasons, instantly usurping experienced internationals and Champions League heroes in the form of Dudek and Hamann. Sissoko's second season was also fairly faultless, but his third was pretty disastrous, as he lost his confidence. Gifted technically, he had a tendency to rush his passes, just as he rushed all over the field to destroy opposition moves. Despite scoring his one and only goal in his 87 games at the start of 2007/08, he lost his form, and his passing grew ever more wayward. But as would later happen with Crouch, Sissoko was sold for a clear profit; moving to Italian giants Juventus for £9m.

Pepe Reina, who once saved seven out of nine penalties in one Spanish season, would also go on to break a number of Liverpool goalkeeping records: incredibly impressive given the keepers who had gone before him, and the legendary defence of the late '70s. Just 22 when he signed, the Spanish international had bags of experience, having already played over 200 career games, including a spell in Barcelona's first team at the age of 18. Like all keepers, Reina has made mistakes and had days he'd rather forget, but on the whole he has proved to be the complete modern keeper: agile, commanding, and possessed of often overlooked qualities with his feet in terms of sweeping behind a high back-line and distributing the ball, which he does better than a lot of outfield players. All he lacks is a couple of inches in height — at 6' 2" he's tall enough, but he'll always find it a little more difficult than keepers of 6' 5" when it comes to getting above the mêlée on crosses. In each of his seasons to date, he has attained the Premiership's highest number of clean sheets; obviously that's as part of a five-man back unit, but the confidence stems from the man between the sticks; field a shaky keeper and you have shaky defenders. Reina surpassed Ray Clemence's record of 53 clean sheets in his first 100 league games; the Spaniard recorded 54. In December 2005 Reina kept his sixth consecutive league clean sheet, against Wigan Athletic, to break the Liverpool club record for successive clean sheets in the Premiership era. Reina also broke Liverpool's all-time, all-competitions consecutive clean sheet record with eleven between October and December 2005. Still only 25 at the end of 2007/08, Reina surely has a very bright future ahead of him. Benítez was certain of the player's qualities: "Reina is a keeper with very strong character, a good personality and is very competitive. Every training session and during the games, he is very critical of himself and he tries to improve on things all the time. He is good in one-against-ones, good in the air, is quick and can start counter-attacks. He is a very modern keeper."

Paul Anderson, a 17-year-old Hull City trainee, was brought in with former England U21 international John Welsh heading the other way. Anderson excelled in the FA Youth Cup success of 2005/06, tearing through teams with his searing pace and direct running, and plundering a few goals. In 2007/08 he went on loan to League One Swansea for the season, where he did extremely well; the small, slight winger toughened up and gained some senior level experience, helping the Welsh club to promotion. In 2008 he moved up a level, going on loan to Nottingham Forest.

Villarreal's Jan Kromkamp was an interesting signing, albeit one that wasn't entirely successful. The Dutch international full-back arrived in January 2006 in a swap deal with Josemi; he was clearly an upgrade on the unreliable Spaniard, but Kromkamp himself wouldn't last long before being 'swapped', albeit indirectly, for Alvaro Arbeloa. Kromkamp, formerly of AZ Alkmaar, put in a couple of excellent displays in his first five months at the club, and never let the team down, but had a stinker in his one and only game of 2006/07; he was offloaded to PSV Eindhoven before the transfer window closed.

The biggest shock of all Benítez's signings was the free transfer of Robbie Fowler from Manchester City in January 2006. It was one of those gambles — talented player past his best — that had the fans purring with anticipation, as Fowler jumped at the chance of a five-month trial with the chance to earn another year at the club. Would the familiar surroundings and crowd adoration restore Fowler to the player he had been a decade earlier, before injuries and alienation robbed him of his confidence and *joie de vivre*? At first it seemed the unique marriage between player and club would prove beneficial. Fowler, who turned 31 in the April of 2006, bagged five league goals in the remaining few months of the season, each strike either winning a game or setting the Reds on course for victory. With a proper pre-season behind him, it seemed anything would be possible in 2006/07, but alas, Fowler still looked sluggish in the ultra-fast modern game. He bagged seven goals, including a sublime dinked finish in the League Cup and two goals in his first ever Champions League start in the dead rubber at Galatasary, but scored only penalties in the league as he virtually vanished from the scene from autumn onwards. But Benítez had given the fans and the player a chance of a proper farewell, for which both will be eternally grateful.

Young Danish centre-back Daniel Agger, who had just turned 21, was another transfer-window acquisition. Bought from Brondby for £5.8m, he would only feature four times in his first season due to problems with injury and with easing in to Premiership life, but he did enough to whet the appetite. His second season was an outright success. The word 'thoroughbred' springs to mind when describing this ball-playing, goal-scoring left-footed centre-back with bags of class on the ball, but he also possesses a winner's mentality and good size and strength. In the Reds' history, arguably only Alan Hansen and Mark Lawrenson have had similar qualities in possession, although neither scored a goal as stunning as Agger's swerving 30-yard piledriver against West Ham in the opening home game of the 2006/07 season, nor as important as the Champions League semi-final goal that enabled progress to Athens in May 2007. What those illustrious forebears have over Agger is years of consistency borne through experience and a wealth of medals, but both played in the outstanding club team of their day, and neither was as young as Agger when signed. Injury meant Agger missed most of 2007/08, playing just five league games before sustaining a metatarsal break that would be aggravated two further times on comeback attempts. If he can stay fit, Liverpool have an absolute gem on their hands.

If Agger was the thoroughbred, Dirk Kuyt, the major summer signing of 2006 at £9m from Dutch club Feyenoord, was the workhorse — a player to whom injury is a total rarity. Lacking finesse, it was often joked that the Dutchman's second touch was a tackle, and that he was the world's first 'holding forward'. But what he lacks in skill he makes up for in sheer work-rate and commitment; at times he is perpetual motion personified as he runs and runs, and often with intelligence to his movement. His first season was a relative success, scoring 14 goals, 12 of which were in the league, as well as hitting the post on six occasions (all with good efforts) and scoring the winning penalty in the Champions League semi-final shootout against Chelsea. All this was achieved while playing behind the main striker, often Peter Crouch. But Kuyt failed to find the net in Europe until the final minutes of the season, scoring a header against AC Milan in Athens that ultimately proved in vain. It was pointed out, as with Peter Crouch a year earlier, that the lack of European goals was the sign of deficient qualities. In his second season Crouch had remedied that situation, scoring six goals *en route* to the Champions

League final, and Kuyt went one better. Alarmingly, the league goals dried up for the Dutchman, but he managed seven in Europe, including absolutely vital first-leg strikes against Inter Milan, Arsenal and Chelsea that tipped each tie in the Reds' favour. By that stage, however, he'd been moved to the right-wing, to a role similar to that in which he'd started his career at FC Utrecht. Kuyt splits fan opinion, but those at the club don't doubt his contribution. In 2008 Benítez stated: "Kuyt has a fantastic mentality and a strong character. He is a winner, a fighter. I am really pleased with him — he is a player you can always trust", while Torres is another fan: "This Liverpool side works its socks off. Dirk Kuyt, for example, is spectacular in how cleverly and how hard he works to make sure I get top-quality possession near goal." To date Kuyt has 25 goals in 96 games, 74 of which have been starts.

Brazilian Fabio Aurelio, a free transfer from Valencia, is a talented left-back. Aurelio had won a title with São Paulo in 2000, before moving to Spain. Under Benítez at Valencia he quickly added a *La Liga* title, and scored eight league goals a season later. Injuries began to dog his time in Spain, and when his contract expired his former manager made a move. "The most important moments I had in my career were with Benítez. He trusted me and he continues to trust me," said the player upon arriving at Liverpool. Injuries have also disrupted his time at Anfield, limiting him to 54 games in two seasons, but by the second half of 2007/08 he was showing his quality on a consistent basis, defending with impressive solidity, and passing and crossing with vision and accuracy. The question is, can he maintain it?

By the summer of 2006, Benítez was well aware of just how important pace was in the Premiership. He still went for technical players like Fowler and Aurelio, when a deal made sense, but the emphasis had to be on pace where possible — however, pace allied to more skill and guile than he was getting from the likes of Cissé and Traoré. However, it would take another year before the manager would find the quality of player he was looking for. In the meantime, several speed-merchants signed in the summer of 2006 did fairly well, but didn't elevate the club to the next level as expected. Benítez needed to strengthen the squad with numbers, but the budget meant he couldn't spend lavishly on any one individual.

Craig Bellamy had just had an excellent season with Blackburn Rovers, and his value had soared to in excess of £10m. However, a clause in his contact came to the attention of Liverpool, the club he supported, whereby a £6m offer had to be accepted by the Ewood Park board. The bid duly arrived, in what was a sensible gamble given the relatively low fee. The Welshman had caused trouble at previous clubs, but at 27 he appeared to be maturing. However, just days before the Round of 16 Champions League clash in Barcelona, Bellamy was reported to have attacked John Arne Riise with a golf club. Benítez did not punish the Welshman there and then. With the preparations for the Barcelona match well underway, and with the striker's pace key to the plans, the Spaniard would have been cutting off his nose to spite his face. Bellamy rose to the occasion, looking to make amends; he scored the equalising goal, and set up Riise (inevitably) for the winner. Little did he know it, but his career at Anfield was already as good as over. He started few games after Barca, and was sold to West Ham for £7.5m in the summer of 2007.

Mark Gonzalez, signed from Albacete, experienced the opposite trajectory to Bellamy in his Liverpool career — however, the pacy winger ended up in the same situation: cast aside after just one season. He started well, scoring on his full debut to put Liverpool into the Champions League proper, and scoring on his Premiership debut. But he struggled to adapt to life in England, and the good start proved a false dawn. He was sold to Real Betis for £4.5m, ensuring a profit on a player whose style suited Spain, where he was soon playing well again and scoring at a fairly prolific rate.

Jermaine Pennant, another fast attacking option, arrived from Birmingham for £7m. Like Bellamy he'd had his disciplinary difficulties in the past, but unlike Bellamy he proved more of a reformed character. Pennant was just 23 when he signed — some seven years after his debut for Arsenal, and following good individual displays at Leeds (on loan) and Birmingham, as both suffered relegation. His time at Liverpool has thus far proved mixed; spells of indifferent form followed by pace and trickery out wide, and plenty of assists. Three goals in 77 games is not a good return, but when on form, as in the 2007 Champions League Final, he can consistently create chances for others.

Gabriel Paletta, bought for £2m from Banfield of Argentina at the age of 20, had a good pedigree with the Argentine national youth teams, but his lack of pace was quickly exposed in English football. Central defence is a perilous position for youngsters, given how any mistake can be quickly punished — but at least those with pace can sometimes get themselves out of any trouble borne of *naiveté* or just bad luck. As with Bellamy and Gonzalez, Paletta lasted just one season, but again, no loss was accrued: Boca Juniors paid £2m (including a swap deal with Emiliano Insua) for a player they knew would serve them well in the Argentine league. He's a player to watch with interest, and one who may return to Europe when he's matured.

In October the Reds signed Nabil El Zhar, a tricky, diminutive winger, recently turned 20. El Zhar had represented France at youth level before switching to Morocco, whom he helped to the semi-finals of the 2005 World Youth Championships, and for whose senior side he has twice scored in just five games. He made his Liverpool debut as a 71st minute substitute against Portsmouth on November 29th 2006, in the first of three appearances that season. The following campaign saw El Zhar score a 25-yard screamer against Cardiff City in the League Cup on his first start, but most of his time was spent in the reserves, where he did well without ever looking a sure-fire hit. However, he featured in the first three games of 2008/09, each time as a sub.

If 2006 proved a mixed bag for Benítez — only Agger excelled — then 2007, from start to finish, will surely prove the year when his judgement, and that of the club's raft of scouts, was at its very best. It coincided with the American takeover, and it's clear that the arrival of Tom Hicks and George Gillett, for all the subsequent problems, enabled Benítez to spend a larger amount of money than had David Moores still been in control. Even so, player sales also boosted the coffers as the manager traded up with improvements, or offloaded mistakes. Benítez signed more than a dozen players who would do very well in either the first team or reserves.

Having worked his way through several right-backs who could pressurise Steve Finnan for his place, Benítez appeared to finally find one who fitted the bill in the form of Alvaro Arbeloa, a £2.6m signing from Deportivo La Coruña. The former Real Madrid full-back, who had just turned 24, excelled in his first start — against Barcelona in the Nou Camp, marking the Argentine *wunderkind*, Lionel Messi; a baptism of fire if ever there was one. A dogged man-marker, Arbeloa was deployed on the left that night, and again in the return leg, and once more kept Messi quiet to the point of anonymity. Pacy without being electric, solid without being beefy, tall without being a giant, good on the ball without being a winger in disguise, Arbeloa offered a bit of everything — he resembled Rob Jones in his running style, and like Jones, was comfortable on either flank; unlike Jones, *he actually scored a goal*. His second season was a bit less successful than his first, as a series of niggling injuries curtailed his progress, while the arrival of Martin Skrtel meant that Jamie Carragher was shifted to right-back on a number of occasions. In the spring of 2008 Arbeloa became a full Spanish international, and played once for his country in Euro 2008, to cap a successful rise from Real Madrid reserve to fully established player at another big club.

Another full-back signing was confirmed in January 2007. Emiliano Insua, a 17-year-old Argentina U-20 international, was lured from Boca Juniors on what was initially a loan. Within a few months, after turning 18, he would make two league appearances, albeit in games that were largely meaningless; a year later 2007/08 he started three such games. While Insua spent his first full season almost entirely in the reserves, he excelled as the second string coasted to the league title. Lacking in height at just 5' 6" — always a concern for defenders in English football — he is a powerful, skilful player who is strong in the tackle and quick to get forward. He seems to have an exceptionally bright future — Benítez said in April 2008 that Insua "is still a young player but he is improving and I think he will be one of the names maybe in the future".

A key transfer-window signing was that of Javier Mascherano, another young Argentine. Still only 22, Mascherano had already played more than 20 times for his country, including games at the 2006 World Cup. His move to West Ham involved a controversial deal in which his registration was retained by a third party, but with the midfielder bizarrely left out of Alan Pardew's plans, Benítez moved to rescue a player many believed to be a world-class holding midfielder from the Hammers' reserves. Within months, the man Diego Maradona once described as a "monster of a player destined for great things" and known in his homeland as *Jefecito* (Little Chief), was marking Kaka out of the Champions League Final. Mascherano was originally signed on an 18-month loan deal, for a fee of £1.5m, but in February 2008 the player moved on a permanent basis, with the addition of £17.1m taking the payment to £18.6m — on a par with other defensive midfield signings, following Claude Makelele's £16.6m move from Real Madrid to Chelsea in 2003, and more recently, John Obi Mikel's signing for £16m, while Manchester United paid in the region of £18m for Michael Carrick (2006) and Owen Hargreaves (2007). Deceptively quick and unquestionably dogged, a fine tribute to his first 18 months at Liverpool came from Cesc Fabregas, as the Arsenal midfielder, frustrated by the Argentine in the Champions League quarter-finals, stated "I could feel his breath on my neck all the first half. I think he is an amazing player."

A number of promising teenage recruits were signed throughout 2007. Francisco Duran arrived from Malaga in January, at the age of 18, having already played four times for the Spanish club. Two subsequent cruciate ligament injuries have limited the talented playmaker's reserve appearances to date, but he retains a lot of potential. Daniel Pacheco and Gerardo Bruna, both slight and skilful, were snaffled from the youth teams of Barcelona and Real Madrid respectively, when they were aged 16. Mikel San Jose, a very highly-rated 18-year-old centre-back arrived from Athletic Bilbao for a reported fee of £270,000, and made the bench in the Premiership match against Chelsea in February 2008. A mainstay of the successful reserve team, its manager, Gary Ablett, said of the defender: "He has an eye for a pass, good composure on the ball, he's physically strong and can compete against the more robust forwards. He can also use his brain to deal with the smaller, quicker ones ... he's going to be a very good player." Two more centre-backs, Ronald Huth (17) and Daniel Sanchez Ayala (16), arrived from Paraguay and Spain respectively. Ayala was the second player the Reds plundered from the

Sevilla youth team, following the capture of Antonio Barragan in 2005. A link-up with MTK Hungaria saw the signings of Andras Simon, 17, and Krisztian Nemeth, 18, while young goalkeeper Peter Gulacsi, 17, was signed on a year's loan with a view to a permanent move. Of the Hungarians, Nemeth was clearly the star prospect. He missed the first half of the reserve's campaign through injury and youth international commitment, but the striker, who had already scored 14 goals in 37 Hungarian league games by the age of 18, would average a goal a game for the remainder of the campaign. His all-round play — close control, intelligent movement, exceptional awareness, the ability to shoot with either foot, and a natural predatory instinct — led Benítez to suggest he might soon be pushing for a place in the first team squad. Reminiscent of Robbie Fowler, the fact that the Reds found Nemeth at such a young age will help him adapt to English football and to be eased into the first team picture.

But the teenage recruit who made the most progress in 2007/08 was Damien Plessis, signed from French champions Lyon at the end of August, aged 19. "He is a good player, big and strong, and we're sure he'll do well for us," said Benítez at the time Plessis arrived in England. Plessis resembles a mix of Momo Sissoko and Xabi Alonso — the physicality and tackling of the former (without quite as much pace), but with some of the passing skills, positional sense and composure of the latter. (His height makes it possible to also liken him to Salif Diao, but thankfully the resemblance ends there.) Almost 6' 4", the central midfielder made his first-team debut a month after his 20th birthday, away at Arsenal in the Premiership in front of 60,000 people and a live TV audience, and looked incredibly assured. While it was a chance handed to him due to Benítez resting key players for the Champions League quarter-final against the same team a few days later, he impressed the manager. The challenge for him now is to go back to playing in front of 800 people and continue his progress in the reserves.

One youngster bought with an eye on the first team squad was Sebastián Leto, who arrived from Lanús in Argentina for £1.85m shortly before his 22nd birthday. At 6' 2", he is unusually tall for winger. Reasonably quick and skilful, he had scored eight goals in 52 Argentine league games, but struggled with the pace and intensity of the English game. He has looked too good for the reserves, but not yet good enough for the first team. Passport issues meant he spent the last few months of the season ineligible to play for the Reds, and with the same problem in 2008/09, he was sent on loan to Olympiacos for the season.

Another South American — one who came with a higher pedigree and who adapted more quickly — was Lucas Leiva, a 20-year-old Brazilian who had already represented his country. For the current Brazilian league's

Footballer of the Year, £6m seemed a very astute investment. His inaugural campaign was promising, but more a case of steady than spectacular. He didn't look out of his depth in terms of ability, but was physically slight for a midfield enforcer and at times easily out-muscled; he doesn't have the physical gifts of Momo Sissoko, who settled far more quickly, but perhaps possesses more long-term potential. At times the Brazilian tired towards the end of matches, particularly on a run of consecutive starts, but for such a young player thrust into the heart of a Premiership midfield he generally acquitted himself well. When Benítez switched to two holding midfielders and freed Gerrard to a position behind Fernando Torres, having sold Sissoko, it meant Lucas was then only competing with Mascherano and Alonso for a place in the side. The emergence of Plessis, a year younger than Lucas, might pose a further threat to regular games, but having featured more than 30 times in his debut season, the Brazilian was satisfied with his first year — as was Benítez.

With Scott Carson loaned to Aston Villa for a £2m fee, the Reds needed experienced back-up for the bench. Charles Itandje, who stood at 6' 4", arrived on a free transfer from Lens. Aged 24 when signed — still quite young for a keeper — Itandje had some good games in amongst his seven starts (all in the cups), and made some very impressive saves, but a tendency to flap at crosses had fans a little wary. It's difficult to judge a reserve keeper who comes into the side cold after months of inactivity, and who might be prone to trying too hard to make an impression, knowing full well that he's likely to face a month or two back in the wilderness.

With Luis Garcia opting to return to Spain, Benítez went into the market to replace like-with-like. Yossi Benayoun, at £5m, cost less than Garcia had three years earlier, and only a fraction more than the little Spaniard, approaching 30, left for. All in all it was a great bit of business. Benayoun has similar traits: the ability to run with the ball and drift past people, an eye for a cunning pass, and a crucial knack of popping up with goals. While Benayoun didn't score as many vital goals as Garcia tended to during his first year, the Israeli had already reached double figures soon after the turn of the year, including two hat-tricks in cup competitions. Starts became rarer in the second half of the season, as Benítez altered the formation, but Benayoun was still an important player, almost always keeping other big names out of the 16-man squad. He played 47 times in his first campaign, but only 26 of those were from the start.

Benítez's need for a pacy, skilful winger was met with the arrival of Ryan Babel, 20, who cost £11.5m from Ajax. French international Florent Malouda had been the original target, but he moved to Chelsea who were offering higher wages. Babel actually performed better than the 28-year-old Frenchman, and scored ten goals to the Chelsea winger's three. While the young Dutchman was frustratingly inconsistent as he acclimatised, he did produce some scintillating displays. His form improved in the second half of the season, once he began getting regular starts, and although he still had the occasional anonymous game, he was a vital part of Benítez's attacking quartet. He was not only having to adapt to a new country, a new style of football, a new team and new ideas, but he was stationed on the flank — something he'd done in the past, but with less onus on defending. Benítez admitted that Babel might get to play in his favoured role as a deep-lying striker further down the line, but right now, apart from the odd occasion towards the end of games, he was needed elsewhere. Reminiscent of John Barnes in physique and balance, and also the way he manoeuvres the ball at pace, Babel was three years younger upon arrival; by the age of 23, if he adapts fully to English football, Babel could be every bit as good. The Dutchman started 26 games for the Reds, but only finished six, coming on as a sub a further 23 times. Compared with Thierry Henry by no lesser judge than Marco Van Basten, Babel has all the raw ingredients to be a Liverpool legend, but he needs to turn that potential into a regular end product.

One signing that Benítez got 100% spot-on, even for a fee that could approach £26m with future add-ons, was that of Fernando Torres; the manager's best signing to date. Less successful was the free capture of Bayer Leverkusen's Andrei Voronin. He started exceptionally well, scoring the winner in Toulouse in the Champions League qualifier, and bagging goals in his early league games; he was also heavily involved in five of the eight scored against Besiktas, showing his intelligent movement and passing ability. But after a bright start his form dipped, and an injury caused him to miss much of the rest of the season. He returned to the side for the run-in and scored a couple more goals, but at times looked lazy, and missed some sitters. Still to win over a number of fans, he has ability and experience, and looked very sharp in the 2008/09 pre-season games, but is likely to remain a cost-free back-up.

Continuing with his run of at least one outstanding signing every year, Martin Skrtel was bought in January 2008, costing £6.5m from Zenit St Petersburg. While it's still early days for the big, rugged Slovakian, his no-nonsense approach, decent pace, aerial dominance, crunching tackles and good distribution quickly marked him out as a fans' favourite — an old-fashioned stopper who can find a team-mate with a pass. "We knew this player when he was 18," Benítez said. "It was funny because some people were going to see Everton against Zenit and were saying this player really has ability. But we already had four or five videos of him which we liked. We had already sent our people over there and we knew he was the player for us." After a difficult start against non-league Havant & Waterlooville he quickly found his composure, and bar the occasional mistake all defenders are prone to, showed great consistency for the remainder of the 2007/08 season, going on to make regular starts and rack up 20 appearances by the end of the campaign. More needs to be seen of him before being too conclusive in judgements, but he appears to have what it takes.

Obviously, signings made in the summer of 2008 cannot be judged at the time of writing. Philipp Degen, an attacking right-back, arrived on a free transfer from Borussia Dortmund. "He is an offensive player with great energy and a winning mentality," Benítez said. "His strength is going forward and I am confident he will be prove to be a quality addition to our squad." Also signed was Andrea Dossena, the Italian left-back, for a fee of £7m. Like Degen an attacking full-back, Dossena won his first Italian cap in 2007 after his impressive overlapping displays for Udinese. Preferring to deploy two holding midfielders, Benítez now has two quick, ambitious full-backs who can supply the width and attacking threat, while the wingers cut inside to forage for opportunities. Next in was goalkeeper Diego Cavalieri, a £3m signing from Brazilian outfit Palmeiras. The 25-year-old penned a four-year contract with the Reds and will act as understudy to Pepe Reina, with Itandje on the move.

French teenage striker David Ngog arrived in July for just £1.5m from Paris St Germain, with his contract at the *Ligue Une* club about to expire. Tall, quick and very skilful, the 19-year-old was immediately earmarked for a place in the Reds' first-team squad. While struggling to score in his debut season in France, as he was eased into first-team life with stints on the wing and as a substitute, his record with the national side at youth level remains very impressive.

The big signing of the summer of 2008 was Robbie Keane, who cost £19m from Spurs (just ahead of going to print). The Irish international, who excels as a 'second striker' (a little in the Peter Beardsley mould), is Benítez's most expensive signing when age is taken into account. Having just turned 28, Keane will have nowhere near the resale value of Torres, who cost a few million more, but the decision was clearly about paying top-dollar for an experienced, reliable player who could slip immediately into the team to link the midfield and attack, while weighing in with a good goal return. On paper Keane looks a great acquisition; but worse players have succeeded at big clubs and better players have failed. Time will tell.

Player	Quality	0.01pg	IN	OUT	FGV	**VALUE**	Ap	Details
Jose Reina	8.93	1.56	-2.1	4.5	5	**17.89**	156	£6m 2005 Value +
Fernando Torres*	9.81	0.46	-7.5	10	3.5	**16.27**	46	£23m 2007 Value +
Daniel Agger	8.03	0.53	-1.9	3.9	3.5	**14.06**	53	£5.8m 2006 Value +
Javier Mascherano	8.88	0.52	-5.8	6.5	3.5	**13.60**	52	£18m 2007 Value +

Ryan Babel	7.56	0.49	-3.7	4.5	3	**11.85**	49 £11.5m 2007 Value +
Martin Skrtel	7.74	0.2	-2.1	2.8	3	**11.64**	20 £6.5m 2008 Value +
Xabi Alonso	8.22	1.63	-3.6	5.2	3	**11.45**	163 £10.5m 2004 Value +
Lucas Leiva	6.39	0.32	-1.9	2.4	3	**10.21**	32 £6m 2007 Value +
Emiliano Insúa	6.00	0.5	-0.3	1	3	**10.20**	5 £1m 2007 Value +
Álvaro Arbeloa	6.78	0.55	-0.9	1.5	2	**9.93**	55 £2.64m 2007 Value +
Peter Crouch	7.63	1.34	-2.4	3.2		**9.77**	134 £7m 2005 Value +
Scott Carson	6.34	0.9	-0.3	2.6		**9.54**	9 £750k 2005 Value +
Fábio Aurélio	6.56	0.54	0	1.3	1	**9.40**	54 Free 2006 Value +
Yossi Benayoun	6.91	0.47	-1.6	1.6	2	**9.38**	47 £5m 2007 Value =
Dirk Kuyt	7.11	0.96	-2.9	2.9	1	**9.07**	96 £9m 2006 Value =
Luis Garcia	7.44	1.21	-2.1	2.2		**8.75**	121 £6m 2004 £3.5m '07 @29
Average	**6.2**		**-1.6**			**8.71**	
Mohamed Sissoko	7.02	0.87	-1.9	2.7		**8.69**	87 £5.6m '05 £8.2m '08
Jermaine Pennant	6.06	0.77	-2.2	1.7	2	**8.33**	77 £6.7m 2006 Value -
All Managers' Average						**7.92**	
Jack Hobbs	5.13	0.05	-0.3	0.6	2	**7.48**	5 £750k 2005 Value +
Andriy Voronin	5.00	0.26	0	1	1	**7.26**	28 Free 2008 Value +
Craig Bellamy	5.78	0.42	-1.9	2.4		**6.70**	42 £6m 2006 £7.5m 2006
Nabil El Zhar	4.27	0.06	-0.01	1	1	**6.32**	6 £200k 2006 Value +
Robbie Fowler (2)	5.89	0.35	0	0		**6.24**	35 Free 2006 Rel. @32 '07
F Morientes	5.17	0.61	-2.2	2.2		**5.78**	61 £6.3m 2005 £3.5m '06 @30
Boudewijn Zenden	5.17	0.47	0	0		**5.64**	47 Free 2005 Rel. 2007
Mark Gonzalez	4.47	0.36	-0.5	1		**5.33**	36 £1.5m 2005 £3m 2007
Sebastian Leto	4.00	0.04	-0.6	0.6	1	**5.04**	4 £1.85m 2007 Value =
Jan Kromkamp	4.82	0.18	-0.6	0.6		**5.00**	18 £2m Sw. £2m Sw.
Josemi Rey	4.24	0.35	-0.7	0.7		**4.59**	35 £2m 2004 £2m Sw.
Antonio Nunez	3.82	0.27	-0.7	0.7		**4.09**	27 £2m Sw. £2m 2005
Gabriel Paletta	3.50	0.08	-0.6	0.6		**3.58**	8 £2m 2006 £2m Sw.
Mauricio Pellegrino	3.44	0.13	0	0		**3.57**	13 Free 2005 Rel. 2005

Key: *See page 51.*

Expensive Folly

Generally, the more money Benítez spends on a player, the better he does. Dirk Kuyt is perhaps the one exception, but even he seems to be reinventing himself — or rather, returning to his roots — as a right-sided attacker. Kuyt's first touch, while not as bad as some suggest, is perhaps not assured enough for a Premiership *striker*, where time on the ball is at such a premium when outnumbered by centre-backs and with shielding midfielders in close attendance. He also lacks the pace to leave defenders behind, which at times stops him getting shots away in a crowded area. But such is his commitment to the cause that he can elevate his team-mates — not with skill, like Torres might, but with his sheer will to win. He is a player who drags those around him up to his level of desire, rather than dragging them down to his weaknesses.

At £6.5m, Fernando Morientes was a bigger disappointment, particularly as he had such a stellar reputation. Unlike Kuyt, Morientes failed to cope with the physical side of the English game, and despite playing with intelligence, his effectiveness was limited. But even then, these two are hardly the kind of costly flops seen recently at other clubs, such as Juan Sebastian Verón (£28m to Manchester United in 2001 and £14m to Chelsea in 2003) or Andrei Shevchenko, who arrived at Stamford Bridge for £30.8m with an even bigger reputation and scored the same number of Premiership goals (eight) as Morientes, in eight more games.

Transfer Masterstroke

Fernando Torres, given his price and pedigree, may seem too obvious a choice. But even so, at the time plenty felt he wasn't suitable for English football, or simply wasn't prolific enough. There was even an ultra-daft notion that because one Spanish striker called Fernando had recently failed, this one would follow suit. By that logic, signing Mark Kennedy should have guaranteed the European Cup in the '90s.

Torres fitted perfectly with the club's ethos, as a world-class player with a world-class attitude and work ethic. Never the most prolific prior to arriving in England, Torres still had all the gifts a spearhead striker needs: pace, strength, bravery, skill, and an eye for goal, allied to a good physique and, at 6' 1", some stature too. Benítez later admitted that he had considered a bid for Michael Owen, but the former Reds' no.10 was becoming increasingly injury prone as he approached his late 20s, as well as being less suited to the targetman/lone striker role. Few people expected Torres to eclipse Owen's best season by the start of April during his first campaign. However, he soon passed Owen's highest Premiership tally of 19 on his way to reaching 24 league goals (making him the most prolific overseas striker in a debut season, beating Ruud van Nistelrooy's 23). Next he moved beyond Owen's best overall tally of 28, and became the first Liverpool striker since Robbie Fowler in 1997 to hit 30 goals in a season; eventually finishing with 33 in all competitions. And all this without taking penalties or free-kicks. It's said of Torres that he never scores the same goal twice; he can improvise in any situation, and make something happen for himself out of nothing, rather than rely on the spoon-fed six-yard poaches that some strikers mop up. The ability to go past players and shoot with either foot (as well as head the ball with precision) enables him to pose every conceivable kind of threat. He can run in behind defenders, or shoot from 30-yards. He can snaffle chances at close range, or rise to head a ball into the top corner. As such he is almost certainly the most complete striker the Reds have ever had. His reputation was cemented by scoring the winning goal for Spain in the Euro 2008 Final in Vienna; the confidence from which he will hopefully take into the rest of his Liverpool career.

One Who Got Away

Daniel Alves, Simao Sabrosa and Luis Figo were all on Liverpool's radar in 2005 and 2006: three skilful right-sided players. In Figo's case, he chose Inter Milan when up for a free transfer from Real Madrid. Simao was close to signing for £10m before Benfica upped the fee to £13m at the last minute, and so the deal fell through; a year later he moved to Atletico Madrid for £15m. Alves, a skilful, quick and powerful (if diminutive) Brazilian right-back, wanted to move to Liverpool in the summer of 2006. His agent, Jose Rodriguez Baster, revealed that, despite the interest of other clubs, Alves had set his heart on a move to Anfield. "I can say that, without any doubts, the player wants to go to Liverpool," said Baster. "Personally I have not listened to any other club, although some have rung and I have passed them on to Sevilla, but what Daniel wants to is to play for Liverpool. The two sides [Liverpool and Sevilla] are getting closer, but we are still quite a way apart." The deal never got quite close enough, much to Benítez's frustration. Two years later, the Brazilian moved to Barcelona for £24m.

Ricardo Quaresma of Porto was another player Benítez spoke with, but the Portuguese winger told him he would not curb his excessive showboating and overelaboration; Benítez admired Quaresma's skill, but without a preparedness to also work hard, he wasn't interested.

Finally, throughout the summer of 2008 Benítez worked tirelessly to capture Aston Villa's versatile Gareth Barry, but no deal had been secured by the time of this book going to print.

Budget — Historical Context

Without doubt, the biggest spenders of modern day football have been Chelsea. The 2007 Champions League semi-final first-leg at Stamford Bridge shows the gulf in spending power. On average, Liverpool's starting XI — Reina, Riise, Agger, Carragher, Arbeloa, Zenden, Alonso, Mascherano, Gerrard, Bellamy and Kuyt — cost just 14.5% of the English transfer record. Adding the seven subs takes the average up a fraction, to 15%. By contrast, Chelsea's 18-man squad averaged out at 42%, and even more tellingly, the team that started the match — Cech, Cole, Carvalho, Terry, Ferreira, Cole, Lampard, Makelele, Mikel, Drogba and Schevchenko — came in at a whopping 51%. So in 'real' terms, Chelsea's team was more than three times as expensive. (This calculation takes Mascherano's fee as the £1.5m paid for the loan, as no permanent deal had been agreed at that point; even taking his value at £18.6m only raises the average cost of the squad to 18%.) With such a gulf, it's not surprising that Liverpool, despite several cup successes against the southerners, have struggled to match Chelsea over the course of a league season. Arsenal, whose spending more closely mirrors Liverpool's, were regularly finishing above their London rivals in the early part of the decade, but since the end of 2003/04 they've only finished below. Only Manchester United have finished above Chelsea in that time.

United's spending also easily exceeds that of Liverpool. The best squads of 16 for each team in 2007/08 (excluding long-term absentees who didn't really feature, like Daniel Agger and Gary Neville), were markedly different in relation to the English transfer record. Despite an extra home-grown player, United's 16 had an average 50% more than Liverpool's. This includes Mascherano at his full fee, with the deal finalised mid-season, but has his fellow MSI-owned compatriot Tevez listed at only £10m, which was the purported cost of his two-year loan deal from the company; a final transfer fee would be around £30m, and as such would increase United's XI to 43.5% of the English record.

RECORD
European Cup/Champions League, 2005
European Super Cup, 2005
FA Cup, 2006
Community Shield, 2006
Champions League Qualification, 2005, 2006, 2007, 2008

	P	W	D	L	F	A	%
Overall	**239**	**134**	**50**	**55**	**395**	**202**	**56.07%**
League	152	83	35	34	233	121	54.61%
FA Cup	12	7	2	3	33	17	58.33%
League Cup	13	8	1	4	25	20	61.54%
Europe	59	34	12	13	99	42	57.63%
Other	3	2	0	1	5	2	66.67%

CONCLUSION
Rafa Benítez will never be regarded as one of Liverpool's greatest-ever managers until he can end the lengthening wait for the English crown. Despite two points tallies — 82 and 76 — that have been enough to win the league in previous seasons, he has yet to finish higher than 3rd. But cup success, at home and in Europe, as well as lifting the Reds to the top of the UEFA rankings, highlight what a good job he has done overall. Unlike the previous three Liverpool managers, he has been able to sell surplus players for a profit after they've served their purpose, and, in relative terms, has on the whole been less able to spend hefty fees on a player. The serious attention paid to the youth and reserve sides has seen them become national champions: the kids in 2006 and 2007, and then, upon graduating to the second-string, many won the reserve title in 2008. This suggests that the manager's best work has yet to bear fruit.

Difficulties behind the scenes hampered progress in his fourth season, but the Reds lost their lowest amount of league games for 20 years, and were within extra-time of a third Champions League Final in four seasons. In amongst the relative failure, there are numerous examples of relative success, not to mention Istanbul — an outright triumph in its own right. If everyone can unite in the coming years, then Benítez's success with Valencia could be repeated in England — although the strength of the other three major rivals will make it no mean feat. Should Benítez finally land the club a league title, then the Spaniard, the first man on the list to win a trophy in each of his first two seasons, will finally stand close to Shankly and Paisley, and arguably eclipse Fagan and Dalglish.

Were he to secure the club's 19th title, then Benítez would become the first of all the managers to win the three most important trophies: European Cup, league title and FA Cup.

"The most important thing is to give the players confidence, to give them answers. If you start saying the right things, and you continue to win, then they will start to have confidence in you."

RAFA BENÍTEZ

"Victory is sweetest when you've known defeat."

MALCOLM S. FORBES

CONCLUSION

All Competitions

	P	W	D	L	F	A	Win %
Dalglish	307	187	78	42	617	259	**60.91%**
Paisley	535	307	132	96	955	406	**57.38%**
Benítez*	239	134	50	55	395	202	**56.07%**
Fagan	131	70	37	24	225	97	**53.44%**
Shankly	783	407	198	178	1307	766	**51.98%**
Houllier	307	158	75	74	516	298	**51.47%**
Evans	226	116	57	53	375	216	**51.33%**
Souness	157	65	47	45	248	186	**41.40%**

* As of June 2008

EIGHT MEN

So there we have it. Bill Shankly, the man who built an empire from scratch; the man who won the club its first FA Cup, and the first manager of an English side to win a European trophy in the same season as becoming English Champions. Bob Paisley, the only manager in football history to win three European Cups, and with the best league-titles-to-years-managed ratio around: six in nine years. Joe Fagan, who oversaw the club's most successful single season, an historic treble. Kenny Dalglish, the club's first double-winner and in his inaugural campaign to boot; followed by the most attractive, free-flowing football the club had ever played. Graeme Souness, winner of the FA Cup in his first season. Roy Evans, who gave the world one of the greatest league games of all-time with a side that rarely lacked for entertainment. Gérard Houllier, who became the first ever manager in English football history to successfully complete every possible fixture in a season when winning three knockout cups, at the same time ending the Champions League exile. And Rafa Benítez, the first Liverpool boss to win trophies in his first two seasons, including the Champions League in the most improbable of circumstances.

Each inherited the club in very different circumstances, and each faced his own unique challenges upon his appointment — whether it was following in the footsteps of a legend, or working with a squad that was limited in quality or getting on in years.

Manager	Average Fee	
Souness	-4.5	(45%)
Paisley	-3.53	(35.3%)
Evans	-3.12	(31.2%)
Dalglish	-2.96	(29.6%)
Shankly	-2.92	(29.2%)
Fagan	-2.5	(25%)
Houllier	-1.96	(19.6%)
Benítez	-1.6*	(16%)

* As of June 2008

Overall, when it came to the eight spending money, the size of the fee certainly did not relate to the quality of player it helped procure. The average cost of a player purchased by Souness was almost half the English transfer record. Perhaps due to the need to fill deeper squads, the two most recent managers have the lowest average, on account of having several cheap back-up players bolstering the ranks (although none of the calculations include young players with no first team experience). But statistics also show how, in more recent years, Liverpool have not been able to stretch to many payments near the transfer record. In 'real' terms, Souness' signings cost almost three times as much as Benítez's.

Manager	Quality
Paisley	7.6
Fagan	6.93
Shankly	6.9
Dalglish	6.32
Benítez	6.2
Houllier	5.59
Evans	5.45
Souness	5.1

While he spent the most in relative terms, Souness bought the worst players in terms of *Quality*. Joe Fagan's purchases were the most steady — nothing spectacular, but almost all of his signings were above average. As can be seen below, Benítez's signings have thus far been better *Value For Money* than those purchased by Dalglish or Fagan.

Manager	Value For Money
Paisley	12.17
Shankly	10.74
Benítez	8.70
Fagan	8.25
Dalglish	8.19
Houllier	6.10
Evans	4.54
Souness	3.45

Comparisons Between Inheritances

In terms of *Quality*, Joe Fagan inherited the best squad and the strongest First XI. But when age is taken into account, to form the *Inheritance* ratings, Bob Paisley was the biggest beneficiary. Regarding *Inheritance*, Roy Evans received the worst squad, and Graeme Souness took charge of the First XI with the greatest age handicap.

	Quality	*Left By*		*Left To*
Squad Average Quality	8.46	Paisley	to	Fagan
Squad Average Quality	8.11	Fagan	to	Dalglish
Squad Average Quality	8	Shankly	to	Paisley
Squad Average Quality	7.2	Benítez	to	? *
Squad Average Quality	6.88	Dalglish	to	Souness
Squad Average Quality	6.74	Evans	to	Houllier
Squad Average Quality	6.73	Taylor	to	Shankly
Squad Average Quality	6.49	Souness	to	Evans
Squad Average Quality	6.07	Houllier	to	Benítez

Inheritance Rating		*Left By*		*Left To*
Squad Average Inheritance	7.46	Paisley	to	Fagan
Squad Average Inheritance	7.25	Shankly	to	Paisley
Squad Average Inheritance	7.05	Fagan	to	Dalglish
Squad Average Inheritance	6.33	Benítez	to	? *
Squad Average Inheritance	5.58	Dalglish	to	Souness
Squad Average Inheritance	5.48	Evans	to	Houllier
Squad Average Inheritance	5.46	Houllier	to	Benítez
Squad Average Inheritance	5.42	Taylor	to	Shankly
Squad Average Inheritance	4.79	Souness	to	Evans

Age		*Left By*		*Left To*
Squad Average Age	27.1	Shankly	to	Paisley
Squad Average Age	26.6	Fagan	to	Dalglish
Squad Average Age	26.5	Dalglish	to	Souness
Squad Average Age	26.4	Souness	to	Evans
Squad Average Age	26.3	Paisley	to	Fagan

Squad Average Age	25.8	Evans	to	Houllier
Squad Average Age	25.6	Benítez	to	? *
Squad Average Age	25.5	Houllier	to	Benítez
Squad Average Age	24.4	Taylor	to	Shankly

Comparisons Between First XIs Inherited

	Quality	*Left By*		*Left To*
First XI Average	8.89	Paisley	to	Fagan
First XI Average	8.8	Shankly	to	Paisley
First XI Average	8.77	Fagan	to	Dalglish
First XI Average	8.23	Benítez	to	? *
First XI Average	8.03	Dalglish	to	Souness
First XI Average	7.64	Taylor	to	Shankly
First XI Average	7.49	Souness	to	Evans
First XI Average	7.46	Houllier	to	Benítez
First XI Average	7.45	Evans	to	Houllier

Inheritance Rating		*Left By*		*Left To*
First XI Average	8.26	Shankly	to	Paisley
First XI Average	7.8	Paisley	to	Fagan
First XI Average	7.7	Benítez	to	? *
First XI Average	7.14	Taylor	to	Shankly
First XI Average	7	Fagan	to	Dalglish
First XI Average	6.78	Houllier	to	Benítez
First XI Average	6.4	Evans	to	Houllier
First XI Average	6.03	Souness	to	Evans
First XI Average	5.67	Dalglish	to	Souness

Age		*Left By*		*Left To*
First XI Average	29.6	Dalglish	to	Souness
First XI Average	28	Fagan	to	Dalglish
First XI Average	26.6	Paisley	to	Fagan
First XI Average	26.4	Shankly	to	Paisley
First XI Average	26.4	Houllier	to	Benítez
First XI Average	26	Benítez	to	? *
First XI Average	25.5	Souness	to	Evans
First XI Average	25	Evans	to	Houllier
First XI Average	24	Taylor	to	Shankly

* As of June 2008

For more statistics from the Dynasty project, visit www.paultomkins.com

*"My idea was to build Liverpool
into a bastion of invincibility."*

BILL SHANKLY

THE GREATEST?

For all the success of the last 50 years, orchestrated by a number of excellent managers, two men — Shankly and Paisley — stand out as a cut above the rest. Directly behind that illustrious pair, Dalglish, Fagan and Benítez vie for third place, with each man's achievements hugely notable for different reasons, while Houllier, had he not systematically undone his own good work, would still be revered by Kopites in the way he was in 2001. Evans and Souness were the only two 'failures', but hopefully their tenures have been put into context, and the things they got right have been acknowledged; Evans, in particular, got within touching distance of a 19th league title, and his side produced free-flowing football, but in terms of trophies he sits at the bottom of the list, with just the lowest-ranked, the League Cup, to show for his endeavours. That pair's main crime was that they just didn't purchase good enough players, and they are the only two to win just a single trophy each. Souness is the only manager to reach just a single cup final, while Houllier is the only man to not lose one.

My own personal rankings would place Dalglish 3rd, Benítez 4th, Fagan 5th, Houllier 6th, Evans 7th and Souness some way back in 8th; should Benítez add the league title, he'll overtake Dalglish in my eyes, particularly because he inherited a side 30 points off the champions and doing poorly in Europe, and given the current strength of the domestic league when compared with the late '80s; also, there's the lower spending power of the Reds in the new millennium to consider. Of course, his reputation could still suffer if, having spent bigger since 2007, he fails to close the gap on the top two. For Dalglish's part, it's not his fault that he could not manage in Europe, but it has to count against him (as an unknown quantity) all the same, as does his poor legacy. And despite the wonderful achievements of Joe Fagan in 1984, the side he inherited was just so good that he cannot receive *total* credit. Without ever having built his own side, he cannot be viewed as having done a 'complete' job.

Shankly, Paisley, Dalglish, Evans and Benítez improved upon the average league points hauls (based on three points for a win) of their immediate predecessors; Fagan, Souness and Houllier saw decreases. Shankly, Paisley, Dalglish, Evans and Benítez also improved the average league position in which the Reds finished. Removing the first season from each manager's record — in order to allow a season's grace if inheriting a difficult situation (for him to assess things and start making adjustments), or for the good work of their predecessor to wear off a little if taking over when the Reds were already the best team in the land — improves the records of Shankly, Paisley, Evans, Houllier and Benítez, but those of Dalglish and Fagan suffer slightly; Souness' suffers heavily after removing the 2nd-placed finish largely established by Dalglish and Ronnie Moran when taking over in April 1991.

But it all comes back to the founding fathers. Choosing between Bill Shankly and Bob Paisley — the pair rightly regarded as the greatest managers in the club's history — is like trying to decide which of Diego Maradona's legs was the more important. Most of the skill was wrapped up in the left, but the right was every bit as crucial; the left obviously becomes useless without it. It takes two legs to run, to jump, to land, and to provide such exquisite balance; while the work of one catches the eye, the other has to be strong, has to carry its partner. Everything Shankly achieved he did so with Paisley at his side. And everything Paisley achieved was as a result of the strength built up during Shankly's time in charge, and what he had learned from his predecessor. The two are inseparable — equals.

Both men had the greatest hand in the other's success. It's like Solomon's decree to split the baby in half — you cannot excise one from the other and achieve any kind of satisfactory conclusion; it makes no sense — as a concept it has no life. While the pair were eventually sundered in 1974, the two can never be separated from each other *in history*; they can never be removed from the partnership they shared, and, more crucially, the influence they had on one another. And as such, it's impossible to judge them independently.

Two great men, one almighty strength.

For tomorrow belongs to the people

who prepare for it today"

AFRICAN PROVERB

POSTSCRIPT: THE FUTURE

It's now 16 years since a club won its 'first' title (first meaning after a gap of at least five years, so that is essentially, if not entirely, a new team) with a side that cost, on average, less than 40% of the English transfer record. In other words, it hasn't happened in the Premiership era, with Leeds United the last inexpensive side to finish as English Champions, in 1992.

Year	Team	% of transfer record
1993	Manchester United	40.1%
1995	Blackburn Rovers	41.5%
1998	Arsenal	43.5%
2005	Chelsea	44.8%

That doesn't mean assembling a side with an average cost in excess of 40% of the transfer record guarantees you the title. Newcastle's 1996/97 side averaged out at 49.7%, but won nothing. Liverpool themselves had a first XI coming in at 43.5% in 1994, and 44.5% two years later.

Liverpool's probable strongest XI going into 2008/09 — Pepe Reina, Andrea Dossena, Daniel Agger, Jamie Carragher, Philipp Degen, Ryan Babel, Xabi Alonso, Javier Mascherano, Steven Gerrard, Fernando Torres and Robbie Keane — averages out at 30%. But unlike the current squads at Manchester United and Chelsea, Benítez's spending is wrapped up almost entirely in his strongest team; the rest of the first team squad — Dirk Kuyt, Fábio Aurélio, Sami Hyypia, Yossi Benayoun, Andrei Voronin, David Ngog, Lucas Leiva, Emiliano Insua, Alvaro Arbeloa,

Martin Skrtel, Jermaine Pennant, Steve Finnan, Diego Cavalieri, Daniel Pacheco, Damien Plessis and Krisztian Nemeth — average out at just 10%, bringing the overall squad cost down to 19.2% of the English transfer record. Even removing youngsters Insua, Pacheco, Plessis and Nemeth, who are only on the fringes, makes a difference of just 3%.

In the '90s, Souness and Evans bought the 1st and 3rd-most expensive set of players out of all eight Liverpool managers, and between them had the club's best-ever collection of youth team graduates to work with. But with ground lost at the start of the decade, it was an uphill climb from then on; the effects of which still abide. Bad investments were made throughout that decade, and too much of a gap opened up. For Liverpool to achieve what all Koptites now dream of — namely overtake Manchester United — we need to look back at how United managed to conclusively overtake Liverpool, back in 1992, and land the title a year later. And the sad fact is, Liverpool fell away *themselves* — dropping to 6th — rather than United having to overtake them. Of course, United had started to slowly improve season on season, but only from the fifth year of Ferguson's reign onwards, and only after assembling a first XI that in 1992 cost 45% of the transfer record. It was a combination of United's financial largesse and Liverpool's own inadequacies that saw a switch in power that year. But at present, United show no signs of weakening, and Benítez's strongest team still cannot match Ferguson's when it comes to outlay.

Look at trying to win the league title as a 4 x 400m relay race, with each year equal to the circuit of one athlete. Barring accident or injury, a runner can only close so much of the gap on each leg if he's racing equally fine athletes. If Ferguson was trailing Dalglish by some distance from 1986 to 1990, and unable to find impetus to even remotely close the gap, then the awful tragedy of Hillsborough was what tripped the Liverpool manager. Dalglish was still ahead when he handed over the baton to Souness in 1991, but vital ground and momentum had been lost; it was a case of stumbling on. Had Kenny Dalglish not suffered from stress following the horrific events of April 1989, things might well have been different.

From that point, every Liverpool manager took charge from a position of weakness; the opposite of Paisley, Fagan and Dalglish, who took control from a position of strength and, at times, outright domination. For those three, even when rival clubs assembled more expensive teams, it was rarely enough to overturn the winning ways and supreme confidence that had been bred at Anfield. But all that changed around the time of the 18th, and final, league title (to date). Returning to the earlier analogy, smooth baton changes with 70 metre advantages were a thing of the past; Souness, with the pack gaining on him, dropped the baton, and now it was United who had the momentum.

In a strange symmetry, Liverpool's dynasty, built by Shankly in the early '60s, was precipitated by another footballing tragedy. Sir Matt Busby's side was clearly set back a number of years by the Munich air crash. Had United still possessed players like Duncan Edwards in 1964, Liverpool *might* never have won that absolutely vital initial title. Shankly's side would still have been excellent, but there was a chance it might not have landed that crucial first honour. Even if it didn't totally deter Shankly's boys, there's a chance that it might have delayed things a little.

When Ferguson retires, United's empire almost certainly won't crumble overnight — as with Chelsea losing Jose Mourinho, if the players are good enough then competitiveness can endure, at least until a complete overhaul is required — but a change of manager, if it means a switch to the wrong man, could unsettle the squad and destroy the balance.

At the very least, United would lose the psychological edge of Ferguson's success rate. Even an equally talented manager coming in wouldn't have prior success *associated with the club he would now be managing*. And let's not forget, for all his acknowledged ability, Ferguson could not break Liverpool's hold or even get close in his first five years. He was an experienced manager when he arrived at Old Trafford, with a decade in the game at that level — the same as Benítez, who was also 44 when he took over at Anfield. Both clubs — the country's two biggest — had gone at least a decade-and-a-half without the league title, so the pressure was incredibly intense. Both clubs were averaging around 4th in the league in the five years before each man pitched up. So the challenges were virtually identical.

In relative terms, Ferguson spent far, far bigger than Benítez in his first four years. And yet for three of those first four years United were marooned in the bottom half of the table. Ferguson made a lot of astute but expensive signings between 1986 and 1989, but those players took until 1993 to deliver the league title. Irrespective of era, teams take time to gel; Shankly's two great sides were the same. But it's clear you need that first league title to instil confidence and create a mythology. While Liverpool haven't won the Champions League since Benítez's first season, the Reds have actually played far better on the whole, and progressed to the latter stages on two further occasions — therefore challenging for *that* title — partly because of the mythology that inhibits the opposition and the belief that bolsters the Reds.

Would Ferguson have been able to create his league mythology and rid the 26-year, 26-ton millstone had a team like Chelsea been on the scene then, with the ability to buy marquee players of the day like Diego Maradona, Ruud Gullit, Michael Laudrup and Marco van Basten (while, say, unsettling United's Bryan Robson in the process), and whose new owner had installed a canny manager like, say, Fabio Capello? Of course, no-one can say for sure. But equally, at a guess, I doubt it.

And would Ferguson have been able to overtake an über-rich new rival in the early '90s *as well* as Liverpool, had the Anfield empire (the equivalent of United now) not self-destructed? Again, at a guess, I doubt it.

With the 50th season since Shankly's arrival under way, it would be poetic if the Reds could end the campaign as Champions once again. But it remains more of a long-shot than a lot of people realise, and to do so with what remains a relatively inexpensive team (when compared with other recent 'new' champions) would make it an extraordinary achievement. If it does happen, it will have been worth the wait.

BIBLIOGRAPHY

Countless sources were referenced during the researching of this book, but those of particular benefit were:

Shankly, by Bill Shankly
The Amazing Bill Shankly, John Roberts
Shankly: It's More Important Than That, Stephen F Kelly
Bob Paisley, Manager of the Millennium, John Keith
Paisley: A Liverpool Legend by Stan Liversedge
Ghost On The Wall, Authorised Biography of Roy Evans, Derk Dohren
Ian Rush, An Autobiography
Souness: The Management Years, Graeme Souness with Mike Ellis
Liverpool Secrets: Behind Shankly Gates
Dalglish: My Autobiography
Dalglish, Stephen F Kelly
Stand Up Pinocchio, Phil Thompson
Fowler: My Autobiography, Robbie Fowler
Jan The Man, Jan Molby with Grahame Lloyd
Who's Who of Liverpool, Tony Matthews

Recent interviews courtesy of www.liverpoolfc.tv

"The best writer on LFC, bar none"

Vic Gill, son-in-law of Bill Shankly, Liverpool FC 1957-62

"Excellent ... A logic, perception and optimism that brings hope
and solace to many fans in this shallow knee-jerk age."

Brian Reade, The Daily Mirror

AN ANFIELD ANTHOLOGY

Articles & Essays
2000-2008

PAUL TOMKINS

ISBN-13: 978-0955636721

www.paultomkins.com